DEREGULATING
DESIRE

DEREGULATING
DESIRE

Flight Attendant Activism,
Family Politics, and Workplace Justice

Ryan Patrick Murphy

TEMPLE UNIVERSITY PRESS
Philadelphia • Rome • Tokyo

TEMPLE UNIVERSITY PRESS
Philadelphia, Pennsylvania 19122
www.temple.edu/tempress

Library of Congress Cataloging-in-Publication Data

Names: Murphy, Ryan Patrick, 1975– author.
Title: Deregulating desire : flight attendant activism, family politics, and
   workplace justice / Ryan Patrick Murphy.
Description: Philadelphia : Temple University Press, 2016. | Series:
   Sexuality studies | Includes bibliographical references and index.
Identifiers: LCCN 2016003227| ISBN 9781439909881 (hbk : alk. paper)
   | ISBN 9781439909898 (pbk : alk. paper) | ISBN 9781439909904 (e-book)
Subjects: LCSH: Flight attendants—Labor unions—United States. |
   Sexism—United States. | Feminism—United States. | Work and family
   —United States. | BISAC: SOCIAL SCIENCE / Sociology / Marriage &
   Family. | HISTORY / United States / 20th Century. | SOCIAL SCIENCE /
   Women's Studies.
Classification: LCC HD6515.A43 M86 2016 | DDC 331.88/113877420973—dc23
LC record available at https://lccn.loc.gov/2016003227

♾ The paper used in this publication meets the requirements of the American National
Standard for Information Sciences—Permanence of Paper for Printed Library Materials,
ANSI Z39.48-1992

Printed in the United States of America

9 8 7 6 5 4 3 2 1

CONTENTS

ACKNOWLEDGMENTS

A central argument of this book is that the pro-business and "pro-family" social movements of the post-1970 period have tried to make domesticity and hard work the central organizing principles of society. These activists have insisted that a renewed commitment to family and work should replace the other affinities that have connected people across space and time. The following pages take the opposite position, however, as a testament to the importance of a multiplicity of friendly, intimate, intellectual, professional, and political relationships. In contrast to demonstrating the value of the atomized individual intellectual, *Deregulating Desire* acts as an archive of dialogue with friends in bars at all hours of the day and night; with my mentors at the Association of Flight Attendants–CWA; with displaced flight attendants in San Francisco, Dallas, Kansas City, and a host of other places; and with my students and colleagues in classrooms at the University of Minnesota, at Earlham College, and in other venues where I have studied and worked. Here I name a few people and programs whose support has been particularly influential to the story I have chosen to tell.

First and foremost, I am humbled by the generosity of dozens of front-line flight attendants who contributed the firsthand evidence and arguments that made this book possible. Although many flight attendants who agreed to be interviewed had lost their jobs, and all struggled to adjust to lower wages, more costly health insurance, and reduced retirement benefits, they took time off work and drove long distances to meet with me, or they cooked me dinner while I rummaged through the archives in their basements. I am particularly thankful to the many former TWA flight attendants who participated in this project, because their journey through the past two decades has been unusually difficult. Paula Mariedaughter and Mary Ellen Miller were immensely generous with their time and with the ideas they shared about the past. Dixie Daniels and Victoria Gray engaged in regular e-mail exchanges to verify the details about collective bargaining, representation elections, and seniority integration. Richard Wagner, Diane Watson, and attorney Bill Jolley also took significant amounts of time from their schedules to contribute to the project. A number of flight attendants, especially Kaye Chandler, Janet Lhuillier, and Ed Sanford, graciously granted me access to their own collections of documents. I am grateful for the support and mentorship I received from my fellow flight attendant activists in AFA-CWA Council 11 in San Francisco, especially Dawn Marie Bader, Christine Black, Dante Harris, Jeanne Heier-Donellan, Stan Kiino, Roxanne Ng, Beth Skrondal, and Terry Sousoures. I also thank everyone who answered phones, sent out e-mail blasts, made picket signs, and handed out leaflets to passengers and coworkers during the ongoing crises of 9/11, the United bankruptcy, and the pension termination, as even the smallest contributions to the movement provided me with the inspiration to tell this story.

My intellectual mentors gave me new tools and ideas that helped enrich my conversations with flight attendants. My undergraduate adviser and friend Peter Rachleff contributed greatly to this book. His lifelong commitment to trade union activism, his immense effectiveness in the classroom, and his ongoing willingness to reinvent both himself and the field of labor history are great inspirations in my own life and career. I thank my graduate adviser, Jennifer Pierce, for her unflagging support for my work. Jennifer's deep knowledge of the intellectual and professional terrain of the social sciences and humanities has been a tremendous material resource for this project, and her encouragement during the 2008–2009 economic crisis is perhaps the most important reason that I have been able to continue working full time as an academic. Thanks go to Kevin Murphy, whose broad, interdisciplinary knowledge has provided a wellspring of ideas for this book. Kevin is both a supportive mentor and one who asks the toughest question on the test. That rigor has added both depth and clarity to the arguments I make herein. I am grateful to all of my teachers who provided generous comments on the many drafts of the manuscript, especially Tracey Deutsch, Lisa Disch, Kale Fajardo, Roderick Ferguson, Karen Ho, Regina Kunzel, Helga Leitner, and Eric Sheppard, whose input has been particularly influential to my work as it has evolved.

I thank those whose generous financial support helped make this book possible. The Graduate School Fellowship and Doctoral Dissertation Fellowship at the University of Minnesota provided the time I needed to research and write. A travel grant from the Tamiment Library at New York University allowed me to conduct in-depth archival research. I am grateful to Macalester College for the research and travel funds it offers visiting assistant professors, which allowed me to take a month-long writing trip that sped my revisions along. Most importantly, I thank Greg Mahler and other leaders at Earlham College who have advocated for material support for research and for the pre-tenure sabbatical program that made the final publication of this book possible.

I am grateful to Janice Irvine, Regina Kunzel, and everyone who has worked on the *Sexuality Studies* series at Temple University Press. Multiple rounds of generous, incisive comments from Janice Irvine and Nan Enstad helped make this a more focused, original book. My editors at Temple offered continuous technical and intellectual support during the publication process. Janet Francendese taught me much about academic publishing and greatly influenced the original structure of the project as I transformed it from a dissertation into a book. Sara Cohen's finesse at providing both support and critique energized my writing in the final phases of the project. I especially thank Michael Needham, whose developmental editing—especially his smart ideas about audience and argument—provided the clarity I needed to finish this book while teaching full time in a liberal arts environment.

Deregulating Desire benefited from the generosity of colleagues at the institutions where I worked during the writing process. Pam Forman and Theresa Kemp offered friendship and support at the University of Wisconsin–Eau Claire. Drinking grappa at Pam's house with Ellen Mahaffy was a fantastic pastime during a cold midwestern winter. I thank Sonita Sarker and Katie Batza for making my visiting assistant professor position at Macalester College one of the best untenured gigs in the academy. My students at Macalester—especially Maxime Goudezeune, Alvin Kim, Maya Pisel, and Emily Pripas—were tremendous, and I am grateful to Miranda Joseph for giving an exceptional talk and class visit that made the year a generative one for my thinking and writing. I thank all of my new colleagues at Earlham College, especially those in the History and Women's, Gender, and Sexuality Studies Departments, which have been fun and stimulating places to work, and everyone who has been involved with the Midnight Manuscripts writing group. Eric Cunningham, Nan Ma Hartmann, Elana Passman, Max Paule, Betsy Schlabach, Wayne Soon, Ted Thornhill, Honghong Tinn, and other Midnight Manuscripts members helped inspire the confidence and creativity that I needed to finish this book. My conversations with students during my first semesters at Earlham, especially with Alex Cook, Iman Cooper, Brian Forman, Stacey Hauff, Laura Honsig, Taylor Jeromos, Sarah Medlin, Jocelyn Sawyer, and Kelly Sullivan, among many others, provided the energy and ideas I needed to sharpen the argument herein.

The friendship and support of many longtime colleagues gave me the confidence to write this book. I met Jason Stahl in 2004, when we worked together on an ill-fated but fun and inspiring campaign to form a union for graduate students at the University of Minnesota. Long nights at Jason and Katie Connolly's dinner table got me through an economic crisis, a sad breakup, and an interminable journey through the job market. Jason's unwavering solidarity and his sharp, original ideas about post-1973 politics helped make this book possible. I am grateful to Danny LaChance for a decade of friendship that has encouraged me to keep reading and writing. On the first day of graduate school, Danny asked me if I had purchased a glossy Rand McNally atlas to enhance my performance in Helga Leitner's critical geography seminar. His humor and our endless conversations during late-night happy hours at Barbette have brought fun and levity to workdays that otherwise would have seemed daunting. I thank Alex Urquhart, whose collaboration during the early phases of this project, and during the production of *Queer Twin Cities,* made me a much better thinker and writer. I hope that we may collaborate again in the future. I am grateful to graduate school colleagues who generously commented on endless drafts of this book: Michael David Franklin, Ryan Lee Cartwright, Pam Butler, Lisa Arrastia, and Adam Bahner; the members of Jennifer Pierce's "Piercing Insights" graduate research group; Marian Traub-Werner, Rajyashree Reddy, Jeff Manuel, and others who participated in the summer reading groups that helped me frame this project; and Liz Ault and Karisa Butler-Wall for their help at the end of my time in graduate school. I am indebted to Jesús Estrada-Pérez, whose untimely death has been a terrible loss for the queer and racial justice movements and for the field of American studies. Jesús's work at the confluence of scholarship and activism was an inspiration as I revised my dissertation and turned it into a book.

I am especially grateful to my students at the University of Minnesota, who engaged me in conversations both inside and outside the classroom that transformed my ideas about my research. Hana Worku's writings on the intersection between family and value deeply influenced the central argument of this project, and Connor Donegan's critiques of the literature on neoliberalism helped make this a more original and more readable book. I thank both Hana and Connor for sharing their ideas and for offering so much fun and friendship during our otherwise turbulent transitions out of the University of Minnesota.

Like the friends I have met as an academic, my family has fostered the intellectual curiosity that drove me to write this book. I owe much of that curiosity to my mother, Mary Lynn (Nelson) Murphy. As we drove around my hometown of St. Paul, Minnesota, when I was a kid in the late 1970s and early 1980s, I would press her with difficult questions. I would ask her why immigrant, Southeast Asian, and black neighborhoods had less money than white neighborhoods; why some people lived on the street; or how you could tell if someone was gay. She would respond in a way that any good teacher does, avoiding easy answers and making her student confront her with new and more complex questions. My dad, Mike Murphy, was also my teacher, one whose specialty lay in the area of aviation, which became the central passion of my life. I am particularly grateful that after he endured a five-day week of work travel during the mergers, delays, pickets, and protests of the first bitter years of airline deregulation in the 1980s, my dad would indulge my pleas to take me to the airport on Saturday mornings to watch the airplanes take off and land. These pages are in part a reflection on what I learned about the airline industry from him. I thank my sister, Mary O'Connell Murphy, for being a tremendous friend and supporter throughout the many turns both of our lives have taken during the creation of this book. Mary provided invaluable research support, offering the expertise she has cultivated as an archivist and manager at the Schlesinger Library at Harvard's Radcliffe Institute, to help me deepen and broaden the collection of documents that uphold this project.

The discursive practice that I call herein the family values economy has been particularly hard on the institution of friendship, because friendship often takes place outside spaces that are marked for domesticity or productivity. Despite its recent devaluation, however, friendship—with both those with whom I have shared domesticity, love, and sex and those with whom I have shared other forms of solidarity—has been the most important material resource for this book. Dan Luedtke's genius and craftiness kept me going as I wrote. Since my adjunct position at the University of Minnesota provided neither an office where I could write nor enough money to pay the insurance on my twenty-year-old Volvo, Dan scouted around and found an amazing space for Madame—which became my office—and signed on as co-parent for the Volvo, which included paying half the bills. The people who made Madame possible, especially Angela Gerend, Jeff Hnilicka, Dan Luedtke, and A-K Thordin, gave this book a home as it was being written. Talking all night with Dan and Anna Tsantir turned the dark nights late in the first decade of the 2000s into a total pleasure. All my San Francisco friends made the city one that I wanted to write about, and evenings at the Phone Booth with Tom DeCaigny, Seth Goldstein, Elena White, Eric Wiesner, Nikki Sidney, Mikey Wallin, Tony Mueller, and a whole lot of other characters made those days many of my happiest. Jimmy Draper made San Francisco a particularly sweet place. Once I moved to Minneapolis, the Revolting Queers—Dan, MDF, Donny, Elliot, Bethany, Walter, Lady Enchantress, Josh, Tages, Emily, and many others—made my life joyous, and their critique of sexuality inspired the ideas in this book. Soniya Munshi has been a friend who proves that long-distance relationships can work. I cherish our annual dinner at Lucien on Second Avenue in New York, and I am so glad our friendship has flourished as we have changed so much over twenty years. I thank Sam Robertson for making Minneapolis a place where I still want to live.

I am greatly indebted to James Andrew for the friendship and companionship that he has given me. At least half of the original ideas in this book came from conversations that I had with James when we were lucky enough to be walking through the rose garden in Buenos Aires or at Point Neuf in Paris or just drinking wine in our tiny apartment in San Francisco. I am so glad that we spent nine years together when we were young, and I am even gladder that, after going in different directions and living half a continent apart, I feel as if I could write another book with the energy and ideas we create when we are together.

This book was completed in large part because of Andy Hamp's love and support. I was stoked when Andy showed up at my Ph.D. defense party just after midnight and even happier when he was still there at 4:00 A.M. dancing with me to "Black Hole Sun" next to Anna and John. Over the next five years, as the chaos of this project and a new career left me sleeping on couches in Jackson Heights, renting a quirky in-law apartment in the Chippewa Valley, and living just beyond the exurbs of Dayton, Ohio, Andy's open-mindedness and flexibility allowed me to follow my intellect. With all the distance in our Delta Skymiles Amex lifestyle, the moments we spend together at the airport, in hotels, in our living room in Minneapolis, and on my back porch in Richmond are precious to me. The tension between movement and personal connection is the central theme of this book, and Andy has helped me transform many moments of uncertainty into moments of pleasure.

DEREGULATING
DESIRE

Beth Skrondal never followed the course that was charted for her as a young white woman in the mid-1960s. When she graduated from high school, most of her peers quickly settled down, married, and had children. Refusing the cultural imperative to domesticate, Skrondal moved to San Francisco and lived in Haight-Ashbury during the summer of love. As the counterculture cooled at the end of the decade, she decided to pack up her things and leave for Miami, where she began a job as a flight attendant for National Airlines. Skrondal became an activist in her new workplace, and in 1973 she mounted a successful campaign for president of her Transport Workers Union local. For the next three decades, Skrondal was on the front lines of cultural and economic change in the airline industry and built a career that took her to Pan American World Airways in 1980 and then to United Airlines in 1985. Skrondal never married, and by the 1990s she had moved back to San Francisco, where she lived on her own in a Pacific Heights apartment just upstairs from her friend Stan Kiino, a gay man who had also spent twenty-five years flying for Pan Am and United and who also spent the majority of his adult life single. Skrondal and Kiino both divided their time among union activism, socializing with family and friends, and working the giant Boeing 747 on trips to Shanghai, Hong Kong, and Sydney.[1]

Skrondal's activism often garnered widespread attention. In 1975, for example, she and her coworkers shut down National Airlines for 127 days when they went on strike to protest long hours and low pay.[2] Although headline-making advances have invigorated Skrondal, she insists that her day-to-day life as a single woman has been the central motivation for her activism. "My little thing has always been single people," Skrondal observed as she described why she continues to build the labor movement. "No 'rights' are ever discussed for single people." Skrondal pointed out that staying single has come with a significant cost for many workers like her. As she began her career in the late 1960s, the employers of teachers, nurses, flight attendants, and other feminized professionals explicitly argued that women's future husbands would meet their long-term economic needs. Most airlines thus paid flight attendants far less than workers in other trades and excluded them from the most lucrative retirement benefits. Despite having full-time jobs in a heavily unionized industry that was recognized for high wages, Skrondal and other flight attendants who chose to stay single would permanently lack the robust pay and job security that the airlines guaranteed to all of their male coworkers. To challenge that disparity, and because they refused to allow corporations to determine their relationship to bedrock cultural institutions such as marriage, monogamy, and domesticity, Skrondal and her flight attendant colleagues built a workplace activist movement to win political power and material resources for people who live beyond the boundary of the traditional family.

Skrondal's lifelong experience as a single person, as a world traveler, and as an activist has certainly been eventful; she has participated in some of the most vibrant and most contentious moments in late-twentieth-century U.S. politics. But her life course is by no means exceptional. By the year 2000, most people's personal lives resembled Skrondal's, as they lived outside the nuclear family. People in all demographic groups were more likely to remain single, to marry later, to become solo parents, and to choose same-sex relationships. Between 1950 and 2000, for example, the percentage of the population living alone tripled.[3] In 2010, a single woman breadwinner headed 40 percent of all families,[4] and half of all children grew up without married parents.[5] Therefore, although Skrondal's journey transgressed the norms of middle-class femininity in the 1960s, a young woman's decision to remain single, to forgo motherhood, and to move across the country to pursue personal and professional opportunities would be unremarkable by today's standards.

While the nuclear family has receded as the dominant form of kinship, the economy has not kept pace with the social transformation. The labor market has changed drastically since Beth Skrondal began her career. In a highly competitive global economy, companies in most industries have phased out the free health insurance, the company-paid pensions, and the high pay that allowed Skrondal's male colleagues to be breadwinners for their wives and children. But instead of replacing the family wage with a new system that meets the needs of today's more flexible kinship networks, most employers have eliminated those material resources entirely. Therefore, as real wages have fallen for all but the most privileged workers since 1970,[6] the vast majority of today's families are struggling to do more with less.

Despite these pressures, critical analysis of the pay, benefits, and time off that all families need is absent from most mainstream political debates. The changing nature of marriage and domesticity has certainly produced a searing controversy over the past four decades. Yet in both conservatives' push for a return to traditional "family values," for example, or liberals' bid for same-sex "marriage equality," labor and work are elusive concepts. These movements indeed make economic claims, as they both argue that marriage and domesticity fill emotional and financial voids in people's lives. Neither side, however, addresses how falling wages, rising insurance costs, and far longer workdays are changing the nature of marriage and the family. For three decades, flight attendants like Beth Skrondal have challenged that erasure and have insisted that for both people who have chosen heterosexual nuclear domesticity and those who have less conventional intimate networks, strong families depend on a living wage and reasonable work hours. Through their unions, and via the coalitions they have forged with feminist and LGBT organizers, flight attendants have built a social movement that has inserted the workplace back into the wider cultural debate about sexuality, family, and kinship in the twenty-first century. That movement—which has transformed the airline industry over the past four decades—is the subject of this book.

"Tell Me about Your Life!": The Political Economy of the Stewardess Past

Marriage, domesticity, and heterosexuality are keywords for flight attendant activists because managers have always used these concepts to assign value to the profession. Between 1930 and 1965, the category of the family helped make flight attendants the lowest-paid employees in the airline industry. The major carriers framed the flight attendant workforce with cultural assumptions that husbands should be breadwinners for their families and that wives should perform unpaid reproductive labor in the domestic sphere. Because top executives explicitly argued that a woman's long-term social role was to be a wife and not a worker, and thus that flight attendants did not deserve a family wage, flight attendants at some carriers made 20 percent less than men in comparably skilled trades.[7] Nevertheless, as the industry boomed in the immediate postwar era, flight attendants worked in one of the most mobile, cosmopolitan, and alluring jobs in the entire economy. That tension—between a vast cultural opportunity and limited economic resources—set the stage for the rise of a dynamic workplace activist movement among flight attendants.

The airlines' explicit use of gender and race as organizing concepts for labor was by no means new in the transport industry. Since the middle of the nineteenth century, for example, the railroads had hired African American men to provide onboard service as Pullman porters. Blackness served two purposes for management in that case. First, as black men performed servile labor for white travelers, those passengers would presumably reap the psychological rewards of white supremacy, which would enhance overall customer satisfaction among whites and thus stimulate demand for train tickets. Second, assumptions about black men's racial inferiority and innate servility helped mitigate the gender and sexual anxieties that would have followed white men doing what was imagined to be docile, unmanly work.[8]

Although airline executives operated in the same system of patriarchy and white supremacy as their railroad counterparts, they used a different calculus of gender and race to staff transportation aloft. From the airline's fledgling days in the 1930s, most airlines hired only young, single white women for regular cabin crew positions.[9] Management's demographic decision stemmed from the most pressing economic problem during the industry's early days: chronic accidents. As the airlines scrambled for market share in a new and unregulated industry, they rapidly deployed untested technology, which caused scores of high-profile crashes. The industry's financial stability in the 1930s thus rested on its ability to prove that flying was safe. As historian Kathleen Barry argues in *Femininity in Flight,* airline managers leveraged the intersection of whiteness and womanhood to make their claim about safety. By making the pilot and flight attendant labor groups all white, the airlines used assumptions that white people are scientific, rational, and technically competent to calm passengers' nerves.[10] Meanwhile, since the dominant culture assumed that middle-class white women were vulnerable and in need of protection, their labor would help turn the airline cabin into a space of safety and comfort.[11] If, managers asked the public, a delicate young white woman could work on an airplane every day, how could a commanding businessman be afraid to take a single airplane ride? Touting those social differences, the airlines chose highly gendered terms for the new profession: "stewardess," referencing a feminized version of elite steamship service work, or "hostess," channeling the white middle-class home. From their earliest days aloft, flight attendants' labor was defined in terms of the cultural categories of femininity and domesticity.

As the airline industry became safer and more successful in the 1940s and 1950s, a tension began to emerge in the story that airlines were telling about their stewardesses. Managers packaged stewardesses with conventional, mid-century ideas about white middle-class femininity. Projecting the stewardess as an attractive but modest "girl next door,"[12] the major carriers clad young women in the conservative attire common in other feminized trades: starched blouses, knee-length skirts, low heels, and conventional hairstyles. But unlike most pink-collar jobs that placed women under the physical oversight of male higher-ups, midcentury stewardesses were self-managed and highly mobile. Though the limited route systems of the 1930s kept stewardesses relatively close to home, subsequent technological advances gave the profession a global reach. In 1953, for example, American Airlines introduced nonstop, coast-to-coast service with the Douglas DC-7. Four years later, TWA took delivery of the sleek Lockheed Starliner, which could carry a stewardess from San Francisco to Paris during a single work shift. While their paychecks were still comparable to those of secretaries, nurses, and teachers, the fast, safe, luxurious airliners of the 1950s gave stewardesses a mobility unimaginable to most other middle-class white women.

The opportunity to travel the world made the stewardess profession highly alluring to young women regardless of its low pay. Georgia Nielsen, who would work the skies for forty-two years, said that she originally chose the job "because it was exciting, and because it gave you mobility." After growing up on a farm in Kansas, Nielsen traveled west, where she ended up working as a bank teller in Colorado Springs and then as a secretary at Denver University. "I was pushing twenty-two and not married, so my options were very limited," Nielsen recalled with a laugh as she described looking for a means to continue her independent life. That opportunity soon surfaced in the airline industry. In May 1960, Nielsen reported for duty at Chicago's Midway Airport as a stewardess for United Airlines. The rhythm of her new career made Nielsen an object of fascination for women friends who had followed a more traditional path through marriage and domesticity. "I transferred to the Los Angeles base so I could fly to Hawaii," Nielsen reminisced. "Then I moved to New York and lived on the Upper East Side. [My friends] had their babies, and they would say to me, 'Tell me about your life!'"[13] By becoming a stewardess, Nielsen was able to remain within the domain of middle-class femininity that otherwise would have channeled her out of the workforce, while pursuing a highly mobile lifestyle that was ordinarily reserved for men.

Although the image of the "girl next door" packaged the stewardess profession in wholesomeness, work schedules that kept women away from home for days or weeks at a time nevertheless threatened the established gender order of the mid-twentieth century. Airline executives attempted to neutralize that threat by offering stewardesses less pay and fewer benefits than they provided for men. Some companies, for example, continued to enforce depression-era restrictions on married women's wage labor, which forced stewardesses to choose between a job and a husband and which artificially shortened many stewardesses' careers.[14] For those who opted to remain on the job, hourly wages at most carriers were lower than those for baggage handlers, ticket agents, and middle managers. Stewardesses lacked the protective work rules that guaranteed male airline workers shorter shifts and more days off and were categorically ineligible for the pension supplement programs that augmented pilots' and managers' retirement income.[15] Because they were denied the longevity pay and the retirement security that allowed airline men to be breadwinners for their families, the most direct route to long-term economic security for many young stewardesses was to leave the airline industry and to get married. Therefore, while stewardesses' unprecedented physical mobility constituted a sexual transgression for young white women, low pay helped ensure that the transgression would quickly end in conventional middle-class domesticity.[16]

By the end of the 1950s, the ideology of the family had left managers and stewardesses in an increasingly untenable position. Pan Am had introduced the Boeing 707, a jet airplane that would double the speed of air travel and drastically reduce its cost. Rapid technological advances allowed the airlines to launch new routes that spanned the globe and to hire thousands of new stewardesses. Downtown layovers in Boston, Brussels, and Buenos Aires aroused new interests and new desires in stewardesses. Inequitable employment policies, however, left stewardesses without the material resources to fulfill many of those desires, pushing them to discard their careers and the new ideas that flying fostered. Many stewardesses accepted that jarring transition in the industry's early days. But as the 1960s approached, and as culture changed at the dawn of the jet age, management's mandate for temporary, low-wage stewardess labor quickly unraveled.

When a 30 Percent Raise Is Still Not Enough: The Social Transformation of the 1960s and 1970s

Space Age brands reveal that the airlines were undergoing a technological transformation in the 1960s. But as American introduced its "Astrojets," as TWA touted its "StarStream 707s," and as Braniff rolled out its "El Dorado Superjets," the industry was also involved in a social transformation. In the major cities where most stewardesses were based, activists in a new upsurge of political movements were exploring new ways of living and loving. They demanded the right to stay single, to cohabitate with friends and lovers, to complement marriage with dual careers, and to forge new identities as feminists, bisexuals, lesbians, and gays. In many cases, stewardesses joined these movements and began to argue that new kinship networks would require new economic resources. By demanding the right to be breadwinners for their families, stewardess activists inverted the argument that airline managers had been making about family since the 1930s. Whereas the major carriers had leveraged marriage, domesticity, and heterosexuality to make stewardesses work for less, the new organizers used the domain of sexuality to secure political power and financial resources for front-line employees.

The new wave of mobilization began as the "sexual revolution" of the 1960s amplified the already significant tension between airline managers and stewardesses. With the explicit representation of sexuality becoming more acceptable in middle-class settings, the airlines made stewardesses' bodies increasingly central to their brand identities. Fashion designers rolled out new stewardess uniforms, tightening blouses, lowering necklines, and raising skirts. Advertisers promoted the racy new uniforms with provocative media campaigns. Beth Skrondal's employer, National Airlines, for example, gave each of its jets a woman's name and then created television spots featuring a stewardess with the same name saying, "Come fly me!" Men in the audience would see the aircraft on the screen but recognize that they were being invited to "come fly" the stewardess.[17] Though titillating new marketing images were in part a consequence of the loosening of conventional ideas about sex, the airlines put even tighter constraints on stewardesses during the sexual revolution. To further increase the likelihood that stewardesses were young, attractive, and sexually available to male passengers, some carriers augmented previous marriage bans with new rules that grounded stewardesses on their thirtieth birthday, a policy that forced workers to sacrifice their careers and forfeit their pensions.[18] By the middle of the decade, as the airlines demanded greater sexual mobility in exchange for fewer resources, the stewardess profession openly transgressed the ideology of domesticity while making young women increasingly dependent on the traditional nuclear family to meet their long-term economic needs.

The emergence of vigorous social movements in the mid-1960s gave stewardesses a new set of conceptual tools to contest these inequities. The women's liberation movement, for example, argued that in a patriarchal society, men exploit women's bodies, restrict their desires, and strip them of economic necessities. Gay liberationists, meanwhile, insisted that traditional marriage and monogamy were outmoded ideals that limited self-expression and curtailed sexual freedom. A nascent transgender liberation movement was denaturalizing gender and providing new critical concepts to challenge the extreme, caricatured version of femininity that the airlines were selling on television. These pointed, comprehensive critiques of sexuality emboldened activists and provided a fresh intellectual framework that undermined management's long-standing rationalization for stewardesses' disparate treatment.

The new stewardess activists had two goals as they brought feminist and gay liberationist criticisms to their workplace. First, they mobilized to end the recruitment and retention programs that had limited employment to single, childless, conventionally attractive, young white women. Front-line activists filed union grievances, built coalitions with feminist and antiracist organizations, sued the airlines, and took their case all the way to the Fifth Circuit Federal Court of Appeals, which in the landmark 1971 ruling for the case *Diaz v. Pan Am* stripped managers of the right to enforce age limits, marriage bans, and other blatantly sexist practices.[19] As they pushed to end overt sex discrimination, activists renamed their profession, discarding "stewardess" and the other gendered terms that management had chosen and replacing them with the neutral descriptor "flight attendant." But even after historic legal advances turned short-term jobs into lifetime careers, new flight attendants still earned considerably less than workers in other airline trades. Closing that pay gap thus became the movement's second goal. Organizers demanded large raises that would far outpace pay bumps for other groups and pushed to end the pension and work rule disparities that had compounded economic discrimination against flight attendants.

By the end of the 1970s, flight attendant activists had delivered on those demands. At Continental Airlines, for example, rank-and-file flight attendants walked off the job during the holiday rush just three weeks before Christmas 1980. Thwarting management's effort to replace union members with strikebreakers, flight attendants ended up winning a 39 percent raise in a new three-year contract that increased top pay to the equivalent of $86,000 a year in 2015 dollars.[20] After similar brinksmanship, front-line workers at American, TWA, Pan Am, and other leading airlines also won double-digit annual pay hikes. By gaining access to generous compensation that had once been reserved for autoworkers, meatpackers, building tradesmen, and truck drivers, flight attendants upended a long-standing relationship between family and work in the U.S. economy. While large paychecks for unionized workingmen had built the modern U.S. middle class in the decades after the Great Depression, they had also reinforced conventional ideas about gender and sexuality because the notion of the family breadwinner helped justify men's dominance and women's dependence.[21] In the airline industry, however, the string of union victories had the opposite cultural consequence.

After flight attendant activists at Continental delivered a 39 percent raise to an almost all-woman workforce, marriage and domesticity were no longer the sole routes to young women's economic security. Higher pay, more time off, and enhanced retirement income gave flight attendants vast new ability to control their relationship to domesticity, kinship, procreation, and sexual pleasure. Therefore, whereas breadwinner paychecks had previously reinforced the cultural ideology of the nuclear family, in the 1970s the workplace was becoming a driving force for social change.

The Family Values Economy

The string of feminist union victories at the major airlines invigorated activists, but it was a deeply threatening prospect for corporate managers in all industries. Flight attendants' large new paychecks proved that the social movements of the 1960s and 1970s could deliver substantive economic gains to much of the U.S. workforce, especially to the women, people of color, and other oppressed groups that had been locked out of the family wage system since its emergence in the mid-nineteenth century. Rapid economic advances for marginal workers were particularly worrying to business leaders because they came at a time when corporations were already facing vast new macro-economic pressures. In November 1973, the U.S. economy entered its longest and deepest recession since the Great Depression. As the economy contracted, and as firms faced new, low-cost competition from emerging economies in Southeast Asia and Latin America, corporate profits fell sharply. Despite the downturn, inflation intensified and interest rates rose as the government continued to borrow to fund a large military and a robust social safety net. By the middle of the 1970s, the postwar boom had gone bust and executives struggled to mitigate soaring operating costs and plummeting revenues.

Recognizing that they faced a cultural and economic challenge in the 1970s, business leaders responded by making a new political argument about both. That argument rested on what managers maintained had been a devaluation of hard work. They acknowledged that the high taxes, generous welfare benefits, and protective government regulation that defined the mid-twentieth-century economy had benefited civil rights activists, feminists, students, and environmentalists. But while those policies helped aggrieved groups surge forward, business leaders contended that they stifled the economy and took opportunities away from hardworking American families. To restore work opportunities for ordinary people, managers and their allies pushed for reforms that would roll back taxes, welfare, and regulation, reforms that they insisted would bolster the bedrock cultural values that had previously made America strong: independence, thrift, deferred gratification, self-denial, and personal responsibility.

Timeless ideals about family and work helped big business produce new momentum for its cause. U.S. corporations had mobilized against taxes, welfare, and regulation for over a century. But as historian Kim Phillips-Fein argues, they enjoyed unprecedented success in the 1970s, when they began to emulate the mass mobilization strategy of the left.[22] By the middle of the decade, corporate executives had built a new, pro-business activist movement that they hoped would appeal not just to elite professionals but also to a wide swath of the U.S. middle class. To make that coalition as broad as possible, pro-business activists framed their agenda not in terms of the benefits it would provide to corporations or high-income individuals but rather as a means to address the pocketbook issues of ordinary families that were struggling in the 1970s. Taxes, they insisted, took money out of breadwinners' much-deserved paychecks and transferred it to aggrieved groups who eschewed the work ethic. Government regulation put fetters on companies and prevented them from creating jobs for responsible people who wanted to work. By making the traditional American breadwinner the rhetorical centerpiece of their movement, pro-business activists were able to frame upwardly redistributive, neoliberal policies—from regressive taxation to deregulation, privatization, and anti-unionism[23]—as pro-family, pro-work reforms.

Big business's appeal to hardworking families resonated in part because of a wider political argument that the family was in jeopardy in the 1970s. That argument originated in a resurgence of conservative religious activism. In Southern California's pristine new megachurches, through innovative media corporations such as Pat Robertson's Christian Broadcasting Network and political organizations including James Dobson's Focus on the Family, a new cohort of evangelical Protestant leaders insisted that the social transformations of the 1960s and 1970s had undermined the nuclear family. Religious activists took an overt and often vitriolic antifeminist, antigay, and antiabortion stance, asserting that radical feminist critiques of marriage, gay liberationist dissent from domesticity, and increasingly permissive cultural attitudes about premarital sex, cohabitation, and single parenthood compromised the cultural values that had provided strength and stability for U.S. society.[24] Contending that social change represented an attack on the family, the new religious movement aimed to build coalitions with allies that would defend the family. By promising to create new opportunities for ordinary people who valued family and work, the pro-business activist movement framed itself as one of those allies.

From radical feminists to religious conservatives, political activists of all affinities argued that the family faced vast pressures in the 1970s. What the emerging alliance between the pro-business and pro-family movements added to the debate, however, was that morality—and not economics—was the root cause of those pressures. Rather than focus on wage stagnation, for example, the new movement talked about personal responsibility and deferred gratification, maintaining that poverty and welfare use were a consequence of families with the wrong values. Rather than discuss work rules, health insurance, or retirement benefits, they talked about independence, self-reliance, and thrift, arguing that families with the right values took care of themselves and had no need for the social programs that high taxes paid for. Whereas the family wage had created the mid-twentieth-century middle class, the new pro-business, pro-family activists claimed that family values would build the middle class of the twenty-first century. For the new coalition, domesticity and hard work would be the organizing principles of a new society. Thus, as historian Bethany Moreton incisively argues, "Family values are an indispensable element of the global service economy, and not a distraction from it."[25]

Although the pro-business activist movement's focus on family values was only one of many interventions in the relationship between family and work in the 1970s, it would have significant political consequences. Perhaps most importantly, framing the workplace in terms of morality and not in terms of economics undermined what had previously been widespread support for the labor movement and for the welfare state among the middle class, particularly among white men in the middle class. According to historian Robert Self, in the decades after 1930, many white men recognized that union contracts, government regulation, and the social safety net delivered the resources they needed to be breadwinners for their families. White racial nationalism, heteropatriarchy, and pro-union, pro-welfare politics all aligned in a mid-twentieth-century paradigm that Self calls "breadwinner liberalism."[26] But after 1970, and in a new formation that Self describes as "breadwinner conservatism," white men began to see state intervention as a threat to their role as providers. Being a successful breadwinner would require eliminating the government regulation that prevented employers from creating work opportunities, as well as cutting the taxes that transferred workingmen's money to poor people with the wrong values. As they began to interpret values-driven policies as aligned with their own interests, a growing number of working-class and middle-class white men joined a political coalition with big business to promote these policies, and they continued to support that coalition even when it attacked the labor movement.

Those attacks were particularly aggressive in the airline industry. In October 1978, after a vigorous lobbying effort from the pro-business activist movement, Congress passed the Airline Deregulation Act, which opened the industry to new competition from upstart airlines that hired low-wage, non-union workers. To bring their operating costs in line with the new carriers, executives at the established companies pushed flight attendants and other employees to forfeit the gains they had made in the 1960s and 1970s. Workers at Eastern, United, Continental, and other airlines struck in protest, and long, bitter labor disputes ensued. At TWA, for example, managers locked flight attendants out of the workplace for almost three years in the late 1980s after union leaders refused to accept a concessionary contract that would have reduced overall compensation by almost 45 percent.[27] The U.S. Supreme Court finally forced TWA to rehire the flight attendants in 1989, but only after they agreed to accept the majority of the cutbacks that management originally proposed.

TWA's unilateral action against flight attendants provided a decisive economic victory for management, lowering the airline's operating costs and weakening its unions. But while it saved TWA money, the campaign against flight attendants also revealed the immense tenuousness of big business's political position in the 1980s and 1990s. The alliance between pro-business and pro-family activists had elevated the concept of domesticity by arguing that thrift, independence, personal responsibility, and other family values would sustain people in a changing economy. Domesticity would, in the words of Christopher Lasch, be a "haven in a heartless world," providing both emotional and economic security.[28] But after the TWA affair, and in the wake of similar events in the mining, meatpacking, and automotive industries, the domestic sphere had become a space of scarcity and pain, as parents and children were forced to adjust to longer workdays and far smaller paychecks. Although big business had justified deregulation, tax cuts, and welfare rollbacks by claiming that they would restore the family ethic and the work ethic, it seemed to most workers that neoliberal reforms had rapidly devalued both family and work. Flight attendants' political task as the 1990s approached, then, was to highlight the striking inconsistencies in corporations' argument about work and family and to offer a different political agenda that would mobilize their coworkers against an inequitable economy.

Flight Attendant Unions and the Decline of the Traditional Family

The disconnect between the story that big business was telling about family and the new pressures on most people's kinship networks provided an opportunity for workplace activists. Corporations made significant economic gains in the 1970s and 1980s in part because they delivered a compelling cultural argument about the past and about the future. Even though economic data clearly contradicted their analysis, business leaders were able to build a coalition because they referenced the moral values that many people held dear. For unions to counteract big business's momentum, they would have to tell a different story about those values, presenting an alternative narrative about the family ethic and the work ethic that would more clearly resonate with the dynamics in people's personal and professional lives. Since the early 1970s, flight attendant unionists had been making just such a case. They insisted that workers need better pay and more time off, not *despite* the fact that the family has changed but *because* the family has changed. Workers deserve new financial resources because they are choosing a wide variety of domestic arrangements; some are pursuing traditional heterosexual marriage like many of their parents and grandparents, and many others are staying single, cohabitating with friends in mixed households, and becoming sole breadwinners for their children. Regardless of which route workers take, flight attendants activists have argued, better pay and benefits help transform the family from a site of scarcity into a site of strength and satisfaction. Whereas the pro-business activist movement has used old ideas about sexuality to justify upward redistribution, the flight attendant activists of the 1990s and 2000s have made new claims about sexuality to advocate for a more equitable economy.

Flight attendants' counterargument about family and work has often delivered concrete economic gains. In the spring of 1997, for example, activists in United Airlines' San Francisco flight attendant base joined forces with local LGBT and HIV/AIDS organizers to demand medical and retirement benefits for workers with same- or opposite-sex unmarried partners. Fifty-one percent of United flight attendants were single at the time, and for decades the company had saved money by using marriage as a means to deny family employment benefits to the majority of the workforce.[29] Unwilling to give up those cost savings, United managers dismissed the flight attendants' overture. For the next twenty-seven months, the grassroots coalition mounted a campaign of street theater and civil disobedience that eventually compelled United to reverse course and offer the medical and retirement coverage. By the year 2000, every U.S. airline had followed suit, which for the first time brought family benefits to tens of thousands of employees who were unable or unwilling to marry their lovers.[30]

The San Francisco coalition overcame immense odds as it pushed a corporation to provide benefits that met the needs of a majority of workers' families.

Workplace activists face undeniable difficulties at the outset of the twenty-first century: the labor movement lost half its members in the 1980s after the rapid implementation of neoliberal policies, and just 7 percent of private-sector workers belong to unions—the lowest rate since management's open-shop drive of the early 1920s.[31] But despite that painful context for activists, the San Francisco campaign was able to overtly politicize the category of the family to deliver material goods that would have been unattainable even at labor's high-water mark in the 1960s. Family benefits were undoubtedly lucrative in the mid-twentieth century, but they were allotted in the narrowest possible terms and available only through legal heterosexual marriage. Therefore, even if companies had kept the same benefit programs from the 1950s, far fewer people would have been able to access them after 1970 because households made up of single, divorced, and cohabitating people had always been categorically ineligible. After the San Francisco case, however, access to benefits rested on signing a sworn affidavit that documented a committed relationship. There was no requirement for a legal marriage, for cohabitation, or for financial interdependence. For the first time ever, the airlines' family benefits programs fit the needs of a highly mobile transport workforce that had always crossed national, cultural, intimate, and sexual boundaries. A sustained, explicit critique of the ideology of the nuclear family helped yield a victory at a historical moment when many other union initiatives had failed.

Flight Plan: Labor Histories, Queer Futures

As it situates the flight attendant union movement in the history of debates about family and work, this book offers both an economic and a cultural analysis. On the first level, the book provides a labor history, theorizing collective bargaining, direct action protest, and the elements of political economy: macroeconomic change, government regulation, and financial organization. The second level addresses how cultural discourse shapes economic policy. Most of the flight attendants who appear in the narrative were active participants in the cultural movements of the late twentieth century, joining such groups as the Kansas City Women's Liberation Union in the early 1970s, living in San Francisco's Castro district during gay liberation, majoring in women's studies while in college in the 1980s, or leading LGBT activist groups such as the Harvey Milk Democratic Club in the 1990s and 2000s. For all of these activists, however, the workplace has been the primary venue to enact feminist and gay politics. This history of flight attendants thus situates post-1970 trade unionism in the history of the women's movement, of lesbian and gay liberation, and of LGBT and queer mobilization.

Chapters 1 and 2 trace flight attendant activists' fight to win a family wage. Placing the flight attendant profession in the context of the cultural ideology of domesticity, Chapter 1 analyzes the causes of the flight attendant upsurge of the mid-1970s. The chapter provides an ethnographic analysis of the early careers of straight, lesbian, and gay flight attendants who worked during the mid-twentieth century, and a labor history of the confrontation between those flight attendants and the airlines that began in 1975. Both the ethnography and the labor history show how ideas about domesticity left flight attendants with lower wages than men and how alliances with the decade's feminist and gay liberation movements pushed flight attendants to confront those disparities. Chapter 2 documents the political economic consequences of flight attendants' activism, chronicling the successful struggle that won both the time off and the money necessary for flight attendants to be breadwinners for their families. The chapter focuses on a grassroots campaign among flight attendants at TWA, United, American, and other carriers in the late 1970s, a movement that ousted the male-led industrial unions, formed independent rank-and-file flight attendant unions, and mounted an aggressive new economic strategy against the airlines. Through their efforts, activists made unprecedented progress in closing the pay and benefit gap between flight attendants and other airline workers.

The next two chapters historicize the rise of the family values economy in the late 1970s and 1980s and show how these new cultural dynamics compromised flight attendants' economic gains. Chapter 3 presents the intellectual foundations of the Airline Deregulation Act of 1978, arguing that its backers justified the act as a pro-work, pro-family intervention in public policy and tracing how their justification rationalized harsh corporate countermobilization against flight attendants. Chapter 4, meanwhile, traces Wall Street's role in the elevation of domesticity as a cultural concept. As the banking industry drastically increased its influence over the U.S. economy in the 1980s, Wall Street financiers took over Eastern, Continental, TWA, and other major airlines, contending that a new injection of capital would leave airlines better able to create work opportunities for ordinary Americans. Once in control of the airlines, the new banker managers cut wages for all workers, reserving the deepest cuts for flight attendants. Chapter 4 analyzes how the ideas about the traditional male breadwinner and women's economic dependency structured the struggle between Wall Street and flight attendants. Both chapters argue that reforms packaged as a means to incentivize domesticity and hard work eliminated the family wage for all but the most privileged workers.

Whereas the middle chapters of the book reveal the dynamics that facilitated the rise of the family values economy, Chapters 5 and 6 focus on the process of contesting those dynamics. Chapter 5 unpacks the new opportunities that have opened up for activists in the twenty-first century. The chapter documents the grassroots campaign among United Airlines flight attendants and LGBT activists in San Francisco that pushed for better pay and better benefits for the flexible kinship networks in which most flight attendants live. Chapter 6 traces the new challenges that activists have faced amid neoliberal reforms, centering on a bitter dispute between flight attendants for American Airlines and TWA when their employers merged in 2001. The struggle between American and TWA activists exposes the enduring importance of feminist commitments to justice to flight attendant activism in the twenty-first century.

Notwithstanding the many examples of rank-and-file workers' political advances in this text, the post-1970 period has by all accounts been an extremely difficult one for trade unions. Organized labor's crisis does not, however, mean that all social movements have receded. For example, the gay and lesbian liberation struggle that had helped deliver watershed advances to flight attendants in the 1970s has given way to the modern LGBT rights movement, which has flourished since 1990. LGBT activists have won lucrative new protections for U.S. workers in an era when many unions have lost the ability to deliver those protections. By the turn of the millennium, almost all Fortune 500 corporations included sexual orientation in their equal employment opportunity statements, and a growing number were providing explicit antidiscrimination language for transgender and gender nonconforming people.[32]

Without a broad-based movement for economic justice, however, cultural struggles like those waged by mainstream LGBT leaders have often failed to address the needs of working people like flight attendants. The rapid string of same-sex marriage victories in the 2010s, for example, delivered both economic security and social acceptance for some LGBT people, bringing legal recognition for relationships and corresponding tax and employment benefits. But by defining the enfranchised LGBT person as married and gainfully employed, these particular gay rights advances reinforced the core logic of the family values economy: that domesticity and hard work should be the organizing principles of society. As Lisa Duggan argues in her widely quoted analysis of "homonormativity," the mainstream LGBT rights framework often "upholds rather than contests the broader neoliberal imperatives of privatization and personal responsibility."[33] Similarly, according to the more recent work of legal scholar Dean Spade, the bid for LGBT protection through hate crimes legislation has often lent political credibility and material support to the system of mass incarceration that has otherwise inflicted widespread racial and sexual violence against queer and especially transgender people.[34] Because of this blinkered agenda, and despite four decades of feminist activism in the airline industry, flight attendants' pressing economic needs have often been invisible in the core agenda of national LGBT rights organizations like the Human Rights Campaign.

Lisa Duggan, Dean Spade, and many others have made these critiques brilliantly, transforming social movements while doing so. There has, however, been far less concrete historical analysis of feminist and queer political mobilization that has moved beyond the marriage rights and equality claims of middle-class families. Over four decades of union activism, flight attendants provide one such example. Whether on the picket line against sexist age restrictions or for a big raise, flight attendants compel feminist and queer activists to take up issues of economic justice. Flight attendant unions have demonstrated that to expand the boundaries of sexual expression and of kinship, activists must push for a fairer overall economy: for a living wage, for safe and dignified working conditions, and for time outside work. In an age when family values have been offered as a substitute for a fair economy, and as flight attendants have challenged that substitution, their activism helps us recognize that domesticity and hard work are the foundational ideologies of an economy that dispossesses not just queer people but all working people. In the context of the flight attendant union movement, labor history contributes to the struggle for justice for lesbian, gay, bisexual, transgender, and queer people. Indeed, when Beth Skrondal reflected on her life and moved single people from the margin to the center of debates about family and work, she imagined a queer future, a time when traditional family values are not the sole organizing principle of society. This book is a history of that future.

I

DOMESTICITY AND
ITS DISCONTENTS

*The Flight Attendant Union
Upsurge of the Mid-1970s*

L abor unrest swept across the airline industry during the long days of the summer of 1976. Flight attendants for the major carriers were demanding double-digit pay increases and shorter hours, threatening to strike during the peak vacation season if managers failed to comply. Though flight attendant contract talks brought unprecedented acrimony that summer, workplace activism was not new to the trade. A decade earlier, flight attendants—whom most airlines still called "stewardesses"—had joined forces with an increasingly vocal and well-organized women's liberation movement to demand an end to overtly sexist employment practices. The coalition prevailed on many of its demands, and by 1975 most companies had been forced to drop earlier requirements that all stewardesses be young, single, childless white women.[1] But rather than placate the workforce, activists' advances stoked deeper grievances among the flight attendant ranks. By the mid-1970s, discontent had spread from its original roots among a relatively narrow group of committed feminists, lesbians, and union militants to a wide swath of workforce. Front-line American Airlines flight attendants, for example, rejected two contract proposals from management in 1975 and 1976, voting to strike in pursuit of large wage increases rather than compromise with the company's executives. During the American standoff, National Airlines flight attendants shuttered their employer with a four-month work stoppage.[2] Six months later, flight attendants for TWA made headlines as they came within hours of a walkout during the travel rush on Bicentennial Weekend, 1976.

Front-line activists embraced militant new strategies as they turned their attention to the vast economic inequities in their workplace. Flight attendants recognized that even after the successful pushback against overt sex discrimination in the early 1970s, workers at some carriers were still paid 20 percent less than the next-lowest-paid group of airline employees.[3] Retirement benefits widened the compensation gap, as flight attendants were denied the lucrative pensions guaranteed to pilots, machinists, and ground crews. Thus, despite management's decision to grant activists some concessions around age limits and marriage restrictions, the airlines remained firmly committed to the gendered disparities in wages, benefits, and work rules that had defined the labor economics of the industry since its fledgling days.

Although the picket line and the bargaining table had become the primary venues for struggle between activists and the airlines, the roots of the flight attendant pay gap lay far beyond the airline industry. Inequitable compensation was a consequence of a set of ideas about gender—in particular, about domesticity—that have organized industrial society for two centuries. With the rise of economies based on wage labor, the cultural value of domesticity became a mechanism to mark the workingman as the primary breadwinner for the family and to frame women as dependent on their husbands for economic sustenance. In her study of the rise of the British labor movement in the first half of the nineteenth century, historian Anna Clark argues that the elevation of domesticity was not a natural consequence of industrialization. Instead, it was the result of the strategic efforts of male trade unionists who hoped to benefit from the emerging bourgeois values of the era.[4] Demanding pay increases that would allow workingmen to support wives and children, labor activists strove to make domesticity both a reward for men's long days in the factory and a mechanism to prove that the working class shared the middle class's commitment to family values such as marriage and monogamy.[5] As domesticity became a payback for hard work and a tool for sexual regulation, working-class women, who could have been imagined as political agents and active participants in the labor movement, were reimagined as passive, dependent wives.

The ideology of domesticity that Clark describes would haunt the U.S. airline industry as workers unionized a hundred years later. In the two decades after 1930, unions made rapid gains in the trades that management had restricted to men: pilots, machinists, ramp service work, and at some carriers, ticket agents. Skill levels varied greatly between those job classifications; most pilots joined major carriers with years of military flying experience, while many baggage handlers were hired straight out of high school with no advanced training. The ideology of domesticity would help union activists win robust wages for airline men on both sides of the skill divide.[6] Leveraging the argument that all men deserved the economic resources to be responsible breadwinners for their families, airline unions secured regular raises, free insurance, and pension benefits for both elite and working-class airline men in the years after World War II.

As domesticity helped activists justify high wages for workingmen, it allowed labor leaders and managers to excuse stewardesses' subordinate position in their workplace and in their unions. Unlike pilots and machinists, who negotiated their own contracts, male higher-ups from the major airline unions represented stewardesses at the bargaining table. At Pan Am, TWA, and Eastern, for example, leaders of the Transport Workers Union sat across from management in stewardess contract talks, while pilot leaders bargained for stewardesses at United, Western, and Braniff. Although collective bargaining entitled many stewardesses to better wages than their counterparts in teaching, clerical work, and other feminized jobs, union higher-ups' and managers' shared cultural assumption that stewardesses were not breadwinners meant that bargaining sessions stopped far short of those for pilots, machinists, and ground crews. Therefore, despite the fact that airlines required most international stewardesses to speak a second language and expected them to draw on the middle-class social skills that came with a college education, they were among the lowest-paid employees on most carriers' property by the 1950s.

With the rise of the women's, gay, and lesbian liberation movements of the 1960s and 1970s, airline managers and union leaders faced a bold new challenge to the stewardess wage gap and to the ideologies of domesticity that upheld it. A new generation of rank-and-file activists—who rejected the gendered term "stewardess" and called themselves "flight attendants"—united around these emerging 1970s critiques of heterosexuality, patriarchy, and domesticity. For the new movement, challenging sexual regulation would require transforming flight attendants from men's economic dependents into breadwinners for their families. A living wage, a pension, and affordable insurance were, activists argued, necessary to sustain the broader forms of kinship that feminists and gay liberationists were advocating. Activists' bid for a family wage touched off a searing new conflict with the airlines in the mid-1970s, since managers remained culturally committed to the ideology of domesticity and to the system of low-wage women's labor that it had justified. This chapter traces the dispute between flight attendants, their unions, and the airlines as it came to an impasse in the mid-1970s.

Stewardess Labor as a Route out of Domesticity

For the activists who confronted their employers in 1976, airline work had always been a reaction to traditional family values. The vast majority of movement participants joined the industry in the decade after 1965. Though Asian American, Latina, African American, and Native American women had picketed, lobbied, and litigated for their right to work the skies, middle-class white women continued to make up the majority of new recruits at the major carriers. Mid-twentieth-century political economy and cultural values would ordinarily have channeled such women toward suburban domesticity. G.I. Bill benefits that guaranteed low-interest suburban home mortgages to white male veterans[7] and union contracts that provided a family wage for white male industrial workers underwrote white women's primary social role as wives and mothers.[8] Although the nuclear family and the male breadwinner were particularly influential cultural forms in the immediate postwar period, historians of the twentieth century have demonstrated a longer-term trend in which a growing number of middle-class white women were staying single, getting divorced, opting not to have children, and otherwise rejecting the conventions of domesticity.[9] Those who worked outside the home, however, often faced a workplace structured around the same patriarchal inequities as the domestic sphere. In nursing, clerical work, teaching, and other feminized trades, women were low-paid subordinates to male higher-ups and had little physical or professional mobility.

The stewardess profession provided an enticing alternative to the other forms of feminized labor. Unlike teaching, nursing, or administrative work, becoming a stewardess gave middle-class white women unprecedented access to an urban, cosmopolitan world, one usually reserved for businessmen. Stewardesses' connection to major cities was a consequence of the operational structure of the airline industry in the mid-twentieth century. Major carriers based flight crews at airports with the highest numbers of flights. While smaller, local-service airlines stationed their workforces in midsized cities, including Portland, San Antonio, and Indianapolis, the vast majority of stewardesses lived in and flew out of the largest cities in the United States: New York, Chicago, Los Angeles, and San Francisco. Given historically low urban real estate prices in an age when the white middle class had left for the suburbs, many stewardesses could afford to live downtown in their domicile city. Freed from the physical and financial responsibilities of home and car ownership and living in neighborhoods with twenty-four-hour services and entertainment, stewardesses could focus time between trips on their social lives. Kathy Lynch, who joined United Airlines' Chicago crew base in the late

1960s, recalls a downtown cosmopolitan world as a key reward of the early days of her career:

> It was a gracious way of life. We had nice apartments. I had a beautiful apartment in a building with a doorman a block from the Water Tower in Downtown Chicago. One of my first trips had a twenty-four-hour layover in Boston—a dream for a kid who had never been out of California. We stayed downtown at the Parker House, in big nice rooms.[10]

Most major airlines gave stewardesses up to four days off in their home domicile cities between trips. But as Lynch indicates, when stewardesses were not home, they were flying trips that lasted between two days and two weeks, punctuated by layovers in other major metropolises both in the United States and abroad. Janet Lhuillier, who worked TWA's European and Mediterranean routes out of New York and Boston in the early 1970s, recalls the pleasure of overseas stopovers between flights:

> We did these trips that went Boston-Paris-Rome-Athens. We had a ball. It was fabulous. . . . They had us eating for free in Athens. There were two restaurants solely paid for by the airline. This little place called the Kasbah. We would just order all these hors d'oeuvres, and the pilots would join us.[11]

Dining with friends and coworkers at a sidewalk cafe in Athens, Janet Lhuillier had been carried by her airline career far beyond the boundaries of domesticity. In an age when the dominant culture steered her white middle-class peers toward the private sphere and the suburban kitchen, Lhuillier spent much of her time in the hotels, bars, restaurants, and airports that most often defined men's urban worlds.

While airline work gave stewardesses unprecedented physical and social mobility, the job also came with significant costs. Most importantly, stewardessing transgressed dominant cultural assumptions that young white women should marry and domesticate, a transgression that implicated both individual stewardesses and the airlines that employed them. Therefore, when airline executives and union higher-ups sat down to negotiate contracts for stewardesses, they used the collective bargaining process to mitigate the anxieties surrounding women's airline work. By paying stewardesses far less than their male counterparts, by discouraging lifetime employment through withholding longevity pay, and by locking stewardesses out of the most lucrative retirement benefits, the airlines could compel individual women to quit their jobs and get married, because doing so would be the only means to long-term financial stability. Union contracts locked these inequities into airline labor economics. In 1972, for example, the average unionized baggage handler at TWA made 24.4 percent more than the average stewardess even though the stewardess job required more education and training.[12]

By 1970, the airlines' strategy had begun to backfire. The low wages and scant benefits that were supposed to regulate stewardesses' sexuality ended up amplifying the profession's transgressiveness. Denied a family wage, stewardesses lacked the economic resources that helped their male counterparts comply with the ideology of domesticity. When the family wage came to the airline industry just after World War II, breadwinner paychecks were meant not just to pay the bills but also to impart cultural values in workers. Earning enough money to buy a house, to save for children's college educations, and to invest for retirement, airline men learned the values of the middle class: thrift, self-denial, deferred gratification, and personal responsibility. Meanwhile, stewardesses were locked out of home ownership and unable to build a nest egg for retirement.

Organizing their lives around limited economic resources and unable to count on lifetime employment, many stewardesses built kinship networks that looked far different from those of male breadwinners or domesticated wives. Staying single, living with friends, and using the household as a space to pool resources, stewardesses often spent what little money remained at the end of the pay period on personal pleasures rather than on planning for the future. Janet Lhuillier describes the social and economic network she built while flying out of TWA's New York base in the early 1970s:

> My girlfriend and I were living with my United friend—six of us in a two-bedroom in Manhattan. But really nice. It was uptown—over by Gracie Mansion. None of us were rich. . . . The problem is that we didn't fly that much so I spent all my money! I was always out doing something![13]

Instead of narrating her household economy in terms of scarcity, Lhuillier recalled sharing a two-bedroom apartment with six friends with great fondness, a time when her life was organized around self-indulgence and fun. Kaye Chandler, who was hired onto TWA's San Francisco crew base in 1968, was even more explicit about the pleasure that came with her departure from domesticity:

In 1968 and 1969 I got really involved with skiing up at Tahoe with some people from the fraternities at San Jose State. When I got based in San Francisco for TWA, I rented a room up at Tahoe and I also rented a house down in Santa Cruz. I would go between the two places and fly in the middle. It was a party. I had lots of cars! Cars were easy, and gas was 25 cents a gallon. I was always involved in my skiing and my sports, and I always had a bit of a different drummer going. When my girlfriends and I would get bored, we would take off and go to Sun Valley or go to Aspen for a week. It was really pretty wild. I didn't think anything of jumping off cliffs with my skis.[14]

Chandler describes a lifeworld normally reserved for men in the late 1960s, one that rejects the responsibilities of domesticity and family in favor of a transient world of sports, cars, and socializing. In a narrative about mobility, adventure, and pleasure, Chandler offers neither an explicitly feminist critique nor an open indictment of the way that sexism limited women's horizons in the 1960s. Nevertheless, Chandler, Lhuillier, and Lynch represent a new generation of women who were using airline work to create social and economic networks that, at least for a time, allowed women to live far beyond the boundaries of the world that traditional family values prescribed for them.

Stewardesses built these networks during a time of rapid social change. Participants in a new upsurge of feminist activism, and in an increasingly visible gay and lesbian liberation movement, were politicizing the decision to stay single, to cohabitate with friends or lovers, and to reject traditional domesticity. The kinship networks of Chandler, Lhuillier, and other stewardesses looked much like those that the new social movements were advocating as a means to challenge the cultural norms of the era. Women's, gay, and lesbian activism would, then, connect stewardesses to a broad cultural debate that would transform their workplace as the 1970s evolved.

The Struggle over Dissident Women's Sexualities in the Airline Industry

With the introduction of the four-hundred-seat Boeing 747 and its eighteen-person cabin crew in December 1969, a growing number of young women chose airline work as a route out of conventional domesticity. But as stewardesses reported for duty at new "jumbo jet" bases such as Miami, New York, and San Francisco, they would do so on the airlines' terms. Managerial policy and union contracts tightly controlled who could be hired, how long a stewardess could remain employed, and how much she could earn. Individual stewardesses thus had little control over the economic resources necessary to sustain the households and kinship networks they built during their first years on the job. As the women's liberation movement made an increasingly bold intervention in political debates, however, stewardesses gained a powerful new means to challenge the airlines' unilateral control of their workplace. By 1970, activists were demanding that front-line stewardesses—and not just managers or male union leaders—shape airline compensation and operational practices.

Particularly visible among these new dissidents was Paula Mariedaughter, who joined TWA in 1968. From her first days at the airline, Mariedaughter was known far beyond her Kansas City crew base. In 1970, she began appearing in a series of glossy, full-page advertisements in the *New York Times*. Wearing false eyelashes and a hairpiece-enhanced bouffant, Mariedaughter smiled for the camera in the first-class cabin of a TWA Boeing 707. She motioned to a lavish spread: platters of appetizers; a full pork roast with candied fruit; a sterling silver coffee service; pies, cakes, and tarts; and a vast selection of wines, spirits, and cordials.[15] Mariedaughter was one of several flight attendants—or hostesses, as TWA still called them—chosen to publicize a redesign of TWA's renowned onboard experience, called "Ambassador Service." To enhance the visibility of the brand refresh, TWA hired the famous Italian fashion designer Valentino to create a new wardrobe for hostesses. Mariedaughter modeled the winter uniform, which included a tight yet angular, deep purple, long-sleeved dress with gold buttons and black lace-up go-go boots. Her image ran in both the *New York Times* spread and glossy internal publications that broadcast Valentino's work to pilots, managers, and other high-ranking TWA employees.

Although advertising agencies used her image to project a sexualized, cosmopolitan version of traditional femininity, Paula Mariedaughter joined the airline industry as part of an intentional effort to reject conventional gender roles. Raised in Miami Springs, Florida, in the 1950s in a G.I. Bill–financed ranch house with married parents and three brothers, Mariedaughter was the child of a father who wanted her "to be a respectable woman and a schoolteacher." The women in Mariedaughter's life, however, provided her with consistent—though clearly subtle—role modeling of alternatives to her father's traditionalism. "My mother was never one of these women who said, 'When are you getting married?'" Mariedaughter recalled. "She wanted me to go to college." Recognizing her mother's insistence that a young woman's life should be more than a rehearsal for marriage and domesticity, Mariedaughter argued,

"My mother wanted to give me wings." In addition to having a close relationship with her mother, Mariedaughter often spent time with an aunt in nearby Miami Beach who always told her to "go out and have a good time and do whatever you want to do." When that aunt's sister got pregnant in high school a generation earlier, the aunt was sent away from her family to avoid the public sexual shaming that would follow her sister. Responding to her aunt and her mother's explicit hope that she would have more opportunities and experience less sexual repression than the earlier generation of women, Mariedaughter quit her administrative job in a Veterans Administration hospital in 1968 and pursued a career as a TWA hostess.[16]

Paula Mariedaughter's arrival in the airline industry would immediately carry her far away from domesticity. At 5'11", Mariedaughter was taller than most women who applied to fly for TWA. Her height provided an initial barrier to employment. Unlike white women of average body size, whom employment recruiters could hire on the spot in any city, unusually tall women—and *all* women of color who sought employment—were subjected to a second and more rigorous round of prescreening by management higher-ups in Kansas City. Mariedaughter passed the second test and quickly turned her height into an asset for mobility in the company. Soon after she was hired, Mariedaughter began taking special assignments that required her to don her uniform and enrich non-airline venues with the style and allure of 1960s jet-setting. When a Miami-based department store rolled out a new makeup line, for example, Mariedaughter and several of her peers got in uniform, sprayed up their bouffants, and posed with the product.[17] By 1970, when she was selected to model for the Ambassador Service rollout, Mariedaughter had built a career that had, in her mother's words, "given her wings," becoming an official corporate representative for that physical, social, and sexual mobility.

As she used the zeitgeist of 1960s jet-setting to her own advantage, Mariedaughter began a personal and political transformation that would soon provide a far greater challenge to the dominant culture than the one TWA sold with her image. From her first days on the job, Mariedaughter openly contested traditional family values. "When I started flying, that book *Open Marriage* was popular," she remembered, referring to Nena and George O'Neill's best-selling 1972 critique of monogamous marriage. "It was about how one person can't meet all your needs, [and how] you could have a wonderful marriage with other relationships. And I was buying into that." Mariedaughter recalls that as she began to push the boundaries of middle-class women's sexuality, having multiple relationships with older and sometimes married men, she began to yearn for more fundamental changes in her life. "I just didn't connect [with those men]," she insisted. "But then women's liberation came along." Mariedaughter argues that the upsurge of feminist activism in the early 1970s shifted her political trajectory, allowing her to build new connections not to businessmen she met on the airplane but to the women she worked with.

The women's liberation movement would help Mariedaughter answer pressing new questions that social and physical mobility were raising. In the early 1970s, many of those questions surrounded a woman who was a friend and coworker from TWA. Mariedaughter recalled the relationship:

> We used to fly together as often as possible. And if we couldn't fly together, we would bring each other presents. She used to bring me these lemon bars. She was tall like me. Had been married briefly and was divorced. She and I took a trip to Atlanta together. We had been out all day, and that evening we came home. I was feeling really close—and excited about being with her. The first thing I know is she wants to call her boyfriend. I felt so left out. That was her priority. But she was enough for me.

Though anxiety and pain surface in her memories of the period, that friendship brought Mariedaughter a new way of thinking about her sexuality and her future. Because of this connection, Mariedaughter began to recognize that she wanted to organize her personal and political life around same-sex desire, intimacy, and camaraderie.

Mariedaughter would soon find those connections in organized feminist activism. In 1973, she attended the founding convention of the Stewardesses for Women's Rights, an organization linking front-line stewardesses to the women's liberation movement. As she volunteered to be the lower Midwest coordinator for the new group, Mariedaughter gleaned two resources: a set of texts that provided a radical and lesbian feminist framework to interpret her life on the job, and connections to principled feminist workers who would be role models for her own leadership at TWA.[18] With those resources, Mariedaughter began what she calls a "transformation" in the workplace and beyond. First and foremost, she did away with the hairpieces, the false eyelashes, and the manicured nails that had featured in glossy magazines just a few years earlier. She began going to work without makeup, presenting her body as it naturally appeared. Second, Mariedaughter changed her name. Paula, after all, was not Paula Mariedaughter when she appeared in the *New York Times* in 1970. She was Paula Nielson then, named after her father. Unlike so many of her colleagues who would leave their airline jobs to marry and to take a husband's name, Paula stayed at work and used her mother's name—Marie—to create a new matrilineal surname. Finally, Mariedaughter began to confirm already widespread workplace rumors about her sexuality and came out as a lesbian. By early 1974, Paula Mariedaughter was going to work as an outspoken, visibly identifiable leader in the women's liberation movement.

Mariedaughter was not alone. At every major airline, a generation of self-identified feminist flight attendants was coming together to challenge the economic and cultural terms of their employment. Their activism would create both new tensions and new solidarities in the airline industry, workplace politics that were particularly evident in Mariedaughter's journey through the early and mid-1970s. Soon after she began her personal transformation, for example, an aggressive, openly antifeminist TWA captain kicked her off his aircraft for insubordination. After departure from Washington National on a multistop flight to Kansas City, the captain berated Mariedaughter for her natural appearance and ordered her to apply lipstick. Mariedaughter refused. Stranded at an en-route stopover in Saint Louis after the captain and the rest of the crew departed, Mariedaughter called her union, and rank-and-file activists soon rallied to her defense. Recognizing the growing militancy of front-line activists, TWA quickly backed down, dismissing the captain's insubordination charge, reinstating Mariedaughter without discipline, and compensating her for the lost flight pay.

Mariedaughter prevailed partially because of the advocacy of Mary Ellen Miller, an increasingly visible and outspoken rank-and-file leader of TWA's flight attendant union. Speaking in clipped, matter-of-fact sentences, Miller recalled that she first applied for a job as a flight attendant as part of an effort to leave a troubled relationship:

> I came [to TWA] because I got married rather than stay in college. I had a scholastic and music scholarship, but I made a bad decision to drop out and get married. It did not work out and was a bad situation. I needed to safely get out and get away.[19]

Soon after she arrived at TWA, however, dominant cultural values about sexuality put her in another dangerous situation, one that sparked her career as a union activist. Miller recalled:

> It was 1972 and I got pregnant. I decided I was going to have the baby. I decided I was going to keep flying—even though we had to inform them right away, I waited so I could keep flying. They grounded me

without pay. I got pissed and started writing letters to the Women's
Equity Action League. I wrote letters all over the place. I had the baby
in 1973 and started starving myself and doing all sorts of dangerous
things so I could get back to work. I had no other income. It just
made me madder.

Because the bodily changes associated with the gestation process would rup-
ture the fantasy of sexual availability without consequences, most airlines
strictly forbade flight attendants from flying while pregnant, grounding them
without paid maternity leave. Miller, like many other flight attendants who
got pregnant, was single and the sole breadwinner for her household. Losing
her paycheck at the moment she needed it most, women like Miller were
forced either to seek abortions, which were still illegal in many states in 1972,
or to turn to families or boyfriends for economic support. Miller refused both
choices and had her daughter on her own. Her anger at being forced to perform difficult physical labor late into her pregnancy and to starve herself to
get back to her company-mandated target weight galvanized Miller to become an activist. As a new single mother, Miller joined the women's liberation movement in Kansas City and got involved with her union to help
defend the workplace rights of the women she worked with.

As Mary Ellen Miller and Paula Mariedaughter became feminist union
activists in the early 1970s, they encountered two distinct and contradictory
political trends in their workplace. On the one hand, activists were energized
from a decade of legislative and legal advances against institutionalized sex
discrimination. Since the late 1950s, rank-and-file leaders had been using
local union infrastructure to file grievances against the airlines' increasingly
restrictive age and marriage limitations.[20] Those efforts got a significant boost
with the passage of Title VII of the 1964 Civil Rights Act, which banned
race- and sex-based discrimination at work. In November 1966, the Equal
Employment Opportunity Commission (EEOC), the new federal agency
formed to apply the Civil Rights Act to the workplace, ruled that sex was not
a "bona fide occupational qualification" for being a flight attendant.[21] With
the ruling, the EEOC formally invalidated airline managers' long-standing
legal claim that only young, single, attractive women were qualified to perform the job. Since the EEOC could not seek direct redress from employers,
and could only recommend that the U.S. attorney general sue companies that
violated the law, relief from overly discriminatory managerial policies came
slowly. Nevertheless, as months and years went by, the legal momentum
shifted in flight attendants' favor. In April 1971, the Fifth Circuit Court of
Appeals finally closed the debate, siding with flight attendants and the EEOC

in the landmark case *Diaz v. Pan Am* and ruling that female-only hiring policies resulted in unlawful discrimination.[22] Although the Mariedaughter lipstick dispute and the Miller pregnancy grounding demonstrate that individual flight attendants would have to continue to fight overtly sexist policies on a case-by-case basis, flight attendants had gained powerful new resources to win those claims.

On the other hand, even as activists were securing the right to marry and to stay on the job after age thirty, the ideology of domesticity continued to shape the political economy of the profession. Flight attendants were often the lowest-paid airline employees and continued to be denied the longevity pay and retirement benefits that had helped lift so many airline men out of the working class and into the middle class in the mid-twentieth century. Therefore, as they sharpened their political skills by fighting overt sex discrimination, Paula Mariedaughter, Mary Ellen Miller, and other women began to focus those skills on challenging the economic disparities that shaped their work. The new cohort of activists would, in other words, fight sexism by insisting that—just like the men they worked alongside—flight attendants deserved to be breadwinners for their families. But as they transformed themselves from passive dependents into active political agents, feminist leaders would face new unrest at work as tensions mounted not just between activists and managers but between flight attendants, their unions, and their male coworkers.

Gay Men, Suspect Masculinity, and the Ideology of Domesticity

Like the many women who became flight attendants in the 1960s and 1970s, a small but growing number of men had been joining the profession because they wanted to live outside the borders of traditional family. Since flying for a living allowed for ample time away from the watchful eyes of friends and relatives, and since downtown layovers across the globe gave flight attendants access to a variety of sexual cultures, many men who had sex with men used the profession to build social and intimate networks.[23] With the emergence of the modern gay rights movement in the 1960s, those men were ever more likely to forge a political identity around those same-sex desires and to mobilize to make the airline industry at least somewhat open to gay men.[24]

Despite the explicit repression of homosexuality and the strict policing of all male flight attendants' behavior and appearance, airline managers included male flight attendants in the lucrative compensation and retirement benefit programs that they categorically denied to all flight attendants who were women. That overtly sexist disparity drove a wedge between male flight attendants and their female colleagues, who were becoming ever more committed feminist activists. Thus, as the gay liberation movement was persuading many gay men to join feminists and lesbians in critiquing domesticity and marriage, male privilege would provide a significant obstacle to solidarity between male and female flight attendants in the early and mid-1970s.

Men were a small but tenuously elite subset of the flight attendant ranks, making up less than 4 percent of the total flight attendant population in the late 1960s.[25] Nearly two decades earlier, major carriers such as American and United had ceased hiring men to work as stewards on domestic routes. As Phillip Tiemeyer demonstrates in *Plane Queer,* Cold War anxieties about male homosexuality and effeminacy led managers to cast doubt on any man willing—or even worse, wanting—to perform work imagined to be docile and servile.[26] Nevertheless, a few carriers, all with prestigious international route systems, continued to hire male stewards during the Cold War. TWA, for example, had been hiring men since 1946, placing them directly into the lead flight attendant position, one many airlines called the purser.[27] Although pursers were not managers and were fully eligible for union membership, they were granted authority that was denied to all other flight attendants: managing in-flight service delivery, directing the cabin crew's response to emergencies, and acting as a liaison between flight attendants, pilots, and management during trips overseas. By the 1960s, when airliners had gotten much bigger and faster due to jet propulsion, and as flight crews grew with the size of aircraft, TWA's international flights were staffed with large groups of women in subordinate positions and with one man who was always the most powerful person on the crew. And because management hired men directly into purser positions rather than selecting them from the existing flight attendant ranks, that man was often the youngest and most junior person on the airplane.

With pursers came both the cultural cachet and the suspicion that followed effete masculinity, an anxious allure similar to that which surrounded male wait staff in the era's five-star restaurants. On the one hand, pursers were assumed to be skilled, technically competent workers. Grooming inductees with the scientific management principles of Fredrick W. Taylor, male purser supervisors clicked stopwatches on in-flight checkrides, timing appetizer deliveries; measuring exact positions of plates, glasses, and silverware on tray presentations; and testing the temperatures of soups, sauces, and steaks as they came out of the galley. On the other hand, pursers' manhood was always under scrutiny. TWA purser Richard Wagner, who joined the airline in the late 1960s, recalled, "I had a particularly harsh supervisor. He would make pursers light a cigarette and then walk across the office smoking it." When the applicant reached the far wall, the test would have one of two outcomes: the label of homosexual, which yielded immediate termination, or no label, which allowed the candidate to proceed through the hiring process. Though Wagner and many of his classmates had sex with men and identified as gay, they had to master nuances that would foreground technical competence while covering up the sexually aberrant properties of their manhood.[28]

Given those aberrations, compensation became a badly needed means for the airlines to stabilize the gender and sexuality of their pursers. At TWA, every man hired was guaranteed the highest possible introductory flight attendant wage and received a pay bump for both international flying and purser flying. Women, conversely, received the lowest possible introductory rate, beginning as regular domestic flight attendants. Thus, on the eve of the unrest in the early 1970s, the starting wage for a purser was $10.16 an hour while flight attendants started at $8.16, a full 20 percent less.[29] Purser's pensions were also artificially inflated, not only because the international and purser bumps were used to calculate retirement benefits for the defined benefit pension plan but also because pursers were provided with a special and separate defined-contribution pension plan to which the company contributed the equivalent of 5 percent of a purser's annual salary.[30] Although pursers' suspect manhood provoked anxiety and ire from individual managers, pursers were still men. Because the ideology of domesticity brought expectations of a family wage, the airlines designed a particular economic infrastructure to maintain that cultural norm.[31]

Special hourly and retirement pay for men presented a political problem for flight attendant unions. On September 16, 1975, just as things were heating up between flight attendants and management over a broad array of social and economic issues, the U.S. District Court for the Southern District of New York began hearing arguments in *McGuire v. TWA,* a class action lawsuit filed on behalf of 2,050 women flight attendants. The complaint alleged that both the company and the flight attendants' union violated the Equal Pay Act of 1963 by inflating the pay differential between regular flight attendants and pursers and then restricting purser employment to men. Though, after pressure from scores of Equal Employment Opportunity Commission complaints, women began being promoted to purser in May 1968, McGuire and the plaintiffs wanted compensation for all the years they flew for TWA while being denied promotions because of their sex.[32]

The case left Peggy McGuire, a flight attendant union activist and the named plaintiff in the lawsuit, in a bitter conflict with Richard Wagner. Along with Arthur Teolis, Buddy Ledger, and many other young men, Wagner had come to a prominent union leadership position through his particular interests as a purser, having helped found and finance an organization called the Purser Benevolent Association for the roughly 5 percent of TWA flight attendants who were men. Many of the association's causes were undeniably legitimate. Since homophobia, for example, prevented pursers from bumping back into regular domestic flight attendant positions that managers cast as more servile and more emasculating than purser positions, junior male flight attendants had nowhere to go during seasonal or cyclical downturns in the international operation, making them disproportionately likely to be laid off.[33] Fifty junior pursers were laid off during the 1970 recession, but the vast majority of them would have kept their jobs if they had been allowed to work one of the other positions on the crew.[34] To McGuire and her peers, however, it seemed that pursers were fighting to defend the jobs they had gotten by using sexism to jump the seniority line and then using sexism again to reap special pay and benefits.

Those privileges infuriated McGuire. Rising to power in the labor movement in the 1960s, she had learned to navigate the mid-twentieth-century bureaucracy in an overtly sexist workplace. Although McGuire had become accustomed to accommodating and ignoring the old-fashioned, often overtly sexist ways of the older men who ran the Transport Workers Union, she abhorred the junior pursers, publicly castigating them with allegations that they purposely allowed TWA to continue making contributions to the special purser pension plan even after junior male pursers were demoted to regular flight attendant positions after 1970.[35] Though some of her characterizations oversimplified pursers' principles and politics, the young men were indeed advocates for their own interests, even when those interests ran directly counter to the needs of their female coworkers.

By the early 1970s, the women's liberation movement was offering a new economic equation that would assuage at least some of the tension between women like Peggy McGuire and pursers like Richard Wagner. Before 1970, the ideology of domesticity had delivered the 4 percent of flight attendants who were men an equitable wage—as long as those men acquiesced to management's gender policing and closeted their same-sex desires. As women like Mary Ellen Miller joined the movement, however, there was an increasingly vocal call for a fair wage for 100 percent of flight attendants. During a broad-based social transformation, both gay liberationists and women's liberationists had provided a bold challenge to compulsory heterosexuality and traditional family values. It was becoming ever more apparent to both pursers and feminist activists that the entire flight attendant group stood to benefit from enriching the practice of trade unionism with the ideas of those movements. Therefore, by 1975, Mary Ellen Miller and Richard Wagner were sitting down together on the same side of the bargaining table, two leaders of a new upsurge that was demanding and winning vast improvements in wages, benefits, and work rules for all flight attendants.

The Long, Hot Summer of 1976

Initiating contract talks with all of the major carriers in the mid-1970s, flight attendants closed ranks around a single goal: ending historic pay disparities between themselves and other airline workers. Though flight attendants were firm in their new commitment, their agenda presented a significant strategic challenge. To close the flight attendant pay gap, activists would have to upend the status quo of collective bargaining in the airline business. As they had in many other industries since labor's watershed advances in the 1930s, airline union higher-ups would meet with company officials to bargain for new contracts every few years. Those agreements had delivered gradual, incremental pay bumps that would help already-high wages cover the rising cost of living. But for a group that had never received the high wages, incrementalism only widened the pay gap between flight attendants and other workers. Thus, flight attendants rejected gradualism at the bargaining table. The new activists leveraged the assertive politics of the women's, gay, and lesbian liberation movements, insisting that they, too, were breadwinners and that they deserved immediate pay and benefit improvements that would deliver a family wage. Flight attendants' ambitious new political economic vision set off a conflict between rank-and-file activists, the airlines, and the union men who had always spoken for flight attendants at the bargaining table.

The industry-wide standoff over flight attendant wage disparities heated up at American Airlines in the spring of 1975. On April 18, Transport Workers Union International vice president William Lindner sent a memorandum to the leaders of the TWU locals at American, those for customer service staff, machinists, and flight attendants. To mitigate the high inflation of the mid-1970s, when a delayed contract settlement would dilute the value of raises, Lindner proposed making a deal with management to expedite bargaining. If all TWU locals agreed to limit contract talks to a short list of disputed items, American would agree to give a robust, standardized wage increase to all union members.[36] Flight attendants balked at Lindner's proposal, recognizing that uniform pay increases would preserve historic pay differentials between labor groups and pointing out that the deal would prevent flight attendants from bargaining for work rule improvements that were particularly important to the rank and file. In mid-June, flight attendants united in opposition to Lindner's initiative, voting down the contract that resulted from expedited bargaining by a 76 percent to 24 percent margin.[37]

Struggling to recover from the rank-and-file rebuke, Lindner scheduled a series of informational "road shows" about the contract. TWU higher-ups hoped that flight attendants would reverse their votes and approve the deal if they learned more about its contents.[38] The problem with Lindner's solution, however, was that rather than being confused or uninformed, rank-and-file flight attendants were abundantly clear about the source of their displeasure—which was the flight attendant wage gap. Back to the polls flight attendants went when the road shows wrapped up, and back down the contract went, failing membership ratification for a second time in early September.[39] Forced out of coalition talks by rank-and-file flight attendants, TWU higher-ups had no choice but to pursue standard collective bargaining with American Airlines in the fall of 1975.

Although the talks were arduous amid mounting tensions between rank-and-file flight attendants, TWU higher-ups, and management, the process received a boost when United Airlines flight attendants locked in a robust new contract just after New Year's Day, 1976. Two years earlier, flight attendants from United and several smaller carriers had ended their subordinate relationship to the Air Line Pilots Association, breaking off and forming their own union, called the Association of Flight Attendants (AFA). In full control of the economic agenda, AFA activists drove a hard bargain against United Airlines management, winning 15 percent and 11 percent raises in the first two years of the contract and securing improvements in work rules and benefits. The United deal was particularly significant because it delivered full "retroactive pay" for the months that flight attendants had spent hammering out the terms of the pact with management. Retroactive pay had been standard for pilots, machinists, and ground crews for decades. But since management had long assumed that flight attendants were not breadwinners and would not need compensation for diluted wages, the group was rarely awarded such compensation.[40]

Energized by the victory on retroactive pay at United, TWU higher-ups intensified their pressure on management in flight attendant negotiations at American Airlines. The union soon reached a tentative agreement that—temporarily—ended the dispute between flight attendants and management. On May 27, 1976, flight attendants went back to the polls to vote on a new pact that offered significant improvements to the deal that flight attendants had rejected in September. Depending on seniority, flight attendants would receive a raise of approximately 12 percent in each of the first two years of the contract and enjoy the single hotel rooms and other work rule improvements included in the United deal.[41] With the improvements, however, came a significant weakness. American flight attendants would receive only 33 percent retroactive pay for the nine-month delay at the bargaining table, far less than the United group, which won 100 percent back pay. Fiercely debating the merits of a contract that would be the best in their union's history while still inferior to that of their United colleagues, a majority of American flight attendants opted to accept the proposal, and the referendum passed by a 61 percent to 39 percent margin.[42] American flight attendants were, nevertheless, closely watching the intensifying conflict at TWA as they went to work and claimed their raise.

Just one week after the settlement at American, contract talks at TWA came to a precipice, one that would mark a new level of contentiousness in flight attendant labor relations. The dispute reached its first breaking point at the New York Sheraton Hotel on Manhattan's Eighth Avenue on the long night of June 4, 1976. At midnight eastern daylight time, flight attendants would walk off the job if union leaders failed to cut a deal with management. Night had fallen at Kennedy, Logan, Dulles, and the other major airports of the East Coast. But it was already morning in London, Paris, Rome, and Athens. Any delay in a truce would push crews to abandon their aircraft and set up pickets in those cities and then, once the sun rose, across the United States.[43] School had just let out for the summer, and a flight attendant strike at New York's largest airline would strand tens of thousands of passengers during the busiest travel weeks of the year.

As reporters milled in the lobby waiting for a verdict, talks slid from tense to hostile in the conference room upstairs. The root of the conflict lay in the presence of three parties at the bargaining table in flight attendant labor relations, rather than the two groups normally involved in contract negotiations pursuant to U.S. federal labor law. On the union side of the table were two constituencies. The first were the elected, rank-and-file leaders of Transport Workers Union (TWU) Local 551. Representing flight attendants who flew international routes were New York–based pursers Richard Wagner and Buddy Ledger. Kansas City–based Mary Ellen Miller and Los Angeles–based Victoria Frankovich negotiated for flight attendants on domestic routes. Rounding out the group was Arthur Teolis, another purser, who served as president of Local 551.[44] Significant divisions existed among the rank-and-file leaders: Wagner, Ledger, and Teolis had been involved in earlier efforts to defend the family wage for pursers only, and the women's liberation movement—especially after Miller's experience with pregnancy discrimination—deeply influenced both women's trade unionism. Nevertheless, all were front-line crew members who had been tasked with a single, unambiguous goal by their peers: closing the flight attendant pay gap.

Next to the rank-and-file leaders were two senior staff from the TWU: International Vice President Fredric Simpson and Vice President for the Air Transport Division Ernie Mitchell. Simpson and Mitchell had come of age a generation earlier as activists in a union that had well-known leftist political leanings and had been committed to cross-racial solidarity among transport workers since the 1930s. Neither had ever been flight attendants, however, and both helped run an organization in which all senior officers were men. But regardless of their personal distance from the sex discrimination that had galvanized a new generation of rank-and-file leaders, Simpson and Mitchell recognized the need to close the flight attendant pay gap. Private correspondence from 1976 reveals that winning a large flight attendant wage increase was the top bargaining priority for the entire union. To achieve their goal, Simpson and Mitchell had hoped to win a large raise in hourly rates at TWA and then use that raise to set a benchmark for Eastern and American Airlines flight attendants, whose contracts became amendable after the TWA agreement.[45]

Across the table from the two-party union delegation was a management negotiating team facing economic pressures as immediate and as intense as those on the union. With a potential strike just hours away, top TWA brass were present, including Chairman of the Board Charles Tillinghast and President Ed Meyer. TWA was indeed a large carrier, flying more passengers than any airline except industry giant United. But it was by no means too big to fail. The airline lost $121 million in 1975 and continued to struggle with fuel prices that remained twice what they were before the 1973 oil shock.[46] With the economy finally emerging from the recession in April 1975, TWA would need to capture the largest possible share of a growing marketplace in order to bolster its revenue streams to cover rising costs. A flight attendant strike during the apex of the U.S.-Europe summer high season would destroy management's effort to build market share. Therefore, Tillinghast and Meyer came to the bargaining table with the company checkbook open. Recognizing that the social transformation of the 1960s and 1970s had emboldened gay and feminist workers, and aware of activists' growing insistence on closing the flight attendant pay gap, Tillinghast and Meyer's team was ready to give everyone a raise and to offer substantive improvements in working conditions. As the deadline approached, management appeared willing to sign a deal that, depending on a flight attendant's seniority, would provide a pay increase of between 29.2 percent and 44.5 percent over the life of a three-year contract.[47]

Impressed with the size of the pay hike, union leaders debated how to respond to two key shortcomings in the proposal. First, despite United and American flight attendants' recent victories, TWA's offer provided no retroactive pay for the fifteen months the union had spent bargaining for the contract. Flight attendants would earn the new wages only starting the day the union signed the new accord, effectively rewarding the company for spending a year stalling at the bargaining table. Second, the contract lacked firm language on work rule improvements, the regulations entitling flight attendants to shorter days, more time off, and guaranteed pay during delays and cancellations.[48] Struggling with the pros and cons of the deal, Local 551 activists took a straw poll on how to move forward, a vote that transcended the ideological positions of the group. Mary Ellen Miller sided with purser Buddy Ledger and moved to compromise with management and accept the deal. Victoria Frankovich, meanwhile, joined forces with purser Richard Wagner and voted to reject the contract and strike. Local president Arthur Teolis stepped in to break the tie, voting with Miller and Ledger to ratify the pact.[49]

Minutes after the rank-and-file activists expressed their willingness to compromise, the sexist culture of airline unionism jeopardized the settlement. As was then standard practice in most flight attendant unions, Fredric Simpson and Ernie Mitchell got up from the table when they received the nod that the elected flight attendant leaders were ready to agree to a deal. They left the room and joined company brass at a separate bargaining table, where they would iron out the final economic details of the fact. Flight attendants were not allowed to witness or participate in those negotiations. Miller, who watched the union and company men walk out of the room that night in 1976, summarized the situation:

> Of course they didn't think women could handle money effectively . . . so our function was really just to let the TWU people know about flight attendant stuff. But it wasn't to talk. It wasn't to negotiate. And it wasn't to make any of the real decisions. That was all done off in another room somewhere with these guys. [TWU staff] were guys in the mid-1970s, and they had the same expectations of women flight attendants as the company. They thought we were going to be hired and not stick around.[50]

Miller argued that although Simpson and Mitchell had grown up on the opposite side of a class divide from Tillinghast and Meyer, their common investment in traditional gender roles led them all to assume that flight attendants' economic stability would lie in their future husbands' wages and not their own. Presumed to be short-term employees, flight attendants had been routinely denied the full voice in contract negotiations that all of their unionized male peers expected. Corporate executives and union higher-ups had been able to justify that disparity in the culture of the 1950s and early 1960s. But in an age when the ideas of the women's, gay, and lesbian liberation movements had transformed flight attendants like Mary Ellen Miller, Victoria Frankovich, and Richard Wagner, the disparity was no longer sustainable.

With history weighing on all parties, negotiations devolved into open conflict when the men returned to share the details from their private bargaining session. Though Simpson and Mitchell had gotten TWA to agree formally to all of the previously promised pay and benefit enhancements, the work rule improvements that rank-and-file leaders thought would be included had been stripped from the deal. Work rules would instead be negotiated as part of a separate side letter to be finalized *after* contract ratification. The glaring problem with that strategy was that if negotiations over the work rules failed, it would be illegal for flight attendants to go on strike in protest, because federal labor law prohibits walkouts when contracts are in effect. If flight attendants signed before midnight, they would forfeit all economic leverage over the work rules negotiations.[51]

All five flight attendants were furious. They immediately rescinded the 3–2 authorization vote and refused to sign the accord. Simpson and Mitchell blew up, loudly and angrily denouncing the activists for threatening to scuttle the giant raise that could be used to force deals at Eastern and American. Exercising their executive power as top TWU officials, Simpson and Mitchell told management negotiators that they would sign the contract and that the dispute was settled. Miller, Wagner, and the others jumped in the middle and yelled back, pointing to the TWU Constitution, which gave Local 551's leaders the right to send the accord to all front-line flight attendants for ratification. Simpson and Mitchell could sign the deal now to avert a strike, but it would not be binding until front-line flight attendants voted on it. It would be perfectly legal, Miller and Wagner's group angrily reminded the union men, for local elected leaders to lobby their coworkers to vote no in the referendum, which would end up sabotaging the agreement.

That, of course, was exactly the strategy that Local 551 activists adopted. Just before midnight, the group poured out of the conference room and into the throng of reporters in the lobby. Flight attendants confirmed that a tentative agreement had been reached, encouraged their coworkers to report for duty, and reassured the public that, at least for the moment, TWA would continue to operate normally. However, as Miller told a reporter from her hometown newspaper the *Kansas City Star*, "The deal is very tentative."[52] Three days later, Victoria Frankovich, Buddy Ledger, Mary Ellen Miller, Arthur Teolis, and Richard Wagner sent a letter to all of their coworkers. Although the activists were circumspect, highlighting the historical value of the pay and benefit improvements, they relayed their frustrations about Simpson and Mitchell's last-minute deal with management. "The tentative agreement does not accurately reflect what the Local 551 negotiating committee believed to have been the understanding reached during negotiations," the activists told their peers.[53] Two weeks later, it was clear that many front-line flight attendants shared the activists' frustration with the status quo of male-led flight attendant contract negotiations. On June 26, 1976, 2,324 flight attendants, or 63 percent of those voting, told Local 551 to reject the compromise and to call an immediate strike to secure better wages and working conditions.[54]

With a strike authorization from the rank and file, core flight attendant activists strategically deployed the threat of labor unrest to exercise maximum economic leverage over their employer. In the process, TWA flight attendants upended the ideology of domesticity, turning the women who worked the front lines from men's dependents into active political agents in their unions. Although federal labor law gave TWA flight attendants the right to strike as soon as the contract ratification failed on June 26, activists opted to delay the strike in an effort to amplify its effectiveness. Miller, Wagner, and the other Local 551 leaders asked their peers to fly their trips during the last week of June and to focus on preparing their finances and their families for a work stoppage. Then, on July 2, 1976, flight attendants would walk out forty-eight hours before the U.S. bicentennial celebration, shuttering Kennedy Airport just as guests arrived for the city's largest gala in two hundred years.

Faced with unprecedented insubordination from the airline's most subordinate labor group, TWA managers responded with an aggressive countermobilization. On June 30, TWA sued Transport Workers Union Local 551, demanding that the union pay the airline back for business lost amid strike threats and seeking an injunction to block a walkout on Bicentennial Weekend. After a federal judge ruled in favor of TWA's motion for an injunction, Miller, Wagner, and the other activists approached management to engineer a compromise. In exchange for TWA's dropping the damages suit, flight attendant activists agreed to give the company at least five days' notice before any work stoppage, blunting at least some of the force of a surprise strike.[55] Nevertheless, flight attendants scored a victory in protecting their overall right to strike during the legal confrontation with TWA.

Invigorated after a strategic advance, flight attendant leaders upped their militancy. During the third week of July, TWA sent a new, slightly improved contract proposal to the union. To the airline's deep displeasure, Local 551 activists rejected the settlement offer outright, refusing to send it to rank-and-file flight attendants for a ratification vote. Instead of compromising, Miller and Wagner's group prepared for a conflict, serving TWA with a five-day strike notice for a work stoppage that could begin as early as August 1, 1976.[56] The timing of the new threat was potentially even worse for the airline than the bicentennial strike. If flight attendants walked out, the carrier would be shuttered during the Republican National Convention in Kansas City.[57] That affair was setting up to be the most important political event of the year because an ascendant Ronald Reagan was mounting an effort to challenge Gerald Ford for the nomination, an outcome that would have drastically shifted the terms of the general election. TWA was Kansas City's largest airline, operating roughly 35 percent of daily flights and controlling two-thirds of the seats from Reagan's home state of California.[58] With the other airlines sold out well in advance of the convention, the delegates who would be so crucial to Ford's or Reagan's nomination would, on short notice, have to take a bus or train or carpool their way across the country.

Faced with the choice between a high-stakes strike and a contract settlement that could derail their political momentum, ordinary front-line flight attendants became political activists. Scribbled notes, formal mailgrams, and reams of petitions were pouring into local and national union offices, revealing both the overall militancy of the rank and file and widespread strategic disagreement among flight attendants. "Working conditions are more important than money," barked a petition from hundreds of Kansas City–based flight attendants. "Tell Mitchell off!" they ordered, insisting that Miller and the other activists hold the line against TWU vice president Mitchell and the other union higher-ups.[59] Other front-line flight attendants were even more pointed in their displeasure with the non–flight attendant union staff. For example, a series of flyers began appearing under flight attendants' doors in TWA's Los Angeles layover hotels, explicitly accusing Mitchell of selling flight attendants out and claiming that he had been witnessed with company brass at posh restaurants.[60] Meanwhile, other rank-and-file flight attendants complained that Miller, Wagner, and the other Local 551 activists were being too confrontational. Material deluged Mitchell's office demanding that he force Local 551 activists to allow the rank and file to vote on TWA's settlement offer from late July. In one of dozens of letters to Mitchell, for example, San Francisco–based flight attendant Judy Marsalis pointed out, "We are a thinking group who wants the chance to decide for ourselves. If it passes, then that is the will of the majority."[61] Concurring with Marsalis, front-line flight attendants sent Mitchell fifty single-spaced pages of signatures on a petition demanding a popular vote on the contract that Local 551 seemed committed to rejecting.[62]

Recognizing the strategic disagreement among their peers, Local 551 proposed a solution that would come to define flight attendant unionism over the coming decade. For thirty years, union higher-ups and managers had been making political and economic decisions for flight attendants. To right that historical wrong, activists decided to let ordinary flight attendants decide the fate of the contract dispute for themselves. Ballots would be mailed to all TWA flight attendants' homes by August 4 and would be due for return no later than August 20.[63] If the referendum passed, flight attendants would work under the terms of TWA's offer from late July. If it failed, flight attendants would walk out immediately.

After three weeks of heated debate over the proposal, a majority of TWA flight attendants opted to settle the dispute. By a margin of 55 percent to 45 percent, front-line flight attendants voted to approve the contract offer on August 20, ending the TWA standoff of the summer of 1976.[64] Though there were few significant improvements in the final deal over the original pact of June 4, the overall value of the raises proved too much for flight attendants to risk in a strike. By the beginning of the contract's final year in October 1977, regular domestic flight attendants would start at $12.58 per hour. With inflation figured in, that would mean a flight attendant flying maximum hours could earn as much as $49,000 a year in 2015 dollars. Even with high inflation rates in the late 1970s, and even though unionized employees in the manufacturing sector made more than this, the equivalent of $49,000 a year was a large sum of money for a group that had been underpaid for decades. The contract's top wage—of $21.70 per hour, or roughly $84,000 a year in 2015 dollars—was even more money.[65] Flight attendants recognized that there was still vast progress to be made, especially in terms of the work rules that guaranteed flight attendants time off, protected them from overwork, and extended flight pay during delays and cancellations. But since the women on the front lines could now expect top pay rates that matched those of many unionized male industrial workers, activists recognized that they had made significant headway in challenging the ideology of domesticity. Regardless of whether they were single, married, or partnered, whether they were parents or childless, whether they were gay or straight, and whether they were women or men, flight attendants cashed their new paychecks and learned how it felt to be a breadwinner.

Conclusion

On July 26, 1976, at the peak of the standoff between flight attendants, their union, and management, TWA's senior vice president of administration, D. J. Crombie, wrote a memo about the flight attendant dispute to the leaders of all of the other unions at the airline. Clearly exasperated, Crombie tried to explain why, even after TWA made a highly lucrative offer to Local 551, ordinary flight attendants were still threatening to walk out on strike. "This is the costliest contract settlement offer we have ever made to TWA flight attendants, and probably the most expensive settlement proposal ever made to flight attendants in the airline industry," Crombie told representatives for pilots, machinists, and ground crews.[66] Crombie had every right to be surprised by the situation, because it stood out in the history of airline collective bargaining. In an era when notoriously hard-bargaining pilots were getting 25 percent raises in three-year contracts, TWA flight attendants came hair-raisingly close to declining a deal that gave many of their peers a 40 percent raise.[67] Crombie appears not to have fully grasped that flight attendants were not thinking about the TWA contract dispute in the context of the history of airline collective bargaining. They were thinking about it in relation to the social transformation of the 1960s and 1970s.

During an era of rapid social change, a new generation of activists was redefining kinship and family values. At the airlines' behest, the stewardesses of the 1960s had forgone traditional domesticity, staying single, moving in with friends, living paycheck to paycheck, and—at least in some cases— spending what little money they had on personal pleasures. By the mid-1970s, many of those flight attendants were mounting a new challenge to traditional family values, but one on their own terms and not the airlines'.

As flight attendants and a whole generation of women's, gay, and lesbian liberationists confronted the cultural foundations of the ideology of domesticity, they raised new questions about its economic foundations. The labor market, the activists insisted, was not keeping pace with social change. How, young people asked, can you stay single and raise a child as Mary Ellen Miller did, or how can you come out as lesbian or gay as Paula Mariedaughter and Richard Wagner did, if a living wage, affordable health insurance, and a secure retirement are channeled through traditional marriage and husband breadwinners? In 1976, flight attendants used the collective bargaining process to force the labor market to provide an affirmative answer to their questions. Robert Callahan, the rank-and-file president of the Transport Workers Union local at Eastern Airlines and Southern Airways, addressed the stakes of the situation. "The idea that we are 'kids,' that we are not breadwinners, allows Eastern Airlines to live comfortably with the low wages and poor working conditions with which we are forced to live."[68] As flight attendants took on the economic roots of heteropatriarchy in the summer of 1976, the airlines could no longer "live comfortably" with those inequities.

Flight attendants, however, raised many more questions than they answered. If, for example, flight attendants were winning the wage increases necessary to turn their job into lifetime employment, why should they continue to be denied the protective union work rules that pilots and machinists had expected since World War II? And if elected rank-and-file leaders could effectively advocate for the most important economic issues, craft a legal strategy to defend themselves against management, and build a communications network to motivate their peers, why did flight attendant activists have to report to male-led parent unions? Flight attendants at American, United, and TWA were energized when they cashed large new paychecks and as they reported to work after winning headline-making labor standoffs. The more they achieved, however, the more they asked these fundamental questions about their workplace. Because they lacked ironclad union work rules, and because their group was made up mostly of women who went home to work a second job providing child care and housework, flight attendants worked more than their male coworkers in the 1970s. As the 1980s approached, flight attendants took on the airlines—and their own unions—as they built a movement to challenge that overwork.

NIGHT FEVER FOR
A NEW ECONOMY

*The Struggle over Time and Money
on the Cusp of the 1980s*

ince the middle of the nineteenth century, the cultural ideal of domesticity has shaped dominant understandings of white women's
labor. Framing white women as their husbands' passive dependents
rather than as active economic agents, domesticity has rendered women's
labor invisible. Although it has obscured their contributions to the economy,
domesticity has often forced women to work harder than men. In the airline
industry, for example, flight attendants earned lower hourly wages, less longevity pay, and fewer retirement benefits than ground crews, pilots, or middle
managers. To make up for the difference in compensation, flight attendants
worked extra flights, adding more hours to their schedules as they struggled
to provide for their families. Additionally, unlike many men who expected to
come home from work and enjoy the domestic sphere as a space of leisure and
pleasure, most flight attendants came home to the "second shift," bearing the
disproportionate burden for unwaged reproductive and emotional labor
within the household.[1] In the mid-1970s, flight attendant activists began to
win many of the economic resources that the ideology of domesticity had
previously taken away. Managers at American, TWA, and United, for example, signed lucrative new contracts with their flight attendant unions in
1976, guaranteeing hourly pay increases that outpaced those granted to pilots
and machinists during the same period.

Aiming to build on recent victories at the bargaining table, and invigorated after a decade of feminist and gay liberationist advances, flight attendants confronted the overwork that domesticity had helped produce. The

intensifying movement against overwork would center on a particular economic resource that flight attendants at all airlines sought in the late 1970s: work rules. Since pilots, machinists, and ground crews first organized in the 1930s and 1940s, work rules had been the foundation of their economic stability. Work rules provided such stability in two important ways. First, regardless of operational irregularities in a highly volatile industry like the airlines, work rules limited work hours and guaranteed that an employee could return home at a specific time. Second, work rules protected an employees' pay even when flights were canceled and crews were sent home without flying. Although airline men took ironclad work rules for granted by the 1970s, most flight attendants lacked such protections. Without stringent work rules, flight attendants were subject to vast monthly fluctuations in pay and in time away from home, irregularities that compromised their ability to provide for their families. By 1977, flight attendant activists had identified work rules as center of a new campaign against overwork.

As flight attendants mobilized for more pay and less time on the job, they practiced what historians have called "labor feminism." According to Dorothy Sue Cobble, labor feminism emerged as a self-conscious political strategy during the Great Depression, when working-class women demanded access to both wage labor and social programs that would help them balance work with family responsibilities. Unlike the middle-class feminist upsurges of the 1910s and the 1960s, which focused on the struggle for equal rights under the law, Cobble argues that generations of workingwomen have made the workplace and the trade union the primary venues for feminist political mobilization.[2] Furthermore, rather than assume that labor feminists had limited their agenda to a bid for equal access to men's jobs, Cobble demonstrates that they aimed to adapt a man's working world to women's particular political economic needs.[3]

Labor feminists' effort to transform male-centered professions involved changing workers' experience with time. In a booming post–World War II economy, large, mostly-male industrial unions had pushed for work schedules that included what United Automobile Workers president Walter Reuther called "lumps of leisure."[4] Trade unionists like Ruther supported long shifts and access to overtime pay in exchange for extended vacations and early retirement. Overtime would allow workingmen to buy the consumer products that would help them join the burgeoning middle class of the 1950s, while vacations and early retirement would ensure that they could enjoy those products with their families. Labor feminists, however, argued that men's leisure on vacation and in retirement depended on their wives' unacknowledged and unpaid domestic labor—toil that was made even harder when the many women who worked for wages did so on the long, inflexible shifts that industrial unions sought. To help women balance their responsibilities in the workplace and at home, labor feminists pushed for shorter workdays, pursuing contractual limitation of hours and federal legislation to reduce work time.[5]

When they mobilized for strict new work rules, flight attendants adapted labor feminists' earlier interventions about work time to the cultural landscape of the late 1970s. When, for example, they sought to limit the duration of the workday, flight attendants' echoed labor feminists' decades-old insistence that most women had to leave their jobs and report for duty on the second shift at home. But by 1976, the household included an ever more diverse array of kinship networks. After landing, many flight attendants would go home to provide physical, emotional, and financial resources to their husbands and their children. Many others, however, lived alone, were single parents, or were the breadwinners for same-sex partners or cohabitating friends or lovers. Activists thus were demanding new economic resources for both nuclear families and the growing number of people who chose relationships that fell outside the boundaries of traditional heterosexual monogamy and domesticity. Supporting these older- and newer-fashioned kinship networks would require an end to flight attendant overwork: access to more time away from the job and more money for hours spent in the air. As they intensified their political commitment to more resources for all flight attendants, work rules became the central goal of flight attendants' activism.

The new campaign for work rules inflamed the already deep tensions between rank-and-file flight attendants, their unions, and the airlines in the late 1970s. Since flight attendants were subordinate members of unions in which male higher-ups set the economic agenda, the bargaining process often paired flight attendants' economic goals to those of their male coworkers. Work rule improvements were thus secondary priorities because pilots, machinists, and ground crews who had already secured their work rules in previous decades tended to focus on hourly pay increases in the 1970s. To bump their own work rules to the top of the list, flight attendants would have to transform themselves into active political agents in their unions, a move that challenged those organizations' male-dominated leadership structures. Meanwhile, for four decades, the airlines had saved money as they withheld the work rules that would have protected flight attendants' pay and time off. Managers bristled at the cost of extending those benefits. Perhaps even more importantly, work rules would turn flight attendants into reliable, stable breadwinners for their families, a change that was politically contentious. Since many rank-and-file flight attendant activists had publicly and explicitly challenged heteropatriarchal power relations in the 1970s, providing flight attendants with new economic independence would further undermine a gendered system that had benefited airline managers and union leaders since the 1930s. Given the weight of that history, the campaign for work rules opened a cultural rift that would transform flight attendant union representation and the political economy of the airline industry on the cusp of the 1980s. This chapter chronicles that economic and cultural transformation.

Night Fever at Tiffany's in Marina del Rey

Although the substantive pay bumps of the spring and summer of 1976 temporarily cooled tensions between flight attendant activists, union leaders, and the airlines, those raises would not cure the institutionalized sexism and heterosexism that were the underlying cause of the dispute. With long-standing tensions looming, conflict reignited soon after the new contracts were ratified. While ties to the women's, gay, and lesbian liberation movements made flight attendants particularly bold in their demand for control over the day-to-day affairs of their unions, rank-and-file insurgency was by no means confined to the airlines in the late 1970s. Instead, and as Nelson Lichtenstein, Peter Rachleff, and other labor historians have demonstrated, the era saw the rise of a new rank-and-file democracy movement across industries.[6] Dissident union activists were rejecting the gradualist, politically blinkered unionism that had been big labor's status quo since the late 1940s. Amid the fierce anticommunism of the early Cold War, George Meany and other conservative trade unionists abandoned the cross-racial, socialist-influenced, arts-inflected 1930s politics of the Congress of Industrial Organizations (CIO), opting instead for a unionism focused on collective bargaining for incremental wage increases. But instead of advocating for a simple return to CIO-style Popular Front politics, participants in the rank-and-file democracy movement took their cues from the social transformation of the 1970s. Coming to the union movement from college campuses and the anti–Vietnam War movement, or after winning access to union jobs through civil rights and feminist activist advances, the new insurgents embraced the principles of those struggles: bottom-up campaign building, participatory democracy, and direct action. As they built those principles into lasting organizations such as "New Directions" in the UAW or the Teamsters for a Democratic Union, rank-and-file democracy activists would become a core of the effort to hold the line against management in the increasingly anti-union climate of the 1970s and 1980s.[7]

In flight attendants' particular case, the push for rank-and-file democracy stemmed from a 1970s feminist critique of their unions' mode of political representation. For dissident leaders, flight attendants' needs would never be met by union men who came of age in conservative Cold War unions, because those men's power and privilege would prevent them from sympathizing with flight attendants' political economic demands. These needs would be met when feminists, young women, single mothers, and lesbians and gays actually ran their unions. By 1977, then, flight attendants at Continental, Pan Am, American, TWA, and other carriers were aiming for more than just lucrative new contracts that would close the flight attendant pay gap. They aimed to take control of their political future by severing ties to male-led union bureaucracies.

Opening up her scrapbook at the kitchen table of her suburban Kansas City ranch home, Janet Lhuillier, a veteran of TWA's New York and Boston international bases, recalled the political and economic foundations of her decision to embrace the rank-and-file democracy movement among flight attendants in 1976. By that time, Lhuillier was no stranger to flight attendant activism, having walked out on strike with her TWA peers in 1970 and then again in 1973. But in both of those cases, strikes were initiated to strengthen the hand of male contract negotiators from the national office of the Transport Workers Union (TWU) who had never been flight attendants. In 1976, Lhuillier was insisting that she and her colleagues—and not union higher-ups—deserved to set bargaining priorities and call strikes.[8]

Rather than wait for orders from her union to begin her activism, Lhuillier joined the movement on her own terms in July 1976. That summer, flight attendants had threatened to shutter TWA during the New York bicentennial celebration if union leaders and managers failed to improve flight attendants' work rules (see Chapter 1). Angry about a June settlement offer that included a raise but few work rule enhancements, Lhuillier headed to the TWA hangar at Kennedy Airport, where an all-domicile meeting was under way between flight attendants and TWU staff. According to Lhuillier, the meeting with union higher-ups was even more disappointing than she expected:

> The little man the TWU sent looked like a beat-up bird. He had a patch over his eye and his arm in a sling. And he showed up with two HUGE bodyguards. And we were thinking, "Why does he need two bodyguards for flight attendants?!" So we kept asking him questions about our contract, and he didn't know anything. He didn't know anything about our work rules. He didn't know anything about what we were trying to negotiate. We were going, "How can this guy fight for us?"

Lhuillier's criticism grew, on the one hand, from a basic 1970s feminist demand for political representation. When over 90 percent of her colleagues were women,[9] and when she and many of her colleagues supported the new upsurge of feminist activism, an older man who had never experienced sex discrimination on the job would inevitably fail to advocate for flight attendants' political and economic interests. Indeed, as Lhuillier described a scenario that sounded like a scene from *On the Waterfront,* one in which union thugs battled corrupt managers to defend the interests of the workingman, she referenced a labor history that most flight attendants understood to be part of their collective oppression rather than a means to their liberation.

On the other hand, and even more importantly for the flight attendant rank-and-file democracy movement, Lhuillier was making an economic argument. Work rules were a center of the debate between flight attendants and the airlines in the late 1970s. In Lhuillier and other flight attendants' appraisals, the "beat-up bird" failed to understand how work rules could protect flight attendants' pay and why work rules were more important to flight attendants than other contractual improvements. Instead, he came to Kennedy Airport that day ready to talk about only percentile increases in hourly pay, the issue normally at the core of contract negotiations involving the other, mostly-male groups in the union. Those increases could be worthless for flight attendants without work rules that guaranteed each flight attendant a minimum number of hours each week and month—work rules that most workingmen already had. Disturbed that top union negotiators failed to understand the basic building blocks of flight attendants' compensation, Lhuillier walked away from that July 1976 meeting sure that she and her colleagues needed a new union. And she was not alone.

Transport Workers Union staff answered criticism from Lhuillier and her colleagues not with a concerted effort to mentor women into top leadership positions or to refocus collective bargaining on work rules, but with an increasingly vigorous countermobilization against dissent. At TWA, union higher-ups recognized that by the fall of 1976, they were facing a full-fledged, well-organized movement for a new union. That movement had a name—the Independent Federation of Flight Attendants (IFFA)—and rumor had it there were IFFA sympathizers among the elected local leaders of TWU Local 551, the flight attendants' existing union. While national union staff controlled flight attendants' economic agenda, elected rank-and-file officers were allowed to run their union on a day-to-day basis, staffing offices, processing paperwork, and filing grievances. Transport Workers Union staff had come to believe that at least some members of Local 551's leadership team agreed with Janet Lhuillier and her colleagues and were conspiring with a plan to sever the local's ties to the TWU. In October 1976, national leaders of the TWU called Local 551's executive board into an emergency meeting. Mary Ellen Miller, who had just finished negotiating the new 1976 contract and was one of the flight attendants summoned to the meeting, sketched out the theatrics that ensued:

> They called us all into TWU headquarters . . . and got really belliger-ent. All these big-name union guys. And they lined us up against this wall. They lined us up and brought out the TWU International Con-stitution. We were supposed to put our hand on it and swear—like a bible—that we would uphold the constitution of the union. [But in-stead] we swore on the constitution that we would support the TWA flight attendants and do what they wanted. Then the shit hit the fan big time. [TWU leaders] told us they were going to throw us out.[10]

Recognizing that their failure to submit to the loyalty oath could lead to their removal from office and ejection from the union, Local 551 activists soon dropped the pretense of support for national union higher-ups and declared their membership in the insurgency. On October 21, TWU Air Transport Division director Ernie Mitchell sent a letter to the officers of Local 551—President Arthur Teolis, Vice President Victoria Frankovich, and Secretary Treasurer Jim Tuller—ordering them to a meeting at the office of TWU International president Matty Guinan on October 26 in New York.[11] Rather than respond to Mitchell, President Teolis publicly addressed all TWA flight attendants the next day, declaring his support for IFFA and urging all of his colleagues to join the movement.[12] The following day, the Transport Workers Union put Local 551 in trusteeship, removing Teolis, Frankovich, and Tuller from office, charging them with "dual unionism," revoking all privileges of membership for the officers, and appointing Barney Spera to run the local in place of the dispatched activists.[13]

Although the cast of characters was different at American Airlines, the situation was equally acrimonious. A year earlier, as front-line flight attendants rejected a series of settlement pacts between TWU higher-ups and American managers, a series of affinity groups had formed to push the TWU toward a more militant stance at the bargaining table. Under banners like "The Com-mittee for a Fair Contract" and, more pointedly, "How Much More Can You Take?" these underground cells funneled information about the negotiations directly to rank-and-file flight attendants while chiding national union leaders for their ineptitude and ineffectiveness.[14] Although most affinity groups were short-lived, their orchestrators had begun to coalesce under the banner of APFA—the Association of Professional Flight Attendants—in the summer of 1976.

The surfacing of APFA brought swift sanctions from the Transport Workers Union. On August 27, 1976, national union staff got the attention of all American Airlines flight attendants when they sacked Patt Gibbs, removing her from an elected position in the Dallas base, revoking her membership privileges, and convicting her of dual unionism.[15] Gibbs was an outspoken member of the women's liberation movement, a lesbian feminist, and a leader of the Stewardesses for Women's Rights, the women's liberationist umbrella group demanding an end to institutionalized sex discrimination in the industry. The move against a highly visible representative of 1970s feminist politics demonstrated the union's willingness to take aggressive and unpopular steps to curb the flight attendant upsurge. Just as they did at TWA, union staff forced all 107 rank-and-file union representatives at American to take a loyalty oath on February 4, 1977, swearing to "bear true and faithful allegiance to the International and Local union." Seventy-seven flight attendants took the oath, but thirty refused it, opting to face ejection from the union.[16] The most visible activists were hit first: Ardell Callas was suspended from the base chair position in Boston, and Kathy Knoop was removed as Los Angeles vice chair on the day of the loyalty oath.[17] Then, on March 7, came a system-wide purge. All rank-and-file leaders in the Buffalo, Nashville, Chicago, Dallas, Los Angeles, and San Diego bases were removed from their positions.[18]

Transport Workers Union officials were responding with increasing force at American Airlines because they were in the process of being formally removed from TWA. After petitioning the National Mediation Board—the federal agency that interprets and implements labor law for airline and railway workers—for an official change-in-representation election, TWA flight attendants went to the polls on February 8, 1977, to decide whether or not to continue their relationship with the Transport Workers Union. The vote was a draw: 44 percent of voters chose the TWU, 44 percent chose IFFA, and 9 percent wrote in the Association of Flight Attendants (AFA)—another woman-led national flight attendant union that had big shops at United and Braniff, among other carriers.[19] Members were clearly divided about how best to move the flight attendant movement forward, about the pros and cons of cutting ties to a relatively wealthy union and the strike fund it controlled, and about whether or not Arthur Teolis, Victoria Frankovich, and other strident activists really represented the worldviews of ordinary TWA flight attendants. But after seven more weeks of campaigning, and after the TWU failed to formally address the issue of work rules that was the centerpiece of IFFA's campaign, flight attendants for TWA chose to go independent. In a runoff election on March 22, 1977, by a margin of 59 percent to 39 percent, the group made IFFA the union that would take TWA flight attendants into the 1980s.[20]

IFFA's upset at TWA left dissident flight attendants at American partying. During the first weekend in April, activists held three simultaneous discos to benefit APFA. Cover charges and bar proceeds from a long night of disco dancing at Faces in Chicago, Truffles in Dallas, and Tiffany's in Marina del Rey, just north of the runways at Los Angeles International Airport, helped fund the new union's get-out-the-vote effort.[21] The parties quickly paid off. On May 3, 1977, American Airlines flight attendants went to the polls in their own change-of-representation election: 75 percent of flight attendants voted, choosing APFA by a margin of 58 percent to 41 percent.[22]

The American and TWA elections were part of a political cacophony from flight attendants in the late 1970s. Save for the decertification of the TWU at the small supplemental carrier Seaboard World in 1965, there had never been a rank and file–initiated flight attendant change in representation in the United States before 1970. But by 1976 they were virtually constant. That year, Northwest Airlines flight attendants—who had abandoned the TWU for AFA in 1971—left AFA for the Teamsters; National Airlines flight attendants dropped AFA for the TWU; and Continental Airlines flight attendants went independent, forming the Union of Flight Attendants Local 1. And just five months after the TWA and American elections, Pan Am flight attendants ditched the TWU, also going independent in October 1977.[23] Even in places where decertification attempts were not made, such as AFA's shop at United or the TWU's at Eastern Airlines and Southern Airways, labor leaders were on notice: a burgeoning rank-and-file democracy movement was under way among flight attendants, one committed to the political agenda of the women's, gay, and lesbian liberation movements of the decade, and one demanding substantive economic gains through progress on work rules. Unions could either deliver those goods or, as flight attendants would say, collect all of their carry-on items and leave the aircraft.

Carrying the Movement Forward with Work Rules

The new unions at Continental, American, TWA, and other airlines understood their comfortable margin of victory in the change-in-representation elections of the late 1970s as a mandate for change and immediately presented management with a new economic agenda. There was a clear continuity between that agenda and the one that drove the unrest in the summer of 1976. The new leaders were, of course, still focused on winning a breadwinner wage for flight attendants by closing the pay gap between themselves and other airline employees. Doing so would force the industry to provide material resources for the diverse spectrum of domestic arrangements among flight attendants, resources that women's, gay, and lesbian liberationists were seeking in many workplaces. But when flight attendants sat down at the bargaining table on their own terms and in control of their own finances, activists offered a clear new focus for their effort to winning more time away from work and more money: contractual work rules.

Leaders of the new unions coalesced around work rules because of the highly unusual manner in which flight attendants are paid. As in many other unionized professions, flight attendants earn income by the hour. But instead of making their wage from the moment they arrive at work until the moment they leave—like the factory worker at the punch clock—flight attendants are paid only while the aircraft is en route. On most modern aircraft, a computer sensor attached to the parking brake system triggers flight attendant pay, starting the clock when the brakes come off and ending compensation as soon as the brakes are set on arrival. Flight attendants are not paid until the approximate moment that the purser says, "Flight attendants, prepare the doors for departure"—when the crew engages the airplane's emergency slides in advance of pushback—and pay stops when the purser says, "Flight attendants, disarm doors for arrival and cross check." This presents a problem for flight attendants because they earn no income while performing some of the most essential and most difficult elements of their jobs: calming down angry businesspeople during boarding when overhead bin space for their overstuffed rolling suitcases runs out, soothing stranded passengers on airport concourses during thunderstorms and blizzards, or simply watching television alone in hotel rooms night after night, away from family and friends. Worse yet, when flights cancel, flight attendants earn no pay at all—even when cancellations come after flight attendants put on their uniforms, get their kids to child care, arrive at the airport, and assist their passengers with boarding.

Work rules help flight attendants remedy the problem of unpaid labor by shifting the economic risk associated with airline operations back toward management. The following two case studies illuminate the economic foundations of flight attendants' push for work rules. Both reference the operational experiences that flight attendants described during interviews for this book. The details of the narratives are then placed in the context of specific contractual work rules that flight attendants sought and won in the late 1970s. For the sake of consistent comparison, I assume that each of the flight attendants makes the same wage: $20 per hour, a round number that is a roughly average starting wage for a flight attendant today.

A Tale of "Duty Rigs"

There are far too many work rules to present them comprehensively, since most flight attendant contracts were over three hundred single-spaced pages long in the late 1970s. The following two examples, however, showcase the work rules that have been most effective in transferring risk away from flight attendants and toward the airlines. The first hinges on a concept called "ratios-in-guarantee," or in industry parlance, "rigs." Designed to ensure a reasonable wage for each day and each trip that a flight attendant works, rigs build a ratio between the number of hours worked and the number of hours paid. United flight attendants, for example, had a "1-for-2 duty rig" by the mid-1970s, which gave a flight attendant at least one hour of pay for every two hours spent on "duty"[24]—when she is at the airport or aboard an aircraft but not necessarily flying.

Duty rigs are particularly important in the predictably unpredictable airline industry. Take a given morning, when a Chicago-based flight attendant checks in for a one-day trip to New York. The trip has the flight attendant working the 8:00 A.M. flight from Chicago O'Hare to LaGuardia Airport, and then working another flight back home, which is scheduled to arrive at 2:00 P.M. Unfortunately for the flight attendant, just as she enters the terminal, a passenger distraught from a business deal gone bust bolts backward up the down escalator without clearing security and vanishes into the terminal. Security clamps down, evacuating the entire airport. At her original departure time, the flight attendant is standing in the airport driveway with twelve thousand of her passengers, going nowhere. When she finally gets back to operations around 11:00 A.M., she finds out that her New York flight is canceled. Crew schedulers order her to work a short hop to Cincinnati that finally leaves at 1:00 P.M. and then will turn around and bring her home before dinner.

Things get worse in Cincinnati. Right before departure for the trip home, at four o'clock on a hot afternoon, a thunderstorm deluges O'Hare, shutting down arrivals from all directions. Ten minutes before they are supposed to close the door in Cincinnati, they get the word about the storm and proceed to sit in the suffocating aircraft full of passengers for three hours. As the storm clears Chicago, it bears down on Cincinnati, but luckily the flight attendant's trip rolls on departure in the tiny window between the sun coming out in Chicago and the squall line coming up the Ohio River valley. Landing finally takes place at 8:30 P.M. Heading to the parking lot, the flight attendant has worked exactly fourteen hours. Here emerges the importance of duty rigs. Under the TWA contract that led to the 1976 standoff, the flight attendant would get paid for only the two one-hour flights to Cincinnati and back. At $20 per hour, her daily wage is $40. But if she were flying under the United contract of 1976, she would be paid under the 1-for-2 duty rig, which, after a fourteen-hour day, guarantees seven hours of pay.[25] Her daily wage would be $140, or 3.5 times that of the TWA flight attendant who earns the *exact* same hourly pay. In this case, duty rigs—rather than an hourly pay increase—would be the most important resource for increasing the flight attendant's standard of living.

A Tale of "Line Guarantees"

Equaling rigs in their fundamental importance to flight attendant activists are another set of work rules called "line guarantees." This set of strictures allows flight attendants to count on a baseline monthly wage. Line guarantees stem from the unique way in which flight attendants choose their schedules and, in effect, their wages. In the middle of every month, flight attendants "bid" on schedules for the following month. The days in that month are laid out in a line, with trips that last anywhere from one day to two weeks beginning on given days of that month. Each flight attendant submits requests—or "bids"—for the "line" with patterns of trips matching her favored dates, favored times of day, favored layover cities, and favored aircraft types. That month-long group of trips, or "line of flying," represents a fixed number of hours if all goes according to plan. Airline work, however, rarely goes according to plan. Storms brew, airplanes break down, and air traffic control delays mount, inevitably canceling some of the trips that the flight attendant originally bid on. The purpose of line guarantees is to lock in the cash value of the line of flying that the flight attendant bid on, setting that value as the particular employee's minimum monthly wage. Even if flights cancel, the flight attendant will be paid what she bid, with the airline thus assuming the full economic risk of the operation.

To demonstrate the importance of line guarantees, I return to the Chicago-based flight attendant, a single mother with two kids. This time she is headed to O'Hare for an international trip, working the 15.5-hour nonstop to Hong Kong. Between a sister and a neighbor, the flight attendant has access to free child care on the weekends, so she bids trips that check in Friday mornings and return on Mondays. Her sister works nights starting Mondays, so our flight attendant must be home in due time for the sister's 7:00 P.M. start.

On a given Friday morning, a supervisor joins the Hong Kong crew for briefing in O'Hare operations, mentioning a "minor" problem with the pressurization system of the airplane they are slated to take to Hong Kong. But as the flight attendants walk aboard the Boeing 747, seemingly dozens of mechanics are on ladders undoing what looks like miles of ductwork. "She's a goner," the captain barks as he makes his way down the staircase from the upper deck, bags in hand and apparently leaving the aircraft. Shortly thereafter, the jetway phone rings, bringing news that the flight is canceled.

As the trip is scrubbed, line guarantees—those in all United Airlines contracts since the 1970s—kick in to govern the outcome of the situation. Though the flight attendant will now go nowhere near Hong Kong, her pay for the trip is protected. The airline, then, may reassign her to another trip. But contractual work rules also mandate that any replacement trip must return within six hours of the originally scheduled Hong Kong arrival, which in this case would be 9:00 A.M. Monday.[26] Crew schedulers immediately recognize that they need flight attendants to cover the following evening's London flight, but since that trip doesn't return until Monday at 7:00 P.M.— four hours past the return deadline listed under the line guarantee work rules—they may not assign any of the Hong Kong flight attendants to the London trip. The only open trip available for the flight attendant, it turns out, is a two-day domestic trip with a Philadelphia layover that returns Monday at 1:00 P.M. Thus, she heads home, gaining two unexpected days off to spend with friends, kids, or as she pleases, and then coming back to work to fly the Philadelphia trip on Sunday.

Now imagine her without line guarantees. Once the Hong Kong trip cancels, all of her weekly pay is in jeopardy. Back at crew scheduling, she is informed about the Philadelphia trip and the London trip. The flight attendant immediately recognizes that she cannot afford to work the Philadelphia trip because at ten hours of pay—versus the thirty hours for the Hong Kong trip—two-thirds of her weekly earnings disappear. So she takes the London trip. But its late arrival on Monday snags her child-care plans. At an airline without line guarantees—Continental Airlines after 1983, for example[27]— she would have to have a child-care backup, since late arrivals would be commonplace without contractual rules to protect against them. She could call a babysitter to pick the kids up at school and stay with them until she gets home. But if she is late coming out of Heathrow, that option will get even more expensive. Either way, the flight attendant without work rules shoulders the risk of the canceled flight to Hong Kong.

Line guarantees dramatically alter this flight attendant's weekly pay. With the line guarantee, the flight attendant is paid the full, thirty-hour value of the Hong Kong trip, even though she flew only the ten-hour Philadelphia trip. At $20 per hour, her weekly wage is $600, exactly as she planned it the month before. But without line guarantees, she would get paid for only the much shorter London trip, which is worth nineteen hours, or $380. Moreover, that extra babysitter cost $50, so pay after special family expenses drops to $330 for a week. With line guarantees, the flight attendant makes almost twice as much as without them at the *exact* same wage. This is why flight attendants were so committed to action on work rules in the late 1970s. Even if management was promising some flight attendants a 40 percent raise in hourly pay, as they were at TWA in 1976, without duty rigs, line guarantees, or scores of other work rules that flight attendants sought, the actual cash value of that raise was up in the air.

As they turned their attention to work rules to free themselves from the economic risk of airline work, flight attendants were demanding only what the workingmen who were members of the UAW, the Steelworkers, the United Food and Commercial Workers, and other large industrial unions had long expected. Flight attendants wanted to know exactly when they could leave work. They wanted to know the exact value of their monthly wage. Flight attendants, in other words, wanted access to the basic middle-class model of employment that followed the successful union upsurge of the 1930s. Activists in the new flight attendant unions were, however, making those demands for a group of people who were increasingly vocal critics of middle-class values. Indeed, for the single people, the unmarried mothers, the feminists, the gays, and the lesbians, work rules were as likely to allow flight attendants to deviate from middle-class standards as to embrace them. With work rules, in other words, flight attendants would have the economic resources to live how they chose, whether that life revolved around marriage, domesticity, and heterosexuality or not. The push for work rules, then, helped flight attendants carry the liberation movements of the 1970s forward—even if those dense contractual formulas share little with gay or feminist activism at first glance. From the push for work rules, it was turning out, flight attendants had created a strategy to move marginalized people out of marginal work.

The Watershed Economic Advances of the Late 1970s

As they handed managers reams of contract proposals for duty time limitations, trip rigs, and line guarantees, the new flight attendant unions presented the airlines with an ambitious program. Although strategies varied among the airlines, all the new unions displayed a labor feminist commitment to ending overwork and aimed to deliver on that commitment quickly. Pan Am flight attendants, for example, focused their activism on traditional collective bargaining. Three months after flight attendants certified their new union, the

Independent Union of Flight Attendants, leaders sent the airline an opening proposal for contract negotiations in December 1977. Consisting of fifty-eight single-spaced pages of detailed, heavily annotated proposals, the opener demanded nothing short of a watershed reworking of flight attendants' pay, benefits, and working conditions.[28] After grinding through seventeen months of back-and-forths with Pan Am managers, and after tensions culminated in a brief strike in April 1979, activists made many of those proposals—and an impressive 45 percent baseline wage increase—a reality.[29] Among the coveted work rules in the new agreement was the industry's strictest international duty time limitation, one that protected flight attendants from fatigue by limiting most workdays to thirteen hours and providing extra staffing to prevent overwork on the few long-haul flights that kept crews on duty for longer periods.[30]

American Airlines flight attendants, meanwhile, led with a more unorthodox strategy. Fired up after their resounding electoral victory, the new leaders of the Association of Professional Flight Attendants refused to wait for the regular contract negotiations cycle to push for improvements in working conditions. Just weeks after the new union's certification, APFA sent management official notice of their intent to pursue unprecedented midcontract negotiations in July 1977. The overture included work rule proposals for a new four-tier "reserve" system that would rotate responsibilities for on-call flying to mitigate burnout, low- and high-time flying options that would allow individuals to maximize time off or earning potential, and increased staffing on American's large fleet of Boeing 727s.[31] Predictably, American slammed the door in APFA's face, blasting Patt Gibbs—the women's liberation movement organizer who was elected APFA's first president—for "undermining the labor-management relationship," for "attempting to coerce the company into adopting APFA's plan," and for preparing a document that was "completely unacceptable for serious consideration."[32] Although the rebuke forced activists at American to wait for regular negotiations to advance their agenda, APFA demonstrated that flight attendants were newly and passionately committed to intervening in the workplace. Even more importantly, activists eventually won many of APFA's 1977 midcontract demands, making multitier reserve rotation, low- and high-time scheduling options, and increased cabin staffing standard by the early 1980s.[33]

While Gibbs and the American Airlines group were combative, TWA flight attendants were calm and calculated, though no less ambitious. Mindful of the infighting and unruliness that had dominated the summer of 1976, TWA flight attendants went into talks for a new contract in the spring of 1978, aiming to innovate not just on *what* would be in a new contract but on *how* they would win an accord at the bargaining table. Preparing to approach

TWA to open negotiations, activists in the newly formed IFFA began with the premise that the very process of collective bargaining in the airline industry was a root cause of frequently disappointing outcomes for workers. Most troubling about airline negotiations was their unfailingly glacial pace. Such slowness was a consequence of the airline industry's unique relationship to federal labor law. While most employees work under the National Labor Relations Act of 1935, a law that was among Franklin D. Roosevelt's most important New Deal accomplishments, the Railway Labor Act (RLA) of 1926 covers workers on the railroads and in the airlines. The RLA was ratified at the apex of management power over unions following the "open shop drive" that rolled back craft union power in the early 1920s.[34] Though management activism had significantly demobilized the labor movement by mid-decade, small pockets of committed employees—especially railroad engineers, firemen, brakemen, and machinists—could still hobble core industries and disrupt the economy. Taking advantage of the anti-union consensus in Congress, elected officials crafted a new law that would maintain a reform-oriented commitment to labor peace while permanently snuffing out labor radicalism in the nation's transportation system. Congress accomplished this by making railroad and airline union contracts endless. Instead of expiring, as they do in all other industries, the RLA mandates that collective bargaining agreements become "amendable" at the end of their term. The lack of a formal expiration date means that airline and rail employees have no automatic right to strike. Employees can still resort to a walkout, but only after a federal panel called the National Mediation Board (NMB) authorizes such a strike. That petition process regularly takes months or even years in the airline industry, a status quo that is lucrative for managers as employees continue to earn the outdated wages of the previous contract as they wait for the NMB to set a strike date.[35]

To counteract the slowness of the RLA process, airline unions—especially the Air Line Employees Association for ground employees at National Airlines and the Association of Flight Attendants units at Alaska and Braniff—designed an expedited negotiations process in the mid-1970s. The new, faster bargaining system was based on a horse trade in which airlines would promise employees total wage increases of at least 5 percent on an annual basis and unions would waive their right to strike in exchange for the automatic raise. Regular pay increases were the quid pro quo for union commitment to labor peace, a trade-off that mirrored the incrementalist unionism that was dominant among the powerful unions of the manufacturing sector.[36]

TWA flight attendants decided to use expedited negotiations as scaffolding for upcoming talks with management in 1978. But given their generation's commitment to direct action protest and member mobilization, IFFA leaders such as Victoria Frankovich, Mary Ellen Miller, and Arthur Teolis refused to agree to any framework that would forfeit flight attendants' right to strike. Since TWA had made a $64 million profit in 1977,[37] and because rank-and-file flight attendants understood that profit to be evidence that the airline could afford to provide work rule improvements, Frankovich and the others recognized that signing away flight attendants' strike threat would have debilitating political consequences for their new union. Thus, IFFA proposed a different horse trade. In March 1978, activists approached TWA with a tight timeline for negotiations. The union and the company would simultaneously submit a bargaining petition limited to twenty-five items. TWA and IFFA would have six weeks to talk over those proposals. If no deal resulted, a federal mediator would be appointed for a month of supervised talks. At the end of that month, parties could either proffer arbitration, a back-and-forth system requiring parties to meet in the middle of their differences, or, presumably, petition the National Mediation Board for a strike release. There would be no IFFA waiver of the right to strike, and TWA would have no responsibility to provide a raise.[38]

Well aware of flight attendants' activist vigor and glad to limit the number of items on the table, management accepted the deal, and IFFA and TWA submitted their openers on April 10, 1978. The details of the opening contract proposals paint a telling picture about the balance of power between workers and management amid the flight attendant unionist upsurge of the late 1970s. Management's opener was detailed and modest, using each of its twenty-five allotments to seek, for example, minor modifications like a reduction in meal budgets for Tel Aviv layovers, elimination of the $2.50 per day en-route laundry compensation, reduction by one day of time off for domicile transfers, and elimination of the pay differential between the Boeing 707 and 747.[39] IFFA's pitch, conversely, was open-ended and expansive. Line items dotted the IFFA dossier, including "revise and increase all elements of pay," "reduce on-duty time limitations," "improve sick leave protection," and "eliminate all discriminatory practices." Although aggressive proposals like the ones IFFA was making would dominate management's bargaining position after the anti-union advances of the Reagan years, it was a union that offered this transformative approach in the late 1970s.[40]

After only twenty months off since the upheaval of the summer of 1976, the IFFA bargaining team—this time Victoria Frankovich, Mary Ellen Miller, Bill Numrich, Arthur Teolis, and Roberto Veitia[41]—was back in marathon talks with TWA. Though private bargaining broke down on May 26, forcing the dispute into government-supervised mediation, the overall pace of negotiations was remarkably rapid. After only ninety-five days at the table—a sixth the length of the 1976 standoff—IFFA and TWA reached a tentative agreement on July 14, 1978. The new pact greatly increased flight attendants' take-home compensation by augmenting their work rules: guaranteeing a new $1.25 per hour per diem for entire trips, extending full pay credit for "deadhead" flights where flight attendants ride to work as passengers, an industry-leading 1-for-3.5 trip rig, and a significant improvement in minimum monthly pay for flight attendants with on-call reserve schedules. The accord also included major symbolic improvements, among them crew meal parity with pilots, a standard rooted in the push for gender equality that was unheard-of in the industry before the 1978 deal. Additionally, the contract included a "reopener clause," giving flight attendants a permanent right to weigh in on the structure and operation of the company in a changing industry by automatically compelling TWA to bargain with IFFA in the event of a corporate merger, route transfer, or change of ownership.[42] IFFA certainly fell short of prevailing in a few key areas, as TWA could still monitor flight attendants' appearance and body size and ground them for missing weight loss targets, for example, and as the union failed to persuade the company to agree to the coveted 1-for-2 duty rig. Nevertheless, the deal was an undeniable victory for IFFA on the grueling terrain of the RLA, the first pact *ever* reached before the amendable date in the history of flight attendant unionism. IFFA leaders immediately endorsed the contract and sent it to the general membership, which ratified the three-year accord on July 30, 1978.[43]

Pan Am, American, and TWA flight attendants were still working in an economy stratified around race, gender, and sexuality as they celebrated their lucrative new contracts. Supervisors could stop flight attendants and inspect their hair, fingernails, and makeup at any time and could fire flight attendants for gaining weight. Nevertheless, the new unions had shown that feminized service employees could make economic gains at work. Activists demonstrated that they could build a social movement around that economic oppression and could use the momentum of that movement to outpace their much more privileged peers in the unions of the manufacturing sector. The new flight attendant unions had thus proved that with an ambitious strategy and an effective organization, those doing "women's work" could win a family wage.

Time, Money, Peripheral Bargaining, and the Night of March 4, 1983

As the ink dried on the robust new contracts at Pan Am, American, and TWA, vast political economic changes swept across the industry that would transform the nature of airline work. In October 1978, President Jimmy Carter signed the Airline Deregulation Act (see Chapter 3). By eliminating government price controls and removing barriers to entry, the act opened the established carriers to new competition from upstart, non-union firms with far lower labor costs. Amid the shock of regulatory reform and because of the deep recession of 1982, many of the largest airlines posted record economic losses. Trying to stop the hemorrhaging, managers turned to unionized workers for pay and benefit concessions. Unwilling to accept employers' proposals that would have cut compensation by as much as 50 percent, unionized workers in all trades countermobilized in protest. Long, bitter strikes ensued at United, Continental, and TWA, and by the early 1990s, once-powerful Braniff, Eastern, and Pan Am had collapsed.

As the turmoil of deregulation intensified, flight attendants' labor feminist program became a focus of the conflict between corporations and workers. Nowhere were these tensions more vivid than at TWA. Although they deeply opposed flight attendants' goals, managers at TWA and other major carriers had begun to understand the substance of activists' politics. They recognized that flight attendant unionism was fundamentally different from pilots,' machinists,' and ground crews' strategy at the bargaining table. Whereas men's unions had pushed a narrow economic program centered on incremental hourly pay increases, flight attendants had broadly challenged the ideology of domesticity, both demanding an end to marriage prohibitions, age restrictions, and other overtly sexist policies and seeking the economic resources to close the flight attendant wage gap. Managers also knew that by the late 1970s, contractual work rules were the primary means through which flight attendants hoped to advance their expansive agenda, because work rules would guarantee flight attendants more money and less time at work.

With the industry in crisis, TWA executives attempted to exploit flight attendants' political and cultural commitments to strengthen their own position against the labor movement. In 1981, managers insisted that IFFA forfeit many of the work rule gains that they had made in late 1970s. Company negotiators calculated that the bid for work rule concessions would have two possible outcomes, both of which would benefit TWA. Flight attendants would either acquiesce to the givebacks, which would save the company money in a weak economy, or they would strike in protest, which would provide a legal opening for TWA to hire permanent replacement workers and break the union. But because management only partially understood the substance of labor feminism, and because they underestimated the importance of economic resources to the women's, gay, and lesbian liberation movements, TWA's strategy backfired.

The new conflict between TWA and IFFA began when the 1978 collective bargaining agreement became open for renegotiation. Hoping to replicate the success of their previous strategy, union activists submitted a proffer for expedited negotiations well in advance of the contract's amendable date of June 30, 1981. With the company's finances deteriorating in a deregulated marketplace, and as the economy slid into recession, managers swiftly rejected IFFA's overture.[44] Unwilling to participate in the narrower, faster negotiations that had benefited the union in 1978, management sent flight attendants a deeply concessionary forty-six-item opening proposal for traditional bargaining on April 1, 1981. The opener came with a stern warning from TWA president Ed Meyer. Like all unionized employees, flight attendants would be required to accept an eighteen-month pay freeze. Furthermore, and in a move that would raise the ire of IFFA members and leaders, Meyer insisted that flight attendants be ready to forfeit the work rule gains they had made in 1978. To demonstrate his seriousness, Meyer let flight attendants know that TWA's top executives would have to sign off on any changes to the flight attendant contract, which was a highly unusual mandate in an industry where company brass usually stayed above the fray of day-to-day negotiations.[45]

IFFA responded assertively to Meyer's warning, although in far more measured terms than they would have used at the peak of the flight attendant upsurge of the 1970s. Maintaining their long-standing opposition to differential treatment for flight attendants, activists indicated that they would join all TWA employees in accepting the eighteen-month pay freeze but that they would refuse to entertain demands for work rule givebacks made solely of IFFA. Company negotiators quickly rejected two proposals from flight attendants that would have traded the wage freeze for work rule protections, declining IFFA settlement offers in June and then again in November 1981. After eighteen months of fruitless talks, and in an effort to prove their commitment to defending their work rules, activists conducted a strike vote on September 22, 1982. At the pit of the recession, and regardless of the highest unemployment rate since the Great Depression, rank-and-file flight attendants overwhelmingly endorsed a walkout if management continued to insist on work rule concessions.[46]

Despite their members' militancy, IFFA leaders pursued a compromise with TWA. On January 26, 1983, flight attendants submitted a proffer for arbitration with management, which would have allowed a neutral referee to settle the conflict between the company and IFFA. Opening the door to arbitration was a conciliatory move by the union; the process aimed to split the difference between TWA and IFFA and would allow the company to realize many of its demands for concessions, including those on work rules. But in a move that rattled activists, TWA swiftly rejected IFFA's olive branch, declining the proffer for arbitration. Absent any progress at the bargaining table, the National Mediation Board declared an impasse between TWA and its flight attendants on February 22, 1983. Thirty days later, the Railway Labor Act would let flight attendants walk out on strike and would allow the airline to implement its demand for a pay freeze plus work rule concessions.[47]

Soon after the impasse, Ed Meyer's management team drastically upped the stakes of the standoff. During the last week of February, the company sent a new settlement offer directly to the homes of all fifty-five hundred TWA flight attendants. They did so without notifying core union activists and without offering to negotiate the deal. Meyer's effort to bypass traditional collective bargaining exemplifies what labor relations scholar Kenneth Jennings calls "peripheral bargaining." According to Jennings, as employers recognized that the political tide had turned against unions in the 1980s, they were more likely to involve parties external to negotiations to increase their leverage against the labor movement. Rather than focus on direct talks with elected union officials, companies lobbied Congress for new antistrike legislation, created eye-catching media campaigns to sway public opinion, and appealed directly to rank-and-file union members as they strove to build a new national consensus against strikes. By creating distracting spectacles, peripheral bargaining strategies helped managers make contract talks slower, more contentious, and less favorable to workers.[48]

TWA's foray into peripheral bargaining shocked IFFA activists. Although the offer that managers sent directly to flight attendants included the work rule cuts that management had sought from IFFA, it came with an hourly pay increase of approximately 30 percent over five years.[49] Over twice the amount that TWA was offering at the bargaining table, the pay bump was particularly valuable because the rate of inflation had fallen sharply after the Federal Reserve raised interest rates in 1981. If economists' forecasts for a long-term reduction in inflation proved correct, Meyer's offer would vastly improve all flight attendants' standard of living. TWA seemed to be serious: managers lobbied individual flight attendants to call their union leaders and urge them to accept the agreement that TWA had sent through the mail.

Although managers refused to explain their peripheral bargaining strategy to flight attendants, IFFA activists made an educated guess about the company's aims. Union leaders speculated that TWA offered the 30 percent raise in an effort to divide rank-and-file flight attendants from the IFFA negotiating committee. Most of Ed Meyer's leadership team had watched Mary Ellen Miller, Victoria Frankovich, and other young activists come of age in the women's liberation movement of the 1970s. They knew that a deep-seated commitment to feminist principles had guided Miller and Frankovich at the bargaining table and within the labor movement. Meyer's team also knew that work rules were the centerpiece of the next phase of their labor feminist campaign. Though most TWA flight attendants wholly endorsed leaders' bid to end sex discrimination and to improve working conditions, managers guessed that core activists had a more sophisticated understanding of political and economic issues than ordinary flight attendants. According to activists, because of TWA's assumption about that difference in sophistication, managers wagered that IFFA leaders would be more committed to protecting work rules than those on the front lines. Managers thus made an offer that coupled work rule givebacks with a large pay increase, a package that they guessed would appeal to the rank and file while remaining unacceptable to union leaders. If IFFA activists rejected the work rule concessions and therefore refused the 30 percent raise, the company hoped that activists like Frankovich and Miller would seem ideological and intransigent to ordinary TWA flight attendants. When the rank and file blamed IFFA and not TWA for scuttling the deal, the union would lose the solidarity necessary for it to negotiate a better contract or to win a strike.

Management's effort to isolate IFFA activists quickly proved to have been an immense miscalculation. For a decade, flight attendants at TWA and most other airlines had pushed for work rules not because they were intransigent ideologues but because work rules were a surefire way to end the chronic sex discrimination that had been endemic to the labor economics of the airline industry for forty years. Work rules would give flight attendants the time and money that pilots, machinists, ground crews, and managers had always expected. In this particular case, a 30 percent raise in an era of low inflation would do the exact same thing—even if it came with rule givebacks. Flight attendants could use the large pay bump to buy a house or save for a child's college education, or they could use it reduce their hours in an effort to better balance family and work. A 30 percent raise would, in other words, give TWA flight attendants both the time and the money that they had been demanding since the mid-1970s. Those economic resources would constitute a substantive political victory for a group of mostly-women union members whose trade had always been defined by low pay and overwork. Furthermore, TWA's offer would help finance the cultural transformation that the women's, gay, and lesbian liberation movements had championed, because it would provide flight attendants with the material resources to live comfortably outside the boundaries of domesticity, marriage, and heterosexuality if they chose to do so.

Recognizing that they were about to beat management at its own game, the IFFA negotiating committee crafted a response to TWA's peripheral bargaining offer.[50] The union would go back into negotiations with TWA and would attempt to persuade company negotiators to rescind some of the work rule givebacks that they had paired with the 30 percent raise. Activists would push the negotiations as far as possible, but even if the company ceded no ground on work rules, IFFA leaders would accept the contract. The moment they uncapped their pens, the negotiating committee would lock in the largest real-dollar raise in the history of their work group.

TWA flight attendants executed their plan just before midnight on March 4, 1983. During what could have been another long night of circular work rule talks, union activists returned from a short recess and sat down at the bargaining table across from TWA's team. But instead of resuming negotiations, the flight attendants made an announcement, one that provoked a shouting match between the company, the union, and the federal mediator who had been refereeing talks during the year of turmoil.

"Okay, we'll take it," the IFFA team announced.

Mary Ellen Miller, one of the five activists who delivered the news, describes the drama that ensued:

"WHAT?!" company negotiators barked. "No!"

According to Miller and others present, TWA's team then grabbed the mailed-out offer and ripped it off the table.

As soon as they did so, the mediator took the lead in yelling.

"NO, YOU OFFERED IT. IT'S A DONE DEAL,"[51] he shouted, ordering TWA to place the deal back on the bargaining table.

The mediator reminded both parties that since IFFA and TWA had formally agreed to mediation over a year earlier, federal labor law mandates that every settlement offer must remain on the table until the opposite party formally accepts or rejects the offer. Miller and the other IFFA activists had certainly castigated managers for undermining the bargaining process when they sent the offer directly to flight attendants' homes and had condemned the work rule givebacks in the deal. But they had never rejected it. The union, therefore, could accept the deal at any time.

As the two parties put their pens to the paper, the deal proved that activists Frankovich and Miller were not the ideologues the company had hoped for. The flight attendant union movement was able to adopt a flexible set of strategies to further its core political goal: ending the economic sex discrimination that flight attendants had borne since the 1930s. Management quickly recognized this, but only after it was too late to change its strategy. Company negotiators were furious. TWA's team was, in Victoria Frankovich's recollection, "crestfallen" and "visibly shaken."[52] "They yelled at us all the way down the hallway afterward," Mary Ellen Miller later recalled. "We made them look bad."[53]

The managers were chagrined, but the front-line flight attendants were elated when IFFA leaders brought news of "one of the most lucrative economic offers recently negotiated by any group in the airline industry."[54] By the third year of the contract, TWA flight attendants with regular domestic schedules would be starting at a wage of $23.81 per flight hour. Assuming that airline crews fly an average of one thousand hours per year—the number most airline unions use to calculate their members' annual earnings—new hires would join the industry making just under $24,000 per year in 1984. With inflation figured in, that means a TWA flight attendant could have made up to $54,000 in 2015 dollars during her first year on the job. To put the new wages in context, new hires in UAW-organized General Motors plants were starting at roughly $56,000 inflation-adjusted dollars per year during the same period.[55] Though wages in manufacturing were already falling in successive rounds of concessionary bargaining during the anti-union upsurge of the Reagan years, flight attendant pay had matched or exceeded workingmen's breadwinner wages by the mid-1980s. Indeed, the top wage for international flight attendants with at least twelve years of experience in the 1983 TWA settlement was $42.64 an hour. With inflation figured in, a full-time, senior TWA flight attendant could have pulled in as much as $97,000 a year in 2015 dollars.[56]

Front-line flight attendants wholeheartedly endorsed the accord in a referendum, validating the contract on April 12, 1983. All TWA flight attendants I interviewed for this book described the 1983 deal as among the most important moments of their careers. Janet Lhuillier beamed as she remembered hearing the news:

> The 1983 contract victory was a fabulous psychological story. I remember sitting there on the Champs-Elysées on a Paris layover having a cup of tea, and I am going, "I am richer than shit right now!" It was absolutely phenomenal because all of a sudden we were paid so much for doing our jobs. People were like, "I can buy my own home. I can buy my own car. I can take care of my son. I can put my kids through school." All of a sudden, flight attendants' self-esteem rose.[57]

Here Lhuillier captures the political and cultural significance of the victory. With the advance at the bargaining table, flight attendants proved that one could access middle-class economic resources without necessarily living in middle-class social locations or subscribing to middle-class values. All of a sudden, just like autoworkers, just like machinists, and just like building tradesmen, flight attendants could buy a house, send a child to the university, or take a winter vacation at the beach. But unlike their labor movement peers, 91 percent of TWA flight attendants in the mid-1980s were women.[58] And even if a flight attendant was a man, his labor was more likely to be dismissed as feminized and servile than read as a sign of his independence and skill. Therefore, although many flight attendants lived in domesticated, nuclear families, those families became far less traditional after March 1983 because they could count on a feminized service worker to be their breadwinner. With the contract advance, flight attendants could—at least for a moment— live middle-class lifestyles outside the boundaries of traditional family.

Conclusion: The Emerging Struggle over Domesticity and Hard Work

As they cashed paychecks that, when converted to today's dollars, delivered an annual wage of nearly six figures, flight attendants acted with historical significance. On the one hand, they helped advance the project of labor feminism. For the first time, the flight attendants made enough money to balance both family and work. Unlike most women workers, flight attendants' first shift provided enough pay to buy more time for the second shift. On the other hand, and even more importantly, as flight attendant unions made these gains for working women, for single people, and for lesbian, gay, and bisexual workers, they made those gains for people who were part of a rapidly growing demographic trend. As scholarly works such as sociologist Judith Stacey's *Unhitched*[59] or historian Elizabeth Pleck's *Not Just Roommates*[60] have demonstrated, and as the Pew Research Center's 2013 analysis of female-headed households has documented, over the past thirty years fewer people have married, those who have done so have married later, and more people have had children outside marriage.[61] By the year 2010, 40 percent of households depended on a woman to be the primary breadwinner, a fourfold increase in five decades; 44 percent of those solo mom breadwinners had never been married, ten times as many as in 1960.[62] For decades, being a solo mom—or even just being single—had marked a woman for poverty. With flight attendant unions' advances, and after similar advances from public employee and clerical workers' unions during the same period, those sexist inequities began to change.

A family wage for flight attendants and for other workingwomen in the late 1970s and early 1980s came on the cusp of a vast economic transformation. As neoliberal reforms became the hegemonic response to the global economic crisis of the 1970s, all workers would face new downward pressures on wages and on working conditions. As union density dropped to levels not seen in a century, and as companies shifted economic risk toward employees and away from corporations, managers in all industries eliminated work rules that had protected people from forced overtime and from unpaid labor. By the year 2000, as real wages continued to fall, the family wage—whether for the traditional husband breadwinner or for a less traditional breadwinner like a flight attendant—was vanishing from the economy. In an age when most new jobs began to offer the pay and benefits of the "women's work" of previous decades, flight attendant activists would face daunting new pressure to forfeit the resources they had just won.

Although neoliberalization would provide new challenges for all working people, the particular cultural dynamics of flight attendants' struggle with the airlines in the 1970s would remain central to the process of political economic change in the 1980s and 1990s. Rather than a 1970s feminist anachronism or a distraction from the bread-and-butter economic issues of neoliberalization, ideas about family, domesticity, and heteropatriarchy would shape corporations' demands for wage and benefit cuts and would influence workers' efforts to resist those cuts. Since the early 1970s, flight attendants had made domesticity and work the keywords of their struggle for fairer labor economics in the airline industry. Contesting the ideology of domesticity, union activists aimed to transform flight attendants from men's dependents into active political agents. Once they took control of their unions, flight attendants confronted a system of compulsory overwork and demanded more money and more time to balance their jobs with responsibilities to their kin. After 1980, the advocates of neoliberal reforms would focus on a new strategy that ran directly counter to flight attendants' agenda, one that elevated domesticity and hard work. More domesticity and more work would, in other words, become the organizing principles of the new economy.

(DE)REGULATING DESIRE

Family Values, Pro-work Politics, and the Airline Deregulation Act of 1978

B y the end of the 1970s, flight attendants had transformed the political economy of their workplace. For the first time in the history of the airline industry, flight attendant pay and working conditions matched those of many of the men they worked alongside, as well as those in the high-wage manufacturing sector. Guaranteeing more money for less work, flight attendants' collective bargaining advances propelled the social and cultural transformation of the decade. Liberated from dependence on husbands' wages as a supplement for small paychecks, flight attendants had the financial freedom to choose a variety of domestic and intimate arrangements. They could stay single and live alone, cohabitate with friends or lovers, have children outside marriage, or join lesbian or gay subcultures. With the economic resources to satisfy a far broader range of personal desires, flight attendants challenged the ideology of domesticity and family that was the bedrock of the mid-twentieth-century economy.

Just as activists at Pan Am, TWA, United, and other major carriers celebrated watershed advances, a significant countervailing trend was developing in the broader economy and culture. By 1978, a tightly organized, well-funded, pro-business activist movement was gaining political traction by providing solutions for the decade's economic instability.[1] Although the economy had officially come out of recession in mid-1975, high interest rates, intensifying inflation, and persistent unemployment were providing challenges unseen since the Great Depression for most working people—including those in the middle class. Pro-business activists argued that while the high taxes, strict government regulation, and generous welfare benefits of the midcentury economy provided protection for African Americans, students, feminists, the poor, and other aggrieved groups, they took opportunities away from hardworking, middle-class American families. The solution, they insisted, was to take the fetters off the economy, allowing big business to provide new chances for people who valued family and work.[2]

The airline industry became an early test case for the emerging pro-work, pro-family political agenda. In October 1978, President Jimmy Carter signed the Airline Deregulation Act. Eliminating strict government controls on pricing and competition, deregulation opened the industry to new, upstart airlines that paid employees far less than the established carriers and that in turn offered lower fares. During the same months that flight attendant unions were winning economic and cultural mobility for women workers, deregulation placed an unprecedented burden on their employers' finances. The consequences are difficult to overstate. In the first five years after deregulation, Braniff collapsed, and Pan Am, Eastern, and others forced drastic wage cuts on all employees. Shortly after the ink dried on lucrative new flight attendant contracts, the new pro-family, pro-work politics pushed managers to break those contracts. By early 1984 at Continental Airlines, for example, where flight attendant pay had previously topped out at $40 per hour, a bankruptcy and a failed strike allowed the airline to cut the maximum wage to $16.47 an hour,[3] returning wages to a level unseen since 1957.[4] Unfortunately for the labor movement, the trend was by no means isolated to the airlines, as wages also collapsed in such heavily unionized industries as meatpacking, construction, telecommunications, and trucking.[5]

This chapter focuses on the deregulation of the airline industry to illuminate the practices and ideologies that converted much of the economy from a high-wage to a low-wage model in the late 1970s and 1980s. It considers how policymakers arrived at a new consensus on neoliberal reforms that made economic sustenance much more difficult for working people, including most of the white middle class. The domain of sexuality provides a revealing lens for approaching that question. I demonstrate that a new constellation of public policy aimed to produce a new sexual subject in the 1980s, a person with a new set of desires that were far different from those of many 1970s flight attendant unionists. Pro-work, pro-family values would define that subject. Those values, commitments like thrift, self-denial, deferred gratification, and personal responsibility, would in turn be the basis for an efficient new economy that would finally end the downturn of the 1970s. As a coalition of public officials, activists, and intellectuals designed and implemented this family values economy, they touched off a bitter conflict with the flight attendant union movement and with other groups that refused to subscribe to this new sexual subjectivity. By analyzing that conflict, we can understand both the foundations of the new economy and why unions—within and beyond the airline industry—have had such a difficult time intervening in an economy that elevates the moral significance of family and work.

Pro-work Politics and the Airline Deregulation Act of 1978

To much of the white middle class, it seemed as if work was being devalued in the late 1970s. As the federal government printed money to pay for an expansive Cold War military and for Great Society social programs, and as energy costs soared after the second oil shock in 1979, the inflation rate climbed toward a worrisome peak of 16 percent in 1980.[6] Trying to chase down inflation, the Federal Reserve repeatedly raised interest rates, which topped out at a painful 18.9 percent.[7] Therefore, even if an ordinary family breadwinner did everything right, building skills and productivity, getting promoted, earning incremental wage increases, and picking up overtime, that person's purchasing power declined throughout the 1970s. Mass consumption and suburban home ownership, the bedrocks of postwar middle-class white identity, were jeopardized in the economic malaise, as rising consumer prices drove up the cost of everything from a boat to a summer vacation and as high interest rates made it difficult for many middle-class families to qualify for a home mortgage. To some suburban whites, the Democratic Party, which had been the handmaiden of the modern middle class in the decades after the war, seemed more focused on addressing the demands of radical movements for social change than on the pocketbook politics of working families.[8] Taking advantage of that discontent, a resurgent conservative movement flourished by the end of the 1970s. Success came as conservative activists centered political analysis on middle-class anxiety about the devaluation of work.

The new pro-work agenda would originate not in traditional venues of bootstraps ideology, including the Republican Party, elite business schools, or corporate boardrooms, but in an ascendant political institution: the conservative think tank. Such groups were by no means new in the 1970s; the American Enterprise Institute (AEI) dated back to the 1930s, and such organizations as the National Association of Manufacturers and the U.S. Chamber of Commerce had spent decades advocating for the interests of big business. What changed in the 1970s, however, was the scope of the pro-business message emanating from conservative think tanks. Whereas earlier advocacy had focused on fighting particular unions or on pushing for specific corporate tax breaks, the new pro-business agenda centered on long-term political economic change. According to AEI, the Heritage Foundation, the Cato Institute, and other ascendant groups, pro-business reforms would help break the inflationary spiral, reduce unemployment, and restore the global competitiveness of the United States. Pitching a newly ambitious agenda, conservative think tanks channeled donations from major corporations and elite private donors to fund the work of those best trained to produce new ideas: college professors from elite universities. Although some of those scholars had carved out a niche as far-right thinkers—such as Richard Laffer at the University of Southern California—many others were widely cited mainstream scholars, including Alfred Kahn in the Columbia University Economics Department, and Harvard Law School's Steven Breyer, who went on to serve on the U.S. Supreme Court.[9]

To engage a broader public than their predecessors, the conservative think tanks of the 1970s retooled their message. As historian Jason Stahl argues in *Right Moves,* think tanks' growing power came as they embraced a new political strategy called "sensible conservatism." Leaders at AEI and other think tanks recognized that the authoritarian, segregationist, anti-Semitic currents that dominated Goldwater-era conservatism had been marginalized amid the social and cultural transformation of the 1960s. Rather than attempt to rebuild public support for the earlier extremist approach, think tank intellectuals focused on "sensible" new issues with broad appeal, aiming to build coalitions between major corporations, small businesses, and middle-class families.[10]

Work became a key venue on which sensible conservatives built those new coalitions. According to historian Kim Phillips-Fein, conservative think tankers drew an ideological line between workers and nonworkers—between self-denying, responsible, hardworking families on the one hand and self-indulgent, irresponsible, nonworking welfare recipients on the other.[11] Aligning a conversation about family with one about work, activists solidified alliances between two growing political movements in the 1970s: evangelical Christians organizing around "family values" and pro-business activists pushing for tax cuts and deregulation. They did so by arguing that progressive taxes confiscated wages from working families and transferred them to people who refused to work, and by arguing that government regulation hamstrung major employers, preventing them from creating jobs for families that wanted to work. According to this line of analysis, progressive taxation, government regulation, and the social safety net were both antifamily and antiwork. To eliminate the barriers that they insisted had been built in front of middle-class families, sensible conservatives proposed a spectrum of policy reforms: tax cuts that would allow workers to keep more of their pay, the curtailment of welfare programs to penalize nonwork, and regulatory reforms that would allow businesses to spend less time complying with government oversight and more time creating jobs for hardworking families.[12]

By the mid-1970s, the ascendant conservative movement had chosen the airline industry as a test case for its pro-family, pro-work, antiregulatory political agenda. The choice is, at first glance, surprising. After all, state oversight had been a foundation of the unparalleled success of the business before 1970, one that had created tens of thousands of high-paying jobs for the middle class.[13] Comprehensive regulation came to the airlines with the Civil Aeronautics Act (CAA) of 1938, legislation that aimed to stabilize a fledgling industry. During the first years of scheduled air service in the 1920s, fatal accidents were all too common as carriers struggled to deploy new and often untested technology to meet competition from a steady stream of new entrants in the business. Facing public outcry after scores of crash-related deaths, and amid the broader economic uncertainty of the Great Depression, policymakers began to insist that federal intervention to limit competition would allow the airlines the economic stability necessary to improve their margin of safety. Linking a long-established pattern of government intervention in the transport industry—the railroads had been federally regulated since Congress created the Interstate Commerce Commission in 1877—with New Deal regulatory expertise, the Roosevelt administration implemented three key regulations with the CAA. First, strict barriers to entry limited service on trunk routes to firms already licensed to fly. Second, price floors and ceilings prevented airlines from launching destructive fare wars and guaranteed each company a reasonable stream of revenue. Finally, government control of each carrier's route network helped ensure a continuous—yet limited—amount of competition.[14] Aviation flourished under the new regulatory framework. The regulated airlines tripled the growth rate of the broader economy—even during the booming postwar years.[15] In just four decades, the airlines had gone from a hopscotch of hundred-mile trips on lumbering thirty-seat propeller planes to a round-the-world network of jumbo jets flying nearly as fast as the speed of sound.

The dynamism of the airline industry began to evaporate in the 1970s, catching the attention of pro-work, antiregulatory activists. In its fourth decade, economists and policymakers began to argue that regulation had become a victim of its own success. Since airlines had to petition the federal government before they could offer a new fare or launch a new route, regulators' workload mushroomed with the growth of the industry. By the late 1960s, the flurry of requests meant that it often took regulators so long to process paperwork that route and fare awards would no longer match the conditions of a changed marketplace. For example, regulators took four years to rule on Pan Am, TWA, and Northwest's 1965 request for new routes to Hawaii and Japan.[16] Worried that regulatory imprecision had hamstrung airline operations, bankers were increasingly reluctant to authorize loans to even the strongest airlines. Actuaries pointed out that while industry revenues had increased sevenfold between 1959 and 1977—from $2.3 billion to $15 billion annually—profits were stagnant.[17] Investors' jitters had particularly troublesome consequences for the airlines, since insurance companies and commercial banks typically financed 85 percent of aircraft acquisitions.[18] Lacking Wall Street's confidence, carriers were unable to borrow enough money to buy the newer, more fuel-efficient aircraft that would help mitigate the high energy costs of the 1970s. Aiming to rebuild investor confidence, a narrow cohort of policymakers and academic economists—many of whom were affiliated with think tanks like the American Enterprise Institute—came up with a solution: lift the government fetters that limited management discretion in deploying their assets and pricing their products.

The pro-business activist movement's solution to the airlines' 1970s problems originated in the scholarly work of Alfred Kahn, the AEI fellow who is widely recognized as the intellectual architect of the Airline Deregulation Act.[19] In his 1970 tome *The Economics of Regulation,* Kahn argued that consumer prices were a key venue for reducing production costs and fighting inflation. If goods were priced according to their "marginal cost"—the amount it would take to make one more unit of that good—consumers would chose the cheapest product, which would in turn reward the lowest-cost producer. In order for consumers to choose the lowest-cost product, however, prices would have to more accurately reflect what it cost to make a product, costs that Kahn believed government oversight hid in regulated industries.[20] Kahn's theory worked when he implemented it as the state of New York's chief utilities regulator in the early 1970s. Falling electricity prices caught the attention of policymakers struggling to control rising consumer prices in the mid-1970s.[21] Although Kahn—a lifelong Democrat—found a receptive audience for his scholarship on deregulation in both major political parties, he also faced strident critics. Unions, which still represented almost 30 percent of the workforce in the 1970s, were lined up against deregulation in all industries. Kahn's application of marginal pricing, labor leaders argued, would spawn a race to the bottom in deregulated industries. Wages would fall and benefits would disappear as consumers flocked to firms with the lowest operating costs. Facing a pushback from organized labor, Kahn and his AEI colleagues would have to find a way to persuade congressional Democrats—and, after January

1977, President Carter—to break with their allies in organized labor if they wanted deregulation to pass.

To meet this challenge, the advocates of deregulation framed their bid not in terms of profit or efficiency but in terms of their broader commitment to pro-work policy. Marking a populist claim that airline deregulation would create new opportunities for working people, pro-deregulation scholars at AEI found their most vocal and unlikely ally: Massachusetts senator Edward Kennedy. A stalwart pro-labor Democrat, Senate Judiciary Committee chair Kennedy convened a series of hearings on airline regulatory reform beginning in February 1975, joining forces with Utah Democratic senator Howard Cannon to write the first of several competing bills that would comprehensively deregulate the industry. Kennedy offered airline deregulation as an innovative solution to address the pocketbook issues of the 1970s middle class, one that would enhance his identity as the champion of the common man while allowing him to distance himself from trade union bureaucrats whose work rule and wage settlements were being blamed for rising consumer prices.[22]

As he took the microphone and welcomed the public to a Senate Commerce Committee meeting in April 1976, Ted Kennedy insisted that federal regulation had tailored the airline industry to the interests of the elite. Because the federal government had complete control over destinations and prices, customer service was the only means carriers could use to woo passengers away from one another. Thus, airlines offered lavish food service and bought Valentino uniforms (see Chapter 1) for their flight attendants when they could have focused on providing a simpler, cheaper, and more efficient product to serve a broader cross-section of the traveling public. Opulence was certainly enjoyable for those who could afford it, but since the airlines could pass the cost of service on to passengers through government-mandated fare increases, the lavish experience aloft not only excluded ordinary people but also fueled the inflation that made it harder for the middle class to get by.[23] The cheapest economy-class ticket between New York and Los Angeles in 1969, for example, cost the equivalent of $1,880 round trip, putting air travel far beyond the means of the average middle-class family even in the high-wage economy of the 1960s.[24] For Kennedy, a deregulated marketplace would spawn competition that would force the airlines to shift focus away from the Valentino uniforms and toward making travel more accessible.

Airline union leaders were quick to chastise Kennedy, insisting that the removal of government barriers to entry would subject living wage jobs to downward pressure from non-union upstarts.[25] Kennedy and the deregulators responded with a tightly argued answer that originated in American Enterprise Institute research on "load factor," or the percentage of full seats on a given flight. The federal government, Kennedy pointed out, set prices with the goal of keeping 55 percent of airplane seats full. If the airlines were allowed to stimulate demand with lower fares, they could fill up all those empty seats and enhance profits without enforcing layoffs or cutting wages, Kennedy argued.[26] In other words, fares would go down *not* because the price of inputs—such as flight attendant wages—would go down but because on full airplanes an airline would use fewer inputs per passenger.[27] Lower fares and fuller airplanes would actually *increase* employment in a deregulated environment, the pro-deregulation group insisted. Airlines would need more ticket agents, more salespeople, more cleaners, and more flight attendants to meet the demand spike after deregulation passed and fares dropped. Publicly scolding the "management of airline unions" for failing to endorse his load factor plan, Kennedy insisted that while a few stodgy trade unionists might not understand deregulation, front-line airline employees stood to reap its benefits.[28] By lowering airfares and creating jobs, deregulation would bring opportunities for work and consumption that were slipping out of the hands of the middle class in the 1970s.

In an era of shrinking consumer purchasing power and persistent unemployment, framing deregulation as a means to reduce prices and create jobs overwhelmed oppositional mobilization from unions and from airline managers who feared losing state protection for their businesses. The Airline Deregulation Act passed Congress with broad support from pro-business Republicans and pro-labor Democrats, and it received President Carter's signature on October 24, 1978. Regulatory fetters would gradually disappear over five years. Fares could come down immediately by as much as 50 percent, and anyone who was "fit, willing, and able" could start a new airline. What had begun as a scholarly effort by a few think tanks to reshape politics around "sensible conservatism" was now a centerpiece of the bipartisan response to the economic crisis of the 1970s. Overnight, revenue streams at the major airlines would begin to evaporate, compromising the economic integrity of the corporations that the flight attendant union movement had made its primary point of political intervention in the 1970s. With Ted Kennedy and think tank conservatives both promising that deregulation would soon create work opportunities for the middle class, a bitter debate would emerge about the nature of those new jobs. Flight attendants would be at the center of that debate.

The Economic Consequences of Pro-work Policy

The Airline Deregulation Act of 1978 was part of a political transformation that aimed to restore the value of hard work. Whether in broader antitax and antiwelfare mobilization that sought to allow middle-class families to keep more of their paychecks or in pro-deregulation efforts to lower prices, stimulate the market, and create jobs, work was assumed to be a cultural and moral good. With all the discussion of work, however, there was little public debate the economic value of work. Most analysis failed to address how antitax, antiwelfare, and antiregulatory reforms would shape the pay, benefits, and work rules that jobs offered. Indeed, the emerging consensus among policymakers that work was the *solution* to the economic anxieties of the 1970s suppressed consideration of how people's jobs could be the *cause* of economic problems for the poor and middle class alike. Absent though it was in airline policy discussions before October 1978, the economic value of work was at the center of controversy in the airline industry as soon as deregulation passed. In the first decade after deregulation, airline unionists staged a series of bitter and often unsuccessful strikes that aimed to contest the rapid economic devaluation of their work. The consequences of pro-work policy, flight attendants and other activists argued, were longer hours and far lower pay.

There was a notable exception to the elision of labor economics from the policy debate about airline deregulation in the late 1970s, an exception that foreshadowed the coming unrest in the industry. On April 12, 1976, Frank Lorenzo, the CEO of a small, local-service carrier from the banks of the Rio Grande called Texas International Airlines, took the stand in front of the House Aviation Subcommittee. A Spanish immigrant's son turned Texas financier, Lorenzo joined the other airline managers in opposing deregulation.[29] But while his colleagues focused on arcane operational complexities, Lorenzo made a concise, hard-hitting presentation about how deregulation would affect employee wages and benefits. Texas International was in a unique position because the Texas interstate air market had always been unregulated. Five years earlier, a Dallas businessman named Herb Kelleher had started Southwest Airlines, a company that provided cheap, convenient flights between Dallas, Houston, and San Antonio. Southwest was drastically undercutting Lorenzo and his established peers, charging up to 40 percent less than Texas International and Braniff, airlines that were prevented from offering such discounts because they also operated outside Texas and were thus regulated by the federal government. Lorenzo insisted, though, that it was not the absence of price controls that allowed Southwest to charge so little. Instead, it was rock-bottom labor costs that made Southwest Airlines an immediate success.[30]

Lorenzo held up a data table for his audience that revealed a disturbing trend for airline workers. The chart compared the wages of six employee groups from Texas International with the same groups at Southwest. At both airlines, pilots earned the most of any class of employee, and at both airlines flight attendants earned the least. Yet for all employee groups at Southwest, wages were at least 25 percent lower than at Texas International. That was only half the story, Lorenzo argued. Focusing his analysis on a comparison of flight attendants, he demonstrated that entry-level wages were fairly high at Southwest. But whereas established lines had given flight attendants annual raises for at least a decade, Southwest crews had received only a couple of pay bumps. With a flat pay scale and no work rules, Lorenzo noted, turnover was high at Southwest. At Braniff and Texas International, however, flight attendant union activists had turned the job into a career and stayed on the job for at least ten years at both carriers. Senior, unionized flight attendants made Braniff and Texas International's labor costs far higher than Southwest's, Lorenzo argued.[31] Thus, Texas International was losing money while Southwest reaped a $2.5 million profit in 1975, earnings funded almost entirely by Southwest's below-market labor costs.[32] Lorenzo argued that if the federal government emulated the state of Texas and implemented deregulation, new entrants like Southwest would pop up across the country and hire young people right off the street, undercutting mature competitors with heavily unionized workforces. The cost savings of deregulation would come, Lorenzo insisted, not from Ted Kennedy's claims about load factor and job creation but from individual airlines' ability to pay their employees less. Deregulation would, in other words, be a tool to confiscate the gains of flight attendant unionism and of other forms of airline activism.

The audience was silent. When Lorenzo finished, deregulation co-sponsor Senator Cannon asked, "Do you think that [deregulation] would be an attack on the labor movement in this country?" Lorenzo's response was quick and sharp: "Yes."

No follow-up questions were asked.[33]

Stark as it was, Frank Lorenzo's testimony did not change the policy debate about work or about government regulation in the 1970s. When the Airline Deregulation Act passed after Lorenzo and his colleagues failed to convince Congress of the reform's pitfalls, Texas International's finances further deteriorated as the airline faced unfettered competition not just in Texas but across its system. Lorenzo's airline was hardly unique. As Midway, Air Florida, New York Air, PeoplExpress, and other new companies with rock bottom labor costs sprouted across the country, airfares plummeted. Southwest, for example, jumped onto the Dallas–Oklahoma City route in April 1980, charging just 69 percent of what Braniff and Texas International had offered the day before. And while Allegheny had been getting $123 to carry people from Newark to Pittsburgh, PeoplExpress added the route at just $40.[34]

As fares tumbled, the negative impact on incumbent carriers and their employees was immediate. By 1981, Western, TWA, and Eastern had petitioned all of their unionized employees for immediate concessionary contract negotiations to reduce labor costs. Texas International was firing pilots for making indignant announcements about the injustice of deregulation aboard their aircraft.[35] Pan Am was trying to escape contractual obligations to flight attendants to negotiate better pay and working conditions and had requested government permission to defer pension contributions the airline had fallen behind on.[36]

As Frank Lorenzo watched airlines with unionized, high-wage employees fail and airlines with young, low-paid employees succeed, he saw a new business opportunity. The major airlines would return to profitability, Lorenzo suspected, if they could cut employee pay and benefits quickly and drastically. Lorenzo knew that union activists would strike to resist such givebacks, but if managers could outlast the rank and file and cut wages by 50 percent or more, robust profits would flow to managers and stockholders. The time was right for Lorenzo to act: the industry's post-deregulation losses had depressed stock prices, making airlines cheap for prospective buyers. Lorenzo was particularly interested in Los Angeles–based Continental Airlines. A medium-sized airline with strong domestic hubs in Denver and Houston and lucrative international routes to Australia, Continental had a highly paid workforce, including flight attendants who, through the feminist-inspired Union of Flight Attendants Local 1, had just won a 39 percent pay increase with a successful strike over Christmas.[37] Recognizing that high labor costs were preventing Continental from matching the fares of discount competitors, and aware that year-over-year first-quarter losses had quadrupled,[38] Lorenzo bought up 48 percent of the company's shares in March 1981.[39] If Lorenzo could gain majority stakeholder status, he could force a sale of the company to himself, firing the existing management team and enforcing deep cutbacks on all employees, including flight attendants. Just eighteen months after deregulation had been justified as a policy reform aimed at enhancing the value of hard work, Frank Lorenzo was intervening to drastically reduce the economic value of airline labor. Although he had joined his colleagues in opposing deregulation in the mid-1970s, Frank Lorenzo about-faced after 1980, embracing deregulation as a powerful tool to cut costs and enhance corporate profit margins.

With all of their jobs on the line, Continental's workers and managers united against Lorenzo. The airline had a new CEO, Alvin Feldman, who had been recruited out of a successful stint at smaller Frontier to help rescue Continental from its post-deregulation woes in the summer of 1980. A Lorenzo takeover, Feldman insisted, would destroy Continental, either because

Lorenzo would sell the airline's valuable South Pacific routes or because he would touch off a costly political dispute with employees when he tried to slash their pay. To thwart the takeover, Feldman initiated merger talks with Western Airlines, another midsized carrier that was burning cash and desperate for a plan to reinvent itself. And if Feldman failed to sell the rest of the shares to Western, employees stepped up to buy the airline, volunteering to cut their own wages in exchange for a 50 percent stake in the company. New shares issued to employees would then dilute Lorenzo's stake to 24.5 percent, blocking him from acquiring majority status.[40]

The standoff came to a head at the Continental shareholders' meeting in Denver on May 7, 1981. Alvin Feldman gaveled down three separate motions to sell Continental to Lorenzo. Each time, employees who had descended on the meeting armed with picket signs and protest chants vigorously cheered Feldman's grandstanding. Immediately following the shareholders meeting, all unionized employees approved the employee ownership plan, with flight attendants ratifying a 15 percent pay cut in exchange for stock in a referendum on June 15. Significant legal questions, however, remained about the plan to block Lorenzo, especially as it was unclear whether or not Feldman had the legal authority to allow the Continental Board of Directors—and not the shareholders—to decide the fate of Lorenzo's bid.[41]

Alvin Feldman and Continental workers' defense against Frank Lorenzo reached a breaking point during the first week of August 1981. The crisis began when the California Corporations Commission, the regulatory body for publicly held corporations in the state of California, ruled that stockholders would be allowed to vote on all offers to purchase Continental Airlines. Because Lorenzo already owned nearly half the company and had the financial resources to entice the remaining shareholders with a deal more lucrative than the offers on the table from Western Airlines and Continental's own employees, the stockholder vote would allow Lorenzo to force a sale to himself. Two days after the California decision, members of the Professional Air Traffic Controllers Organization (PATCO) walked out on strike to protest what they insisted was a culture of chronic overwork in the nation's air traffic control system. Branding the action an illegal wildcat strike and using the standoff as a test case for a new federal commitment to curbing trade union militancy, President Reagan locked strikers out. The administration's bold intervention widely disrupted air travel and forced controllers who remained on the job to cut capacity by at least 25 percent during the initial months of the lockout. Capacity cuts would compel Feldman to reduce service on the few remaining profitable Continental routes, which would in turn make the company even less attractive to a good-faith buyer like Western Airlines.[42]

Feldman's next move was one he could never take back. At seven o'clock in the evening on August 9, 1981, Alvin Feldman committed suicide in his office at Los Angeles International Airport. He left a series of notes that exposed and reflected on his desperation, thoroughly explaining the agony of a personal and professional life from which he saw no way out. Friends knew that Feldman was still reeling from the tragic day a year earlier when his wife had passed away. Now, both Frontier and Continental, the two airlines he had helped build into stalwarts of the regulated era in the 1960s and 1970s, were spiraling out of control in the third year of deregulation. Feldman left behind three college-age children and everyone at Continental Airlines, people distraught at the loss of one of the industry's most popular leaders and dreading what would come next.[43]

In the wake of the Feldman tragedy came Frank Lorenzo. After the collapse of the proposed employee buyout and Western Airlines merger following Feldman's suicide,[44] and amid widening losses during the PATCO affair, the last defensive shareholders folded, selling out to Lorenzo on July 13, 1982.[45] Lorenzo was clear in his message to all employees as soon as he arrived. Deregulation, as Lorenzo had warned the Senate in 1976, was a policy reform that had drastically reduced the economic value of airline labor. For heavily unionized incumbent carriers such as Continental, minor or incremental labor cost reductions would not be enough. Instead, the established airlines would have to convert their model of employment to match that of the booming service sector, hiring young workers, sloughing coverage for older and sicker employees onto the social safety net, and tailoring pay and benefits to incentivize short-term rather than lifetime employment. Lorenzo's demand was, expectedly, a nonstarter for flight attendant activists. Refusing to even discuss Lorenzo's proposal for a 60 percent reduction in pay and benefits, flight attendants mobilized defensively during the first year of Lorenzo's tenure.

Lorenzo ended the stalemate on September 24, 1983. In what is perhaps the most aggressive management move in the history of collective bargaining in the airline industry, Frank Lorenzo filed for bankruptcy and closed Continental Airlines, grounding all flights and stranding crews and passengers without warning. Sixty-five percent of employees got immediate pink slips and were escorted off the property.[46] Those left on the job were sent a short contract with two check boxes and a signature line at the bottom. The contract was called the Emergency Work Rules. If a flight attendant signed it, she would agree to reduce her top wage from over $40 to $16.47 per hour; to eliminate duty rigs, line guarantee, and all other work rules; to terminate pension benefits; and to extend the workday to sixteen hours.[47] If she refused, she would be terminated on the spot. Compiling a list of all those who signed, Lorenzo restarted Continental three days later. The new airline aimed to run the bulk of its pre-bankruptcy schedule with just forty-two hundred of its twelve thousand former employees.[48] With all unionized groups on strike— machinists had walked off the job in August, and pilots and flight attendants called a strike once the Emergency Work Rules were administered—the build back was slow. But even by the end of the first full week of operations on October 4, Continental was, depending on the day, running between 10 percent and 20 percent of its normal operation.[49] By early 1984, over half of Continental's flights would be flying again, staffed by a mixture of supervisors and rank-and-file crew members who signed the Emergency Work Rules, crossed the picket line, and reported for work.

As union activists salvaged what little they could and drew the strike to a close, two distinct consequences emerged in the Continental affair. The first and most obvious consequence involved employee pay and benefits and affected all airline employees. Airline deregulation, the progeny of pro-work policy reforms, rapidly eroded the economic value of airline work. Both Ted Kennedy and the AEI scholars were right about deregulation, as load factors shot up after the reform, which in turn created more airline work. The problem for airline workers, however, was that fewer workers would perform much more work for far lower pay. The second political consequence stemmed from family values. Although deregulation brought a new, low-wage model of labor to the airlines, older, patriarchal ideas about the value of men's work and women's work governed the economic outcome of the strike. After a 60 percent pay cut, almost no Continental employee could be a breadwinner for his or her family, which effectively ended the family wage system in the airlines. But the residue of the family wage system, the idea that workingmen deserved extra remuneration to fulfill their role as breadwinners, helped redistribute the few remaining resources at Continental away from flight attendants and toward pilots.

The ghost of traditional family values appeared as flight attendant leaders joined forces with pilots in an attempt to force a settlement with Lorenzo. Leaders from both unions approached Lorenzo and submitted a proffer of arbitration—a set of bilateral talks with a neutral facilitator—in an effort to compromise on the pay and benefit cuts that Lorenzo implemented with the Emergency Work Rules. Lorenzo's response horrified flight attendants and made the outcome of the strike far more divisive. In a pattern that would repeat itself at TWA in 1986 (see Chapter 4) and would shape contractual settlements throughout the 1980s, Lorenzo agreed to arbitration with the pilots but rejected flight attendants' proposal outright.[50] The new regulatory regime would mean cutbacks for everyone, Lorenzo insisted, but traditional ideas about gender and family would inform the severity of those cuts. For pilots, a group whose work had always been imbued with ideas about skill, manhood, heterosexuality, and breadwinning, there would be a future, and one in which the union could continue to engage management even while its power was constricted. But for flight attendants, who had long been presumed to depend on men, there would be no future for their union movement. There would be no family benefits, no work rules, and no longevity pay: all of flight attendant unionists' 1970s gains would be confiscated.

The Continental Airlines upheaval would have been disorienting to all but the closest analyst of the U.S. political debates in the late 1970s and early 1980s. The resurgent conservative movement had scored substantive advances—including the election of President Ronald Reagan in 1980—by promising to reverse the devaluation of work for the middle class. Pushing to reduce taxes and cut government red tape that had blocked self-reliant, independent, hardworking American families from getting ahead in the 1970s, the new, right-leaning coalition coalesced around pro-work values. But in headline-making labor disputes that followed pro-work reforms in industries from air transport to mining to meatpacking, hardworking people were being dispossessed, ejected from lifetime, middle-class jobs. For workers who found new careers after setbacks like that at Lorenzo's Continental, most would make only a fraction of the wage from their former unionized career. By the middle of the 1980s, it had become clear that as pro-work political culture intensified, hard work had stopped paying the bills. To understand widespread support among policymakers—and among much of the public—for neoliberal reforms that made people work more for less, I now turn to the discourses that helped manage the vast contradictions that ran through pro-work culture in the 1980s.

Family Values and the Moral Properties of Work

As they pitted workers against nonworkers to justify the Airline Deregulation Act and other sweeping reforms, the resurgent conservative movement transformed the national political debate about work. By 1980, conversation had shifted away from the economic properties of work and toward work's moral properties. Rather than a means to distribute such material resources as pay, health insurance, and a pension, work was most important because it produced moral values, marking a person as either a deserving, responsible family member or a slothful, indolent nonworker. Labor reforms, then, were important not because they would provide more or less money for workers but because they would produce moral subjects with the right or wrong kind of values. Elevating morality while eliding economics, the resurgent conservative movement opened a space to pass reforms that, while lauding work as a social good, would make it much more difficult for working people to make ends meet.

Framing work in terms of moral and cultural values was by no means a new phenomenon in the 1970s. Rather than cut their argument from whole cloth, conservative activists updated a long-standing tendency in U.S. political and social thought that conflated hard work with moral goodness. As Janet Jakobsen has demonstrated, the booming nineteenth-century U.S. industrial economy depended on the morally regulated activity of the laboring body—the labor that Max Weber calls "worldly asceticism."[51] In other words, the free market flourished because people followed their moral compass, denying indulgence in worldly pleasures and making hard work an end—and not a means—in their life. Jakobsen incisively argues that although the work ethic was derived from Calvinist religious beliefs, it became the basis for secular free market society in the nineteenth century.[52] Nevertheless, even though hard work remains a foundation of contemporary, secular, liberal capitalist society, work is still understood to define a person's moral worthiness. Kathi Weeks, for example, argues that the work ethic defines not just how someone behaves but who they are. The work ethic, Weeks insists, "takes aim not just at consciousness, but also at the capacity and energies of the body, and the objects and aims of its desires."[53] Weeks shows us that according to the work ethic, hard work makes people desire the right things.

Grounded though the work ethic was in two hundred years of social thought, pro-work activists would nevertheless face a significant challenge in making their case to renew the ethic of hard work in the 1970s and 1980s. During the previous fifty years, social movements had transformed the work ethic. In the mid-1930s, for example, a coalition between Popular Front radicals and industrial unions won unprecedented resources for working people, securing a living wage, work rules, paid vacations, and company-paid pensions. For the first time, those who had grown up among the immigrant and working poor could work to live rather than live to work. A generation later, the social movements of the 1960s and 1970s gained access to those resources for some African Americans, Latinos, single women, lesbians and gays, and service and agricultural workers who had been locked out of the advances of the 1930s. Fifty years of organizing had inverted the relationship at the core of the work ethic, as people's physical, emotional, and material desires determined the amount and intensity at which they worked and not the other way around. Flight attendants' succession of victories for working women in the late 1970s was, therefore, running with the current of the mid-twentieth century and not against it.

To once again reverse that current in the 1970s and 1980s, pro-work activists would turn to a category that had always buttressed the work ethic: the category of family. As Weeks goes on to argue, the family ethic had historically served as a supplement to the work ethic; politicians and reformers promoted family values as a "crucial adjunct" to work discipline.[54] Family values, in other words, would serve as another sign of a person's dedication to work. After both the work ethic and the family ethic were thrown into question during the social transformation of the 1960s and 1970s, the Reagan administration and its allies among pro-business and pro-family activists reiterated the symbiotic relationship between the two. In a report on the state of the American family, for example, the Reagan White House argued that "neither the modern family nor the free market system could exist without the other."[55]

From the renewed attention to the mutually constitutive relationship between work and family came the primary political justification for the pro-work reforms of the 1970s and 1980s. Tax cuts, welfare rollbacks, and deregulation were necessary not because of what they would do to people's paychecks but because they would restore traditional family values. Focused on the family, the pro-work movement was able to shift the conversation away from deregulation's negative impact on working people like those at Frank Lorenzo's Continental Airlines and toward the presumed gains that a return to traditional family values would bring to the wider American middle class. To make that shift, pro-work activists framed family in specific terms in the 1970s and 1980s, using sexuality—and the long-standing intersection of sexuality with ideas about race, gender, and poverty—to make the case for pro-work reforms.

Nowhere were those racialized and gendered ideas about sexuality more visible than in the pro-work scholarship of Charles Murray. Just a few months after Frank Lorenzo cut Continental flight attendants' wages in half, Murray published his watershed text *Losing Ground* in 1984. Murray had a Ph.D. in political science from M.I.T. and would end up joining pro-deregulation scholars at the American Enterprise Institute in 1990. During the 1980s, Murray traveled in high-profile conservative intellectual circles in Washington, and he wrote *Losing Ground* while on staff at the Manhattan Institute, another conservative think tank. Murray's work rattled mainstream scholars and policymakers with what was, at the time, an extreme prescription. Save for a very short-term unemployment insurance program, Murray advocated a complete dismantling of the social safety net for working-age adults, jettisoning Medicaid, public housing, direct cash transfers, and all other forms of public assistance.[56] Rather than a means to protect society's most vulnerable, Murray insisted that social programs were the cause of deep cultural pathologies that in turn trapped people in a cycle of poverty. Tearing away the social safety net—and forcing people to take responsibility for themselves and their families—would be the only way to lift people out of poverty.

Murray's pro-work analysis rested on an argument not about middle-class people like flight attendants or other workers at Continental Airlines. Instead, Murray shifted the conversation to focus on people who, by and large, lacked the money, the political connections, or the legal resources to challenge him: poor women on welfare, particularly poor black women on welfare. Murray regurgitated long-standing, racist ideas that black people are self-indulgent while white people are self-restrained, that black women are sexually aggressive while white women are chaste, and that black women are domineering and emasculating while white women defer to men's authority. While poor black women appeared on page after page of *Losing Ground* without their consent, racial and economic privilege protected flight attendants and other middle-class workers from subjection to Murray's scrutiny. It would thus be unfair to make a direct linkage between a normatively white airline workforce and the women in *Losing Ground* or to assume that policymakers would think about the sexuality of flight attendants in the same terms that they would think about the sexuality of black women on welfare.

Where a precise connection should be made, however, lies in Murray's approach to work. For Murray, jobs—even very low-wage jobs—mandate responsible behavior that leads to strong families and strong economies. His critique centers on changes to U.S. welfare policy that Murray insists discouraged both traditional family and hard work. Before 1960, if a woman went on public assistance, she was barred from supplementing her income with money from a husband or lover. Most women chose both a relationship and work over welfare since the income from two jobs was worth far more than one welfare check. Domesticity and hard work were, therefore, the dual foundations of low-income women's economic security.[57] This changed in the mid-1960s, when the federal government began allowing welfare recipients to supplement their income with cash from friends or lovers as long as the woman was not married to the person providing the money. After the reform, poor women could maximize their income by staying single and staying on welfare.[58] By taking low-wage jobs and marriage out of the equation for many poor women, Murray argued, the Aid to Families with Dependent Children (AFDC) reforms of the mid-1960s created a sexual culture that valued immediate sexual gratification over long-term commitment, and illegitimacy over the nuclear family. To reverse that trend, Murray proposed eliminating welfare in an effort to move domesticity and hard work back to the center of poor women's lives.[59]

Murray's focus on morality and family helped remake economic policy debates in the 1980s, shifting analysis away from the economic impact of welfare cuts and helping build a new consensus among policymakers that pro-work reforms were in the interest of both the poor and the middle class. For Murray and other antiwelfare activists, trimming the social safety net was important because it would produce a new sexual subject, a person committed to family values such as self-denial, deferred gratification, and personal responsibility. Public policy, Murray and others argued, should penalize the person who stayed single, who cohabitated with lovers, or who had children outside marriage. If Congress obliged Murray's cohort and passed pro-work reforms, it would remake the economy into the family values economy, one in which domesticity and hard work would be the foundations of cultural and economic life. Domesticity and hard work are, of course, the bedrock values of the middle class, which helped Murray, the pro-deregulation AEI fellows, and other pro-work scholars frame their reforms as keys to the restoration of middle-class prosperity in the 1980s.

Lost in this conversation was that the reorganization of the economy around domesticity and hard work would shrink the middle class and jeopardize its quality of life. Sexualized racism helped Murray and other pro-work activists avoid those economic conversations because some of the white middle class would assume that only poor and immigrant women of color would have to take the low-wage jobs that the family values economy was creating. The Continental Airlines strike of 1983 demonstrated, however, that race and class privilege would not protect the middle class. For as policymakers were drawing up the Personal Responsibility and Work Opportunity Reconciliation Act, a reform that would enshrine Murray's antiwelfare theory in law and make poor women of color the hardest hit in the conversion to the family values economy, they were also deregulating core industries and passing right-to-work laws. Therefore, and despite the prominent role that middle-class values played in justifying these reforms, economic sustenance would become much more difficult for most of the middle class after 1980 because low-wage labor had become the dominant feature of the labor market.

Conclusion: Alternative Families and the Crisis of the Labor Movement

In the wake of the Airline Deregulation Act and a constellation of other pro-work reforms, a contradiction emerged between the growing investment in traditional family values and the proliferation of families that were anything but traditional. After Frank Lorenzo became the first executive to convert a major airline from living-wage to low-wage labor, Continental Airlines flight attendants were compensated much like the mostly-female workforce in the burgeoning service economy. Like workers in hotels, restaurants, and retail, post-strike flight attendants made a straight hourly wage that included no work rules, no monthly pay guarantees, no company-paid defined benefit pension, and the ability to be discharged at any moment without explanation. As workers lost control over wages and scheduling, the domestic space of the family became a place to make up for the uncertainties of work. Husbands, wives, and older children could pool wages from multiple low-wage jobs to pay the bills and could rotate work schedules to care for younger children when other family members were on the job. When those resources were insufficient, neighbors, friends, and extended family could chip in to make ends meet. In none too ironic terms, as the traditional breadwinner husband and dependent wife disappeared as economic forms, many more middle-class families grappled with the instabilities that Charles Murray so vehemently condemned in poor black women's lives.

That alternative families were a defining feature of the family values economy does not mean that traditional patriarchal values had disappeared after the 1970s. On the contrary, with self-described "pro-family" activists driving the pro-work reforms of the 1970s, traditional patriarchy became even more important to politics. The evangelical Christian organizations that made up the pro-family movement mobilized for a rigidly defined traditional family— a strictly monogamous, married, domesticated unit where a man was the primary decision maker in the home and where women and children deferred to men's authority—and against any challenge to that family from feminists, gay activists, single women, or sex radicals. Indeed, even as the economic and cultural form of traditional family vanished, it remained an enduring ideal. That residue was evident in Frank Lorenzo's final settlement with the Continental Airlines workers, one that tried to figure pilots as breadwinners and flight attendants as men's dependents even as all living-wage union contracts were pounded to smithereens.

The tension between family values and alternative families proved to be a daunting challenge for union activists, both among flight attendants and in all sectors of the economy. As trucking, telecommunications, and other industries were deregulated and an antilabor executive, legislative, and judicial branch dealt more setbacks to unions during labor disputes, real wages continued to fall in the 1980s. With low-wage work replacing the living wage, families were stretched thin, looking more and more like the female-headed "broken" homes that the pro-family movement scorned.[60] After a decade of framing work in terms of morality—the dominant approach that think tankers like Charles Murray, evangelical groups like Focus on the Family, all of the Republican leadership including Ronald Reagan, and "new Democrats" like Bill Clinton had all taken by 1990—much of the public assumed that nontraditional families were the *cause* rather than a *consequence* of people's newfound poverty. Restoring the middle class, then, would require a campaign to restore society's moral values and not one to improve wages, benefits, and work rules. In that shift, unions lost a long-standing point of leverage as the economics of labor faded to the margins of the public debate about the crisis facing the American working and middle classes in the 1980s.

Labor's challenge would only intensify in the airline industry as the 1980s progressed and pro-work reforms continued to gain momentum. Shortly after the Airline Deregulation Act was ratified, Congress initiated a decade-long deregulation of the banking industry. After those reforms allowed a far greater percentage of banks' profit-making activities to occur beyond the scope of government oversight, Wall Street boomed. In a deregulated financial marketplace, airline managers could access vast new sums of capital to underwrite their effort to extract wage and benefit concessions from front-line employees. Such efforts touched off a new round of unrest, and bitter strikes shut down United in 1985, TWA in 1986, and Eastern in 1989. Family values would organize the terms of public debate about that unrest. Since flight attendants had both rejected the pro-family movement's renewed commitment to traditional patriarchal values and resisted the threadbare uncertainties that most families in the family values economy faced, their unions would be front and center in those debates.

FINANCIALIZING FAMILY VALUES

Flight Attendants and the Wall Street
Revolution of the 1980s

"Stewardesses aren't breadwinners," Carl Icahn told Victoria Frankovich during a bargaining table standoff in August 1985. "They don't have dependents like the men do." The newly elected president of the Independent Federation of Flight Attendants (IFFA) at Trans World Airlines, Frankovich was locked in concessionary negotiations with the Wall Street financier who would soon own her troubled employer. Hoping to build on a series of corporate takeovers that he had recently staged in the technology and steel industries, Icahn had publicly promised to lower TWA's operating costs and to return subsequent profits to investors who backed the deal. Demanding a 40 percent reduction in compensation from pilots, machinists, and ground crews, Icahn would cut all employees' pay as he trimmed TWA's budget. Flight attendants, however, would receive a special benchmark for givebacks. Because 91 percent of flight attendants were women, and because he argued that women do not need a family wage, Icahn insisted that Frankovich accept deeper cuts than those coming from other employee groups. Furthermore, unlike the temporary concessions that Icahn was seeking from the other unions, the flight attendant givebacks would be permanent. If Frankovich signed the deal, flight attendants would forfeit the gains they had made a decade earlier in coalition with the women's, gay, and lesbian liberation movements. With Icahn's proposal, it seemed that restoring corporate profitability in the 1980s would require rolling back the social transformation of the 1960s and 1970s.[1]

The double standard in concessionary bargaining at TWA was a consequence of a broader political economic transformation that scholars have called "financialization."[2] By the mid-1980s, free market reforms had drastically elevated the power of the banking industry relative to other sectors of the economy. Insisting that strict federal financial regulations passed during the Great Depression had exacerbated the economic crisis of the 1970s, pro-business activists helped convince policymakers that eliminating those regulations would be necessary for an economic recovery. They argued that if Wall Street could design new financial products that coupled higher levels of risk with higher interest rates, investors looking for better returns would provide new capital for starved credit markets. As the financial services industry boomed amid successive run-ups in the junk bond, derivative, and mortgage-backed securities markets, Wall Street stockbrokers, hedge fund managers, and investment bankers became the most powerful actors in the economy and short-term stock performance became the most important benchmark for corporations' success.[3]

The new focus on stock and bond prices would present an unprecedented challenge for working people. Before 1980, labor, financial, and environmental regulations made companies accountable to a wide array of stakeholders, from employees to suppliers, customers, and neighbors.[4] Union activists were able to leverage that accountability to make concrete economic gains for their constituents. That changed after financial markets became more important to the economy in the 1980s. Since Wall Street reacts favorably when companies trim labor costs,[5] managers could drive up corporate stock prices by cutting wages and laying off workers. Armed with a new economic incentive and new capital, corporate leaders took aim at the labor movement. As management's anti-union campaign succeeded, financialization helped bring low-wage labor to heavily organized industries that had once been the bedrock of the middle class.

Given the economic inequality that accompanied Wall Street's rise to power, new cultural work would be necessary for big business to sell financialization to the public. Taking up that task, businessmen framed financialization as a means to rescue hardworking American families that were struggling in a weak economy. Before 1980, the financiers argued, government regulation had hamstrung corporate leaders. Labor law, equal employment opportunity enforcement, environmental regulation, and safety oversight had limited executives' control of corporations. With management held in check, environmentalists, community organizers, people of color, and feminists had made advances in the workplace in the 1970s. In the wake of those gains, some single mothers, women of color, and even welfare recipients were able to provide for their families. While marginalized people moved forward, the resurgent conservative movement argued, most hardworking American families had moved backward. To reverse that trend, Wall Street offered a solution: cut government fetters on capital. With new financial resources, managers could jumpstart the economy and provide new opportunities for family breadwinners. As regulation vanished and the economy recovered, businessmen and workingmen could reclaim their natural power over the workplace and over the household.

Wall Street's sales pitch put flight attendants in the crosshairs of financialization. As the airlines singled out flight attendants, using conventional ideas about domesticity to dismiss their need for a livable wage, activists confronted the contradictory foundations of a financialized economy. On the one hand, the architects of financialization espoused patriarchal ideals, promoting businessmen's authority at work, workingmen's authority at home, and the self-reliance of the husband-led nuclear family. But on the other hand, as financialization helped corporate executives cut up union contracts, wages collapsed for all workers. Consequently, as businessmen appealed to traditional family values by asserting that "flight attendants aren't breadwinners," financialization would strip both flight attendants and workingmen of a family wage. As trade unionists with a commitment to feminist and gay liberationist activism, flight attendants refused Wall Street's economic agenda and its cultural justification. Because of their activism, the airline industry took center stage in the debate over Wall Street's rise to power in the 1980s.

Hostile Takeovers, Junk Bonds, and the Problem with the Three-Martini Lunch

Financialization confronted TWA flight attendants as they were jarred awake with news of a crisis on the morning of Friday, June 14, 1985. Newscasters interrupted regular programming to announce that Rome-bound TWA flight 847 had been hijacked after takeoff from Hellinikon International Airport in Athens and that the jet was under siege in Beirut. Five New York–based flight attendants would spend three harrowing days aboard the aircraft as gunmen ordered the pilots to fly back and forth between Beirut and Algiers and murdered one of the passengers at the front of the Boeing 727's crowded, fetid passenger cabin.[6] As they grappled with disturbing live television feed of the standoff, flight attendants picked up morning papers and found a second piece of news about TWA. Bold headlines announced that Texas financier Frank Lorenzo would buy the airline for $795 million.[7] TWA flight attendants were all too familiar with Lorenzo after his intervention at

Continental Airlines in 1983, which eliminated two-thirds of the carrier's employees and cut wages in half for workers who remained. As they pored over details of the Lorenzo transaction, and as the hijacking provided a vivid reminder of the airline industry's vast instability, flight attendants were perplexed. Why, they asked, would a businessman with an unwavering commitment to corporate profitability want to buy a company that had lost hundreds of millions of dollars since deregulation?

The answer to the flight attendants' question begins with a core component of financialization: the corporate mergers and acquisitions boom of the 1980s.[8] With Lorenzo's announcement, TWA became one of thousands of companies targeted that decade for a "hostile takeover," a forced sale also called a leveraged buyout (LBO). Hostile takeovers begin when a wealthy suitor wagers that a company's stock is undervalued. In TWA's case, the company owned a cache of valuable assets, from facilities at Washington National, New York–LaGuardia, and other capacity-restricted airports, to treaty-protected access to lucrative global hubs such as London-Heathrow. The airline had floundered since the passage of the Airline Deregulation Act in 1978, however. Recording net losses in four out of the first five years of deregulation, TWA shed twelve thousand employees and cannibalized 30 percent of its operation.[9] Initiating an LBO, Lorenzo gambled that TWA's low stock price reflected the post-deregulation turmoil and not the overall value of the facilities and routes, assets that presumably would be worth far more if managers had been more effective. Given that assumption, Lorenzo prepared to make TWA shareholders an offer too lucrative to resist. Rather than pay the current, depressed market value for the shares, Lorenzo would buy stock at above-market prices, paying a rate that investors would have gotten if the post-deregulation crisis had never happened. Once Lorenzo owned more than 50 percent of the voting shares of stock, he would control enough votes on the board to make executive decisions by fiat. Exercising that unilateral authority, Lorenzo would fire the existing management team, take the reins of the company, and retool operations to maximize efficiency. Except for the sacked former managers, everyone theoretically wins, as the original shareholders liquidate their once-depressed stake at a profit and as competent new executives put assets to better use, which in turn leaves the firm better equipped to meet the challenge of the marketplace.

Reeling from Lorenzo's hostile takeover of Continental Airlines, union leaders from across the industry insisted that in an LBO, not everyone wins. Because the prices of fuel, airplanes, and facilities are largely fixed, the only way for new managers to achieve promised operational efficiencies is to cut wages. Indeed, after the Lorenzo takeover, Continental flight attendants topped out at $16.47 an hour while their peers at TWA were earning almost three times their wage—$42.64.[10] Recognizing that Lorenzo or any other financier could try to replicate Continental-style labor cost cutting at a different airline, and aware of takeover rumors at TWA, Eastern, and Pan Am, a coalition of activists from multiple trades and carriers mobilized against LBOs. Their initial strategy involved leaning on pro-labor Democrats to convene congressional hearings on the consequences of LBOs in the airlines. The coalition hoped to persuade elected officials to regulate hostile takeovers, creating oversight that would drive up the cost of transactions and make them less desirable to financiers.

Although they provided an audience for flight attendant testimony that underscored the inequitable consequences of LBOs, congressional hearings also allowed bankers to make the case for the political and cultural merits of financialization. Most eloquent in that defense was Wall Street financier Carl Icahn. Notorious for his confrontational approach to business, Icahn would soon inspire Michael Douglas's performance as Gordon Gecko in Oliver Stone's 1987 film *Wall Street*. Icahn first testified on June 6, 1985, the same week that the *Wall Street Journal* reported that he had joined Frank Lorenzo in buying up shares of TWA. Journalists speculated that if he could outbid Lorenzo for control of the airline, Icahn could leverage TWA in a sequence of LBOs he was engineering. He would finance the TWA deal by borrowing against the resources of ACF Technologies, a previous takeover target that Icahn now owned, and then use TWA's unencumbered assets to launch a follow-up raid on steel giant USX.[11] When he took the witness stand, however, Icahn avoided arcane financial analysis and instead engaged the public by insisting that high-stakes financial risk taking was necessary to restore the global economic competitiveness of the United States.

Leading his audience through the economic history of the 1970s to explain his interest in hostile takeovers, Icahn worked to manage a contradiction surrounding Wall Street's growing political and economic power in the 1980s. As they mobilized against welfare and against government regulation, the pro-business activists of the 1970s continually reiterated that hard work is the bedrock of American culture (see Chapter 3). Restoring the power of the free market would, for the pro-business movement, restore such enduring values as self-denial, deferred gratification, and personal responsibility. For more than a century, however, those same pro-work values had also been the foundation of a populist critique of banking, one that condemned Wall Street for its self-indulgent, irresponsible, immoral excess.[12] Indeed, as it drove a financial boom that would soon produce Gordon Gecko's "greed is good" speech as a cultural leitmotif, Wall Street seemed to undermine the pro-business movement's goal of reorganizing the economy around traditional family and hard work.

Reframing that debate, Icahn insisted that hostile takeovers would reinforce pro-work values by teaching corporate managers to work hard. By the mid-1970s, Icahn argued, managers had strayed from the work ethic. Tight credit markets, government regulation, union contracts, and a weak economy had restrained corporate leaders, making non-intervention—rather than aggressive leadership—a survival strategy for those at the top of big firms. With corporate executives choosing inaction over action, Japanese competitors had lapped U.S. firms in the 1980s. LBOs, Icahn insisted, would break that cycle. Hostile takeovers would subject upper management to the forces of the free market, making business leaders either take charge or face ejection in a Wall Street–engineered buyout. Selling financialization as a moral mechanism to transform managers into responsible workers, Icahn accomplished two political goals. First, he undermined flight attendants' effort to claim the moral high ground and in the process moved the labor question to the periphery of the public debate about financialization. Second, he aligned Wall Street with the moral foundations of the family values economy, turning hostile takeovers into means to retool the economy around domesticity and hard work.

The congressional hearings about the TWA buyout seemed to underscore Icahn's point about flagging corporate leadership. TWA president Ed Meyer took the stand early in the process. "If you don't mind, I'll read my presentation," Meyer began, seeming intimidated by the intensity of the venue and keeping his head down in prewritten text. When Icahn was called, however, he spoke directly to the gallery without notes, offering vivid testimony. "Mister Meyer is flat wrong," Icahn boomed as he began.[13]

Rather than offer a narrow rebuttal to Meyer's nuts-and-bolts presentation about airline economics, Icahn launched a broad critique of dominant management practices at U.S. corporations in the postwar era. Bad management was the negative side effect of an immensely stable banking system in the mid-twentieth century, Icahn and fellow financiers argued, one that channeled funds into General Motors, General Electric, U.S. Steel, and other established, stable firms. That banking system was fundamentally risk-averse. If investors recognized that a management team at a given firm was failing, for example, it was extremely difficult for them to gather the capital necessary to eject managers in a hostile takeover. The big banks and insurance companies of the 1960s would not, in Icahn's appraisal, want to dirty their books with the risks associated with buying a failing company, and they had no stomach for the negative publicity that would come with the ejection of well-known and well-liked managers.[14] Executives at brick-and-mortar companies were, therefore, protected from the market forces that would ordinarily force them to innovate.[15]

As he problematized mid-twentieth-century capital formation, Icahn also launched a distinct cultural critique of the era's managers. Because of their insulation from the market, there were few incentives for executives to claim managerial authority or take the risks necessary to build an innovative, adaptive, competitive business. Instead, managing had been relegated to the short blocks of time between three-martini lunches and departure for the golf course. Icahn painted a vivid picture of this culture for the House Subcommittee on Telecommunications, Consumer Protection, and Finance:

> [Managers] are sort of like the fraternity brother in college. The fellow that you elected to be president of the fraternity in college was certainly not necessarily the best and the brightest or the guy that you would have run your company or your funds or your money. . . . He was the good guy, the guy you liked to go drinking with. . . . And that is the guy that gets into the corporation today, a likeable guy. He gets football tickets for the guys on the board and he goes drinking with them when they come in for a board meeting. And what happens is, the CEO likes him and the CEO decides to retire or become chairman emeritus, he makes this fellow, who has been there 20 or 30 years, he makes this fellow the CEO, and this is what evolves. What happens as a result, we have, I believe, poor management today.[16]

Castigating the not-so-smart-frat-brother-turned-CEO, Icahn took control of the debate with TWA's Ed Meyer. The underlying cause of Meyer's opposition to the takeover, Icahn argued, was his unwillingness to part with a mid-twentieth-century managerial culture. Meyer was afraid to lose a lavish lifestyle, one that came with unlimited free rides on TWA flights with gourmet cuisine and attractive flight attendants in Valentino dresses. "It is just fear of the unknown," Icahn taunted, "fear that I am going to oust them."[17] Antagonizing Meyer, Icahn turned the conversation to morality. Because of managerial inaction, Icahn argued, the United States put its productive capacity to a terribly inefficient use. That bloat was the cause of the economic woes of the 1970s, those that had jeopardized the American Dream in a cycle of high unemployment and runaway inflation. Using LBOs to bring back the discipline of the market was, therefore, a way for Icahn to put American families back to work.

What was most challenging about Icahn's line of argumentation for his opponents at TWA was that, at least in operational terms, Icahn was correct.

The management teams of Ed Meyer and his predecessor, Charles Tilling-hast, had, after all, failed to read the tea leaves of a historic reorganization in the global economy in the 1970s. The major airlines had entered that decade making money by cherry-picking revenue off the postwar boom in manufac-turing. In the spring of 1974, for example, U.S. airlines offered more seats on Chicago-Pittsburgh—a route linking the capital of the world's steel industry to the financial center of the Midwest—than Chicago-London and Chicago-Paris combined. Columbus, Indianapolis, and Saint Louis were as important to TWA's route system as Zurich, Milan, and Hong Kong. But after 1973, the U.S. industrial economy withered amid intensifying international competi-tion and relentless inflation. Going forward, it would be much more difficult for the airlines to make money carrying coal, steel, and auto executives be-tween industrial cities.[18] Instead, companies would have to build networks that connected what Saskia Sassen calls "global cities," those with command and control functions over finance, insurance, real estate, communications, and technology. This meant that each major carrier would have to redeploy assets to gain a top position in the East Coast megalopolis, connect traffic through a hub in a large midwestern city with a diverse economy, and then link that traffic to the burgeoning California corridor.[19]

TWA managers failed to meet that challenge. The airline was unable to capitalize on its once-strong position in the most economically important city in the middle of the continent: Chicago. In the mid-1970s, either TWA or American Airlines could have occupied the number two position at O'Hare International Airport behind giant United. In April 1974, for example, Amer-ican and TWA's Chicago stations were the exact same size, with each offering approximately one hundred flights to twenty-five destinations. But as the 1970s progressed, TWA failed to hold the line against American. TWA had almost no ability to borrow by mid-decade, because of both painfully tight lending practices and its own precarious finances. Bad credit made it difficult for TWA to buy new aircraft, leaving the carrier particularly vulnerable to the oil shocks that occurred in 1973 and 1979. American, however, had ded-icated more capital to technological advancement and scooped up most of Braniff International's fuel-efficient 727s when that airline collapsed after deregulation.[20] Thus, when American put the squeeze on TWA in Chicago, it did so with far lower energy costs. In 1979, for example, TWA still flew a full third of its Chicago schedule with fuel-thirsty 707s while American cut its use of the older jets to just 15 percent.

Lacking the right aircraft for the market, TWA gave up. On the eve of the Icahn affair in 1985, when American connected Chicago to the world with nonstops to fifty-seven cities, TWA served just eight airports from O'Hare, three of which were in its hometown of New York City.[21] Meanwhile, TWA built up operations at Pittsburgh and Saint Louis, escaping American's challenge in Chicago but placing itself front and center in the crisis of deindustrialization in the Midwest. Therefore, despite the underlying value of TWA's global route system, TWA's stock price was in free fall while American's had stabilized.

TWA's declining stock price made the carrier particularly attractive to financier suitors like Lorenzo and Icahn. Confirming speculation that he was buying up shares to counter a Lorenzo takeover bid, Icahn went public with an offer to buy TWA for $18 a share on May 22. But with Lorenzo's higher offer for $23 a share on June 14, Icahn faced an immediate choice. He could let the sale close, selling his 32.7 percent stake in TWA to Lorenzo for a robust $78.6 million profit.[22] Or he could stay in the game and counter Lorenzo. All signs pointed to the second option: Icahn had been publicly adamant that TWA's assets made it a good buy and that it would make him far more money than the $78 million that Lorenzo had put on the table.

Carl Icahn formally met Frank Lorenzo's challenge on August 6, 1985, when he raised the Texas financier's bid by $1 and offered $24 a share for TWA.[23] To Icahn's consternation, Lorenzo immediately counteroffered, matching Icahn's bid. Recognizing Lorenzo's determination, Icahn invited Lorenzo into a private meeting in his Manhattan office the following week. Icahn offered Lorenzo a one-time cash payment of $50 million to walk away from TWA, apparently hoping that the opportunity for immediate profit would dissuade Lorenzo from continuing his increasingly risky, increasingly arduous hostile takeover attempt. Lorenzo refused the payment, instead demanding $70 million to withdraw his offer. Exploding in frustration, Icahn threw Lorenzo out of his office.[24]

Abandoning the effort to pay Lorenzo off, Icahn retooled, aiming to secure additional financing and close the sale before Lorenzo raised the price with another counteroffer. As Icahn returned to Wall Street, the most important player in the LBO process emerged: Icahn's investment bank, Drexel-Burnham-Lambert. A driving force in the corporate mergers and acquisitions boom of the mid-1980s, Drexel was working with both Icahn and Lorenzo, preparing to assist in financing either man's purchase of TWA. The investment bank was able play both sides of the TWA bidding war because few other financial institutions were willing to bet on deals as risky as the TWA takeover. TWA, after all, was burning cash, losing market share, and posting net losses. Conventional wisdom said that a lender would be foolish to further leverage a firm that was already hemorrhaging.

Drexel-Burnham-Lambert thought otherwise. The investment bank specialized in identifying undervalued stocks and then funding LBOs of those firms. Most of these transactions were financed with high-yield securities commonly known as "junk bonds." With a rating of BB-plus or lower from Standard & Poor's, or BA1 or lower from Moody's, junk bonds are securities that are backed by little or no collateral but that advertise much higher interest rates than those paid for more secure investments.[25] The junk bond business was small, just $16 billion out of an $800 billion credit market in 1984.[26] But it was red hot and growing, and by 1985 investors were trading as many junk bonds as they were stocks on the Dow Jones.[27] Under the direction of its aggressive CEO Michael Milken, Drexel-Burnham-Lambert helped lead the charge toward the riskiest sectors of the bond market. The investment bank had a growing list of private and institutional investors willing to gamble that TWA would survive the leadership change and become a leaner, more agile, and more profitable company, one that could pay interest rates far exceeding those available from most other stocks and bonds.

By the end of 1985, Drexel had shifted the advantage in the struggle for control of TWA toward Carl Icahn. The investment bank helped Icahn put together what had become the most securely financed buyout offer and to acquire the majority of the voting shares in the company. Like more and more transactions in a junk bond market steaming toward boil-over, however, the deal came at a steep price. The financier was about to pay $24 a share for TWA stock that—given the airline's overall financial performance—was trading at $15 on the eve of the closing. Icahn would in fact have to borrow another $750 million from Drexel just to keep TWA flying once he took over. Nevertheless, short-term economic challenges were no match for Icahn's broader pro-work cultural vision, and the financier closed the sale on the freezing day of January 6, 1986.[28] Using the new financial tools of a deregulated banking industry, Icahn executed a heavily leveraged deal that gave him control of an airline that, for more than a decade, had been home to the industry's most mobilized flight attendant union.

Concessionary Bargaining Family-Style at Trans World Airlines

Soon after Carl Icahn became TWA's chief executive, tensions rose in response to the story that he and other Wall Street bankers were telling about financialization. Regulatory reform in the banking sector, Icahn had argued, was about the future. Financialization would allow companies to move out of the stasis of the 1970s and into a new age of global competitiveness, one that would bring new opportunities for workers who had been frozen in place by a weak economy. The problem with financiers' analysis was that companies like Continental and TWA were dynamic places in the 1970s. Flight attendants had their own vision for a better economic future, one that stood in stark contrast to Wall Street's narrative and guided their unions as they challenged the status quo of airline labor relations. Activists focused on closing the pay gap between flight attendants and other airline workers and had won wage and work rule improvements that allowed union members to be breadwinners for their families.[29]

Icahn and other financiers rejected flight attendants' plan for the future. Echoing religious activists, the pro-business movement that had propelled Wall Street's rise to power in the 1980s pushed for economic changes that would help self-reliant, independent, responsible families. Traditional notions of domesticity defined the family for these activists, who argued that financialization would provide new resources for breadwinning husbands, caregiving wives, and dependent children.[30] A flight attendant movement that delivered big raises to single people, to female-headed households, and to gay, lesbian, and feminist-identified people was thus suspect to Carl Icahn and his colleagues. Insisting that flight attendants are not breadwinners, Icahn designed a targeted package of givebacks that stripped flight attendants of a family wage. Therefore, while all unionized workers faced disheartening setbacks in the 1980s, the renewed cultural commitment to family values provided a cudgel for Wall Street to force flight attendants to take deeper economic concessions than any other airline workers.

The deteriorating situation at TWA in the second half of 1985 demonstrates how family values left airline workers on a divergent path through financialization. That divergence surfaced as all TWA employees scrambled for a response to Carl Icahn and Frank Lorenzo's simultaneous hostile takeover attempts. The 1983 crisis at Lorenzo's Continental disturbed TWA employees, who heard the stories of the surprise bankruptcy, the mass firings, and the 50 percent pay cut blowing across the airline. Motivated by fear, pilot, machinist, and flight attendant leaders quickly arrived at a strategic consensus. Union leaders would try to preempt a surprise attack on employees by engaging Icahn in bilateral talks before the sale of TWA. By promising Icahn expansive labor cost savings, activists could protect themselves from the even more extreme cutbacks that Icahn might design without their input. Meanwhile, Icahn could use concessionary pacts with unions to woo investors looking to cash in on labor cost savings. Guaranteed pay cuts would strengthen Icahn's hand against Lorenzo, thereby reducing the chance that employees would face the notorious Texas financier.

Workers' initial unity vanished as soon as pilots, flight attendants, and ground employees began negotiating with Icahn. Talks with the mostly-male employee groups moved quickly. On July 5, 1985, just three weeks after his first formal buyout offer, pilots announced an accord with Icahn, and a bitter pill it was for any aviator who had built her or his flying career at TWA. Pilot leaders offered a 20 percent across-the-board cut in hourly wages, givebacks that when coupled with work rule and benefit concessions would reduce TWA's total pilot costs by 40 percent. The deal came with a humiliating and ominous caveat: as long as Icahn honored the proposal, cockpit crews would cross the picket lines of any other group that opted to strike rather than take concessions after the buyout. With their livelihood on the line, and without skills that were easily transferable to other industries, pilots abandoned the union coalition in exchange for solidarity with Icahn.[31]

Well aware that ground employees were also close to a deal and recognizing that the pilots' picket crossover agreement had further weakened their leverage against Icahn, flight attendant activists pushed for a compromise. Los Angeles–based flight attendant Victoria Frankovich led her colleagues through that process. Vowing to take the Independent Federation of Flight Attendants (IFFA) in an activist new direction, Frankovich had recently defeated IFFA co-founder Arthur Teolis in a bid for union president. Frankovich had built a reputation as a determined negotiator and sharp communicator in the 1970s and was adamantly committed to protecting the gains that she and other IFFA leaders had won during the upsurge. Nevertheless, Frankovich conceded that the hostile takeover had backed IFFA into a corner and that concessionary bargaining with Icahn was a necessary survival strategy for flight attendants facing financialization. Therefore, on August 2, 1985, she sat down with Icahn in a private, one-on-one meeting in New York. As they began to talk, Frankovich had two basic goals: come away with a deal that would shield TWA flight attendants from further cuts after the takeover, and design the agreement to spare flight attendants from the deep hourly wage cuts forced on much higher-paid pilots. To achieve this goal, Frankovich offered to match the concessionary agreement that the International Association of Machinists and Aerospace Workers (IAM) was finalizing with Icahn, one centered on a 15 percent reduction in hourly pay. Locking in wage givebacks that were smaller than pilots' would preserve flight attendants' longstanding commitment to closing the wage gap between flight attendants and the mostly-male employee groups.[32]

Icahn scuttled Frankovich's overture, refusing to entertain a universal agreement that would standardize IFFA and IAM concessions. "I'm going to need more from the girls," Icahn told Frankovich, rotating the terms "girls" and "stewardesses" when he spoke about flight attendants, as he often did in public presentations. According to Frankovich, Icahn made an explicit argument about gender, sexuality, and family as he laid out a concessionary agenda that would, on a percentile basis, hit flight attendants harder than any other TWA employees. Icahn began by claiming that flight attendants were unskilled. "I can get nineteen-year-old girls off the street to do this job," Icahn told Frankovich. Even though hiring credentials— including college credit and foreign language proficiency—were stricter for flight attendants than for aircraft cleaners, ticket agents, and many others in the IAM, flight attending was, for Icahn, a job that any woman could do. Because of his assumption that all women are naturally good at homemaking, caregiving, and entertaining, the financier insisted that the airline could tap an unlimited applicant pool even if it drastically lowered wages. Icahn then deepened his analysis, using traditional family values to insist that flight attendants *deserved* to earn less than everyone they worked with. "Stewardesses aren't breadwinners," Icahn told Frankovich. "They don't have dependents like the men do." Invoking the family wage system, Icahn insisted that it was fair and appropriate to put a floor under mechanics', custodians', and customer service agents' wages, as those workers needed to fulfill their responsibilities as husbands and heads of households.[33] Regardless of how many flight attendants were the sole providers for friends, lovers, and children, Icahn insisted that no such floor should exist under IFFA bargaining.

Though he dredged up timeworn clichés about "women's work" as he dismissed Frankovich, Icahn made a historically specific argument about men's and women's labor in the 1980s. He instrumentalized widespread sentiment among white men that radical feminists' and gay liberationists' 1970s advances had undermined traditional manhood. To defend ordinary men, Icahn vowed to use the LBO and the collective bargaining process as tools in a countermovement against the culture of the 1970s. Thus, the financier proposed a new alliance between management and pilots, machinists, cleaners, and clerks around a common commitment to restoring men's authority at home and at work. Icahn referenced that solidarity as he described to Congress his plan to sack failed managers: "I am not talking about the real employees, the real guys doing the work, I am talking about what I consider the top layers in these companies that have built up bureaucracy on bureaucracy, and these bureaucracies really throttle up the productive engine in this country."[34] By naming the "real guys" as his allies and by couching the LBO as a means to restart the economy's "productive engine," Icahn described his involvement with TWA as an effort to restore the mobility for workingmen that had vanished in the 1970s. Rather than making an inequitable bid to upwardly redistribute wealth, the Icahn buyout would protect the interests of the "guys doing the work."

As he framed financialization as a means to restore the value of a hard day's work, Icahn took aim at the gains that women had made in the labor market in the 1970s. In an interview with *Cosmopolitan* magazine, Icahn focused on flight attendant labor relations as he explained the importance of his managerial strategy. Perhaps because Helen Gurley Brown's publication had long provided a space to talk about gender while dismissing feminism, Icahn was particularly candid as he argued that flight attendants were overpaid and that financialization would help him cut women's wages:

> I have been able to build a successful airline because I was willing to confront the task, to stand up to unpalatable situations. When I looked at the unfavorable contract we had with flight attendants, I said, "I am not going to live with this." The top management told me they'd handle it, that they always negotiated a deal. I asked, "What happens if the flight attendants won't negotiate?" They said, "Well, we have to work with them." But I said, "We have a training school. Why don't we start training new people so we have some leverage just in case?" You don't have to be a genius to figure that out. We live in a world based on supply and demand. The flight attendant chose to be one, and she's in a business where there are a lot of flight attendants willing to work for a lot less."[35]

Traditional manliness—a willingness to "confront the task" and to "stand up to unpalatable situations"—allowed Icahn to bring financialization to TWA. That process included aggressive new anti-union tactics, which, in turn, unleashed market forces that pushed flight attendants to work for "a lot less." As IFFA's bargaining power evaporated, management confiscated the economic resources that had allowed flight attendants to be breadwinners for their families. The financial revolution of the 1980s would, in other words, roll back the cultural revolution of the 1970s.

Events at TWA in the fall of 1985 helped Icahn deliver on his commitment to changing the value of men's and women's work. On Monday, August 5, Icahn settled with IAM-represented employees, signing the agreement that he had rejected from Victoria Frankovich forty-eight hours earlier.[36] As he compromised with workingmen, Icahn remained unyielding with flight attendants. To secure their jobs at the new TWA, activists would have to come up with a set of givebacks that would lower the airline's total flight attendant costs by at least 44 percent. Furthermore, and contrary to his approach with the pilots or IAM-represented groups, Icahn was not open to "snap backs" that would end the most painful flight attendant givebacks after TWA reorganized. Finally, and once again in a demand made only of IFFA, flight attendants would have to forfeit their "dues checkoff" agreement, a change that would force union leaders to collect monthly dues on an individual basis rather than expecting TWA to deduct the correct amount from paychecks.[37] Instead of rallying their members around key political issues as pilot and IAM leaders could continue to do, IFFA activists would have to spend long hours collecting and processing union dues once checkoff disappeared.

The situation further intensified on November 1, when activists opened major newspapers to see that, in the middle of a corporate downsizing, TWA was hiring flight attendants. The small print in the advertisements revealed that the job postings were a strategic move on Icahn's part. New recruits would earn $1,000 per month in base pay, about half of what the union contract guaranteed flight attendants in their first month. The discrepancy meant that new flight attendants would earn their wings only if existing crews called a strike, taking to the skies as permanent replacement workers.[38] As Icahn continued to harden his position against IFFA, front-line TWA employees were in vastly different situations by the time he completed the hostile takeover in January 1986. Though Icahn had pared down machinists', pilots', and ground workers' wages, he was legally bound to take the knife no deeper. Flight attendants, however, would have no such certainty: by springtime, a hotel full of strikebreakers in Kansas City would be ready to help Icahn confiscate the spoils of flight attendant unionism.

"We Are Breadwinners": Culture, Political Economy, and the TWA Flight Attendant Strike of 1986

Flight attendants crafted a hard-hitting response to Carl Icahn's unprecedented challenge. Instead of sidestepping the political debate about the nature of work and family that Icahn had helped initiate, IFFA intervened in that debate. Making themselves rather than Icahn the center of their campaign, flight attendants rolled out a simple, three-word slogan: "We Are Breadwinners." Claiming their economic role at the head of the household, flight attendants refuted the story that conservative activists were telling during that decade. IFFA activists argued that as it had pitted hardworking American families against single mothers, female-headed households, and nondomesticated relationships, the pro-work political movement of the 1980s had levied a cultural judgment against independent women. Activists insisted, however, that the economic reforms based on that judgment would force every front-line employee to work for less. After a 40 percent pay cut and benefit givebacks, every flight attendant, every machinist, every ramp service worker, and every pilot would have a harder time providing for her or his dependents. As they made their own families front and center in the campaign against concessions, TWA flight attendants demonstrated that there is no way to contest financialization without confronting its cultural underpinnings. There is no such thing as fighting pro-work politics, flight attendants argued, without fighting "pro-family" politics.

Flight attendant leaders had little time to prepare for this cultural confrontation. On his seventeenth day on the job, Carl Icahn formally rejected all flight attendant alternatives to the agreement sitting on the table, demanding a 44 percent cost reduction, no snap backs, and the end of dues check-off.[39] As talks collapsed, the IFFA's executive board extended its long-standing commitment to rank-and-file democracy and sent the Icahn proposal directly to flight attendants for a ratification vote. On February 1, 1986, 98 percent of flight attendants who went to the polls in a referendum voted against Icahn's terms.[40] Even in the face of nearly unanimous opposition, however, activists hedged, figuring that stalling was preferable to a walkout, given the number of replacement workers ready to take flight attendants' jobs. Continued bargaining would delay a concessionary contract or a risky strike.

Icahn quickly called IFFA's bluff and petitioned the National Mediation Board (NMB) to formally declare an impasse in the TWA conflict. Since anti-union Reagan appointees controlled the NMB in 1986, Icahn hoped the board would endorse his effort to force concessions on flight attendants by rejecting IFFA's plea for more time in mediation. With an impasse declaration, Icahn would be allowed to implement wage cuts in thirty days and to replace any flight attendant who struck in protest with one of the strikebreakers in training in Kansas City. On February 5, the board obliged Icahn, thwarting IFFA's bid for more time in mediation and beginning the countdown toward a strike: midnight on Friday, March 7, 1986.[41]

That moment passed without a deal. Any flight attendant who came to work on Saturday morning would do so on Icahn's terms. Refusing to comply with Icahn's demand, flight attendants abandoned their aircraft en masse, grounding TWA as the sun rose across the eastern end of the operation in Bombay, Tel Aviv, and Cairo and rolling like a wave all the way west to Honolulu. With operations halted, flight attendants in the middle of trips would have to stay on friends' couches or hitch rides home on other, unionized airlines. After Icahn cut off payments to strikers' layover hotels, IFFA chartered a series of jumbo jets to perform "sweeper flights," hopping across Europe, the Mediterranean, and the Middle East to pick up stranded crews.[42]

Once back at their domiciles, TWA flight attendants picketed around the clock in front of passenger terminals, maintenance hangars, reservations centers, and ticket offices. All signs they carried included the IFFA logo and the "We Are Breadwinners" slogan. To draw out the theme of the strike, activists included the image of bread in all strike paraphernalia. There were, for example, the scores of picket signs with Icahn as Dracula, wielding a cleaver to hack off pieces of bread marked "wages" and "pensions" and "job security." There were the larger-than-life Styrofoam slices with fang bites missing, presumably lost to the Dracula/Icahn on the posters. There was actual bread at every demonstration, with ready-to-eat baguette, ciabatta, and sliced Wonder Bread serving as both a political prop and free food for protesters. Finally, there were the agit-prop bread deliveries. Activists had sought out moles among unionized clerical workers, banquet waiters, and hotel desk staff with access to Icahn's schedule and whereabouts. Acting on secret tips, flight attendants would barge into meetings and present Icahn with whole wheat, caraway, rye, and pumpernickel, disrupting his business dealings by condemning his claim that "stewardesses are not breadwinners."[43]

With bread at the center of their protests, flight attendants reminded their audience that the labor movement had always been both an economic and a cultural project. Referencing the century-old union slogan "bread and roses," IFFA activists pointed to generations of workers who walked out on strike to meet their *needs* and their *wants,* demanding economic security and the time to pursue personal pleasures. Breadwinning also helped flight attendants make a particular cultural intervention about the 1980s. Naming their position in the crosshairs of the "culture wars," breadwinning allowed flight attendants to frame the strike as a conflict between their own feminist commitments and the visceral antifeminism of the "pro-family" movement. Unwavering in their seriousness, flight attendants nevertheless used humor to respond to their opponents. For example, strikers frequently pumped their fists in the air and roared as they posed for picket line photographs. Skewering dismissive, objectifying press coverage that labeled the strike an angry feminist protest rather than a rational workplace dispute, the fist pumps quoted Helen Reddy's 1972 hit "I Am Woman, Hear Me Roar," which was both an anthem and a cliché by the mid-1980s.[44]

Fist pumps were often accompanied by flying bras. Posing for the camera while walking the picket line outside TWA's Kansas City overhaul base, a flight attendant launched her bra toward an imaginary "freedom trashcan."[45] That trashcan, which gained notoriety in a feminist protest outside the 1968 Miss America Pageant, had been vastly overrepresented in media accounts of the women's liberation movement, accounts that ended up being used to label 1970s feminists "bra-burners." On the same picket line, another flight attendant reclined in a lawn chair and theatrically read a copy of *New Woman* magazine while being photographed, a pose that humorously characterized the strike as a rejection of traditional femininity.[46] Flight attendants' most dramatic performance came in a series of "We Hate Carl Wienie Roasts."[47] As they cooked, sliced, and speared hotdogs, bratwursts, and Polish sausages, all while photographing their knife work, activists' satirized the "pro-family" movement's dismissal of feminism as irrational, obsessive, and castrating. Throwing a few Rocky Mountain oysters on the grill, flight attendants theatrically identified as ball busters.

As they made the history of feminism and the sexual revolution germane to the picket line, TWA flight attendants rejected the dominant cultural approach to working people in the late twentieth century. In mainstream discourse about "working families" and "defending the middle class," workers were defined by their commitment to traditional family values. This pro-family framing came from both anti-union and pro-union constituencies. The business lobby, for example, exalted white working-class "Reagan Democrats" for sticking to moral traditionalism and voting against the cultural agendas of people of color, feminists, and gay activists.[48] Defending the working class against anti-union attacks, the labor left often used the same ideas, offering procreation, domesticity, and moral traditionalism to portray the working class as innocent and dignified.[49] Urban liberals, meanwhile, used the concept of family values to scorn the white working class, dismissing it as reactionary, sexist, homophobic, and racist.[50] With a double entendre about castrating Carl Icahn, flight attendants separated working families' struggles from the moral traditionalism and sentimentalism that elite critics often imposed on those struggles. By taking control of the conversation about breadwinning, flight attendants demonstrated that mainstream invocations of traditional family values were, more often than not, a means to dispossess the working class.

Humor-driven, pointed cultural criticism gave TWA flight attendants momentum on the picket line. But a good campaign would ultimately fail to counteract Icahn's strategic economic advantages. First and foremost, the vast majority of flight attendants' peers on the front lines failed to offer their solidarity. Once flight attendants struck, pilots followed the no-strike clause in their pact with Icahn and crossed IFFA's picket lines. And although 75 percent of front-line IAM members sided with flight attendants and walked out on the first day of the strike, IAM higher-ups showed no more sympathy than pilots. IAM International president William Winpisinger refused to grant a strike authorization to his members at TWA, abandoning the TWA local when Icahn—successfully—sued to force IAM members back to work five days after the flight attendants walked out.[51] Both pilots and IAM leaders knew that the family wage system had guaranteed immense wage premiums to the mostly-male groups at TWA. As that system collapsed in the 1980s, traditional bread-winners among machinists and pilots recognized that they had farther to fall than lower-paid employees such as flight attendants. Facing the prospect of losing that privilege, pilots and machinists were paralyzed with fear.

Meanwhile, Icahn was making good on his threat to hire "nineteen-year-old girls off the street." At the end of the first month of the strike, 1,850 replacement flight attendants worked for TWA, a process expedited when Reagan's Federal Aviation Administration obliged Icahn and reduced the airline's flight attendant training program to eighteen days. The new group—which strikers pejoratively called "eighteen-day wonders"—earned half the wage of those they replaced but could jump the industry's infamously long seniority line. Once they pushed through chanting picketers and entered the terminal, strikebreakers would walk onto jumbo jets bound for Paris and Zurich and Cairo, trips that required twenty or more years of seniority before the strike. Additionally, as they watched a constant stream of replacements take more and more of their jobs, one thousand existing TWA flight attendants made the decision to give up on the strike and cross the picket line. Watching the non-union ranks swell, Icahn showed little interest in finalizing a deal with IFFA and thus kept the bar just above what flight attendants offered. When Frankovich floated a new proposal on April 28 that would lower TWA's flight attendant costs by 28 percent, for example, Icahn spontaneously conjured 30 percent as the new benchmark for flight attendant concessions.[52] That intransigence came at a high price for Icahn: TWA burned $3 million a day during the strike and posted its least profitable quarter ever, a loss of $186 million for the first three months of 1986.[53]

Despite TWA's losses, and even though the "eighteen-day wonders" could never replace the experience of thousands of their older peers, it became clear as spring led to summer that the numbers were not adding up for the strike. Staying on the picket line would, it seemed, only give Icahn what he wanted—an excuse to permanently replace all unionized flight attendants. IFFA leaders thus exercised their rights under the Railway Labor Act and called off the strike. Frankovich's stoically crisp yet clearly morose prose communicated the intensity of the situation to all TWA flight attendants on May 17, 1986:

> Last night at 10pm IFFA made an unconditional offer to return all striking flight attendants to work immediately. This does not mean our fight is over—that decision is up to you. What this does mean is we are no longer withholding our services. Therefore when the company calls you to return to work, you must return. This is a strategic move on our part which is designed to prevent TWA from further attempting to replace us with scabs and new hires.[54]

With Frankovich's message, pickets came down and flight attendants headed home to pack their crew bags and to wait for crew scheduling to call with a flight assignment.

TWA never called. With that silence began the longest—but for flight attendants the most successful—part of the campaign. Hoping to take advantage of a rightward shift in the judiciary of the 1980s, Icahn filed a lawsuit in the Federal District Court for the Western District of Missouri that aimed to dissolve IFFA's union security clause.[55] Perhaps the most important section in any collective bargaining agreement, the security clause requires that managers assign all work to union members who earn a union wage. If the court voided IFFA's security clause, Icahn would be able to continue hiring permanent replacement workers to staff TWA's operation. With the lawsuit, Icahn aimed to set another anti-union precedent in the age of financialization. An Icahn victory over flight attendants would make it easier for employers to permanently replace union members with younger, cheaper workers.

Backing up their effort with a grassroots solidarity and media campaign called the "Boycott of Conscience," IFFA activists carried their case all the way to the U.S. Supreme Court. In the landmark case *TWA v. IFFA,* the justices blocked Icahn from shredding IFFA's union security clause, mandating instead that all new flight attendant positions be assigned to union members returning to work. Although the decision allowed Icahn to retain all the strikebreakers he had already hired, the financier was forced to fill all new positions with IFFA members with full collective bargaining rights and with their full date-of-hire seniority. Thus, in the fall of 1989, the last striking IFFA member returned to the skies at TWA. Despite work rule givebacks that returned flight attendant real-dollar compensation to levels not seen at the company since before the modern flight attendant union movement, the "Boycott of Conscience" and the *TWA v. IFFA* decision guaranteed that all flight attendants could continue to use their union as a check on Wall Street's political and cultural power.[56]

IFFA's Supreme Court victory notwithstanding, financialization had made the 1980s the most devastating decade in the history of airline labor. Whereas airline unionists, from IAM strongmen like Northwest's Guy Cook to feminist insurgents like American's Patt Gibbs, had written the industry's economic equation in the 1970s, the commitment to mere defense of the status quo had become an unachievable goal by 1985. Once an economic asset and political organizing tool for the labor movement, the strike was blunted in its effectiveness. Though United employees used a walkout to defang management-imposed concessions in 1985, workers at Texas International, Continental, Eastern, and TWA were forced to call off long, painful strikes and return to work on management's terms. Workers who voluntarily complied with airlines' giveback demands fared little better, and Pan Am collapsed after employees tried in vain to save the company by cutting their pay. Even for those at the strong firms United and American, new pressure from the ultra-low wages that followed failed strikes forced employees into concessionary contracts. Indeed, after the social movements of the 1970s had brought new horizons for marginal workers like flight attendants, deregulation and financialization turned the tide of political economy toward management. "It felt like the ground was washing out from under us," TWA flight attendant Dixie Daniels commented as she recalled returning from the picket line to work at Carl Icahn's TWA.[57]

Financialization and the End of the Family Wage System

Although every unionized TWA employee struggled to cope with longer hours and lower pay after the hostile takeover, the adjustment was particularly difficult for flight attendants, who bore the deepest concessions. The concessionary contracts recycled the old inequities of the family wage system, returning flight attendants to their familiar position at the bottom of the airline pay hierarchy. But as they forced flight attendants backward in time, Icahn's concessions also did something very new to the airline workforce of the 1980s. After the hostile takeover, all TWA labor became temporary, contingent, and low paid. Icahn, in other words, made everyone's work "women's work." After Icahn's cuts, mechanics, aircraft cleaners, ramp servicemen, and even junior pilots lived much more like flight attendants. No longer capable of being the family breadwinner, TWA's workingmen began taking second jobs to supplement their income and struggled to balance household responsibilities with a working partner and working children.[58] Thus, despite Icahn's success in selling the hostile takeover as a means to save American manhood, financialization brought the end of the workingman as we knew him. Far from an airline anomaly, the proliferation of women's work was even more pronounced in the service, agricultural, and temporary employment sectors, where the lack of unions left workers more vulnerable to management's agenda.[59] By 1990, and even as big business's allies in the "pro-family" movement underscored men's natural roles as husbands and breadwinners, Wall Street had eliminated the family wage system.

With the ink dry on the concessionary contracts, Icahn shifted focus to designing a new set of mechanisms to redistribute wealth away from workingmen and women and toward owners and investors. On June 23, 1987, for example, Icahn announced a deal to privatize TWA, buying out the other investors who had helped finance the 1986 hostile takeover and making the airline his personal possession. To fund the privatization, TWA would spend $1.2 billion to purchase all outstanding company stock, including Icahn's 73 percent stake, at $40 per share. Like a home mortgage refinancing, TWA was both the buyer and the seller in the deal. Icahn, however, would be the primary beneficiary, as the deal would yield the financier $440 million in cash and 90 percent of the new TWA's stock. Investors who became Icahn's business partners in the original LBO stock swap also made a healthy profit, selling shares they had bought at $24.50 just eighteen months earlier for $40. The parties cashing in on Icahn's privatization insisted that the deal was fair, a simple compensation for "saving" TWA from "out of control" labor costs in 1986. However, even the relatively conservative *Wall Street Journal* was putting such "salvation" in quotation marks by the summer of 1987.[60]

While another $1.2 billion in debt jeopardized TWA's future, the airline's insolvency was nevertheless a strategic tool for Icahn. As he blamed union wages, pension benefits, and work rules for TWA's crisis in the 1980s, Icahn insisted that Wall Street's high-risk capital markets were the only lifeline for struggling old-line firms like TWA. On the surface, Icahn was right, because TWA was able to make its interest payments only because Icahn's name and reputation allowed the airline to borrow even more money. On July 2, 1989, for example, when TWA was nearing default on its existing debt, Icahn floated a $300 million high-yield note to investors. Since all hard assets were already leveraged at Icahn's TWA, the new bonds were backed up by the airline's dwindling inventory of consumables, from paint to light bulbs to cleaning solution. The unusual collateral earned the securities the nickname "light bulb bonds" from the *Wall Street Journal*. Icahn's latest proposition seemed absurd to lay observers, like asking someone to invest in the food in your refrigerator or the gas in your car. Light bulb bonds, however, allowed private investors access to the famously high returns on Icahn deals, which in this case promised 16.5 percent annual interest.[61]

In those robust profits for wealthy private investors lies the upwardly redistributive mechanism of the financialized economy. After Icahn implemented the post-strike wages and working conditions, he paid TWA flight attendants $110 million less in 1989 than he would have if the previous contract had remained in place. That same year, Icahn made $475 million in interest payments to investors.[62] Hence while flight attendants were forced to learn the art of deferred gratification, financialization ushered in an age of immediate gratification for the three big winners in the hostile takeover of TWA: for the investment bankers who arranged it; for the hedge funds, bond traders, and other elite private investors who bought in; and for the lawyers who wrote the contracts to define it. Light bulb bonds and similar securities demonstrated that financialization had redefined who would get to indulge after a hard day of work.

The indulgence of financialization came, of course, with consequences. By the fall of 1989, the market for junk bonds was in free fall. During the first week of October, the highly anticipated hostile takeover of United Airlines collapsed. Los Angeles billionaire Marvin Davis put United's stock in play in early August, offering $240 a share for the carrier and touching off a bidding war that ran share prices up to $300.[63] Davis had recently made a run on Northwest Airlines, ratcheting up the stock price until fellow California billionaire Alfred Checci won control of the Minneapolis-based carrier and then enforced deep concessions on unionized employees. But when the United Board of Directors accepted an offer from a labor-management coalition that was trying to fend off Davis's latest conquest, the buyers choked as the banks pulled the funding amid fears that the offers for United were too high.

The Dow Jones Industrial Average shed 7.4 percent of its value on the United announcement, intensifying widespread speculation that the corporate mergers and acquisitions boom of the 1980s was unwinding.[64] Drexel-Burnham-Lambert was, after all, already in bankruptcy. In late 1988, after Drexel pled guilty to scores of felony counts of securities fraud and insider trading, paying the federal government $650 million in fines and sending its leader Michael Milken to jail, a run began on the investment bank from which it would not recover.[65] Although less eye-catching than Milken being hauled out of Drexel in handcuffs, the most costly consequence of the downturn in the junk bond market came from the small "savings and loan" (S&L) banks that had begun buying junk bonds after financial deregulation. By 1991, eight hundred S&Ls had gone bust, due in part to bad investments in the risky financial products that became so central to their business in the wake of deregulation. The S&Ls' failure left taxpayers on the hook for, by the federal government's own estimate, $132 billion worth of insured deposits.[66] In the deeply unpopular taxpayer S&L bailout that helped sink George H. W. Bush's reelection effort, the go-go 1980s went bust.

Conclusion

A poster boy for the culture of hedonism that squandered hardworking families' money during the S&L scandal, Michael Milken drew scorn from the American people. Scorn, however, would do nothing to change the political economy that Wall Street ushered in during the 1980s. Light bulbs and toilet paper would disappear as collateral for investments after 1990. But mortgage-backed securities would soon provide even more liquidity for capital markets than junk bonds, a financial trend with consequences far more dire than Icahn's dealings. Perhaps more importantly, the S&L scandal prompted no reconsideration of Wall Street's intervention in the labor market in the 1980s. Rather than temper their anti-unionism, employers became even more aggressive in the 1990s. TWA, for example, filed for bankruptcy not once but twice during Icahn's tenure, extracting new wage and benefit givebacks from workers both times. The situation was similar at larger and stronger airlines, where management made the concessions enforced during the 1980s crisis permanent. At industry-leading United, for example, flight attendants' starting hourly real wage in 1996 was roughly 45 percent lower than it was at TWA fifteen years earlier.[67] Therefore, it was working people—not the scorned Wall Street bankers—who were forced to learn a bitter, permanent lesson about self-denial and deferred gratification in a financialized economy.

As financialization hobbled the labor movement, the political economic formula that brought flight attendant unionists unprecedented success in the 1970s no longer worked. Before deregulation and financialization, flight attendant activists built a principled commitment to social justice by pursuing their own economic self-interest. When APFA, IFFA, or other unions won an hourly pay bump or a new trip rig, they delivered economic resources to the single women, the unmarried mothers, and the mixed families who had been locked out of the family wage system. An economic victory for a flight attendant union meant a social advance for the women's, gay, and lesbian liberation movements. Carl Icahn and Frank Lorenzo could never take those political commitments away from flight attendants. They could, however, make it much more difficult—and in some cases impossible—for flight attendants to pursue their economic self-interest. When the union's ultimate goal was a smaller pay cut rather than a larger raise, it was far more difficult for activists to mobilize their coworkers for protests and pickets. In the age of financialization, the labor movement withered as collective bargaining became an ineffective means to enrich the struggles against homophobia, sexism, and racism that remained central to U.S. social movements.

The task for the activists of the 1990s, then, was to craft a new strategy to engage new events on the ground. The flight attendant union movement had always been one with broad cultural horizons. The narrow strictures of collective bargaining had, however, been the primary means for flight attendants to put their politics to work. After 1990, flight attendants would have to build new connections to movements for economic and social justice, connections that would deliver the wages, benefits, and work rules that had always been important to flight attendants and would help circumvent the tight new restrictions placed on collective bargaining.

UNITED AIRLINES IS
FOR LOVERS

*The Politics of Domesticity and
Partnership in the 1990s*

The political economic reforms of the 1980s presented vast new challenges for flight attendants at work and at home. After managers
forced union activists to forfeit many of the work rules they had won
in the late 1970s, flight attendants spent more hours in the air and had fewer
days off. Crew schedulers cut layover times on domestic and international
trips, which made it more difficult for flight attendants to adjust to jet lag and
to decompress from the emotional intensity of the job. More takeoffs, land-
ings, boardings, and beverage services did not, however, bring larger paychecks. Instead, flight attendants' earnings declined sharply as hourly wage
rates fell in the second half of the 1980s. To compensate for shrinking incomes, flight attendants worked overtime, took second jobs on the ground,
and leaned on spouses, partners, and children for a greater share of the family income. Upping their hours, cutting their expenses, and pooling resources
with their loved ones, flight attendants turned the household into a space to
perform the economic balancing act that declining real wages required.

Flight attendants were by no means alone as they struggled to adjust to a
leaner economy. In an age when a well-funded, tightly organized pro-business activist movement had built a public policy consensus around pro-work
cultural values, the labor movement was in free fall. Trade unions lost half
their members in the 1980s,[1] and people who remained organized faced intensifying pressures for pay and benefit concessions as non-union wages became standard. A mere decade after the flight attendant union movement had
won access to the family wage, one in which a worker could be a breadwinner

for her or his entire family, the family wage was vanishing in all sectors of the economy.

Organized labor's crisis does not mean that workplace activism disappeared after 1990. On the contrary, front-line employees continued to make successful political and economic demands on their employers. Those advances, however, would require a new set of strategies to supplement the contract-based collective bargaining that had been the dominant practice in previous decades. Particularly effective were the economic claims of lesbian, gay, bisexual, and transgender organizers. By 1990, an ascendant LGBT rights movement was transforming corporate employment policies. As sociologist Nicole Raeburn has demonstrated, the movement won valuable new resources for LGBT people and their families as activists pushed many of the largest corporations to include sexual orientation in their Equal Employment Opportunity statements and to offer the medical and retirement coverage for same-sex couples that organizers called "domestic partner benefits."[2]

Contradictory ideas propelled the LGBT movement's economic advances in an era when most workers faced setbacks. On the one hand, LGBT leaders channeled the radical critiques of the women's, gay, and lesbian liberation movements of the 1970s. Activists, for example, staunchly and vividly confronted the "pro-family" movement with a mass demonstration on the National Mall in Washington, D.C., during the summer of 1993, demanding not only legal equality for lesbian, gay, bisexual, and transgender people but also public funding for AIDS research, abortion rights, and racial justice. On the other hand, by touting the LGBT community as a lucrative emerging consumer market and by framing workplace activism as a demand for benefits for the committed, domesticated partners of deserving, hardworking LGBT employees, a growing number of LGBT rights organizers worked to accommodate the dominant cultural politics of the 1990s. Indeed, by embracing niche marketing and domestic partnership, activists turned the LGBT person into a hard worker, a faithful partner, and a brand-loyal consumer, a formulation that upheld—rather than contested—the dominant pro-work, pro-family ideology of the late 1980s and 1990s.

Flight attendant unionists would intervene in the contradictions of 1990s LGBT activism as they helped bring the movement to the airline industry. During the spring of 1997, a group of flight attendants from San Francisco began collaborating with LGBT leaders who were pushing the airlines and other corporations to offer domestic partner benefits for their employees. When managers at the major carriers refused, flight attendants and their allies responded with direct action political mobilization. Borrowing militant, theatrical protest strategies from the decade's dissident queer groups such as AIDS

Coalition to Unleash Power (ACT-UP), activists organized in gay bars, staged mass union demonstrations, initiated civil disobedience at protests, and launched a consumer boycott against the largest U.S. carrier, United Airlines. This chapter analyzes the political and economic ideas driving a protest movement that, by the end of the decade, had won new medical and retirement benefits for tens of thousands of airline workers and their lovers.

As they mounted a successful challenge to the airlines' anti-union and antigay agenda, flight attendants provided a new direction for organized labor and for LGBT activists at a moment when both movements were at a crossroads. Although unions continued to shed members in their historic stronghold in manufacturing, the labor movement had proved that it could grow on its margins in the late twentieth century.[3] Public employees—many of who were African American women—organized en masse in the 1960s and 1970s. Two decades later, seventy-five thousand Los Angeles–based home healthcare workers voted for union representation as the Service Employees International Union joined forces with the Chicano/Latino and immigrant rights movements. In both of those cases, unions succeeded because they built a political and economic agenda around the needs of nontraditional families. Racism, after all, had locked most Latino and African American men out of family wage jobs, which meant that their households had never counted on a sole male breadwinner. Unions thus would help Latina and African American women provide additional resources for families in which women, men, and children had always worked outside the home. During the domestic partner benefits campaign, flight attendants pushed the labor movement toward a new group of families that had also been locked out of the family wage system. Lesbian- and gay-identified people in same-sex relationships were systematically denied the economic privileges extended to middle-class white straight families in the mid-twentieth century and rarely counted on the wages of a traditional male breadwinner.[4] Flight attendant unionists confronted those historic disparities during the domestic partner benefits campaign, in the process helping unions deliver badly needed benefits to their members in an age when collective bargaining was failing to deliver such goods.

Collaboration with unions, meanwhile, helped shift the agenda of the LGBT movement. Many flight attendants were deeply suspicious of the pro-family, pro-work ideas that some LGBT organizers—especially those in mainstream political organizations such as the Human Rights Campaign (HRC)—espoused in the bid for domestic partner benefits. For the mainstream movement, aligning LGBT people with the family values of domesticity and hard work was a means to defend the community against religious conservatives who had attacked queer people for deviating from traditional family values. But at Frank Lorenzo's Continental Airlines and at Carl Icahn's TWA, the very family values that the mainstream LGBT movement was embracing had helped justify managerial efforts to strip flight attendants of health and retirement benefits. As they joined mainstream LGBT organizations in the streets of San Francisco, then, flight attendants demonstrated that contesting corporate homophobia would require not an embrace of family values but rather an explicit challenge to both the family ethic and the work ethic. Connecting the domestic partner benefits campaign to the long-standing push for more money and less work for a broad spectrum of families, flight attendants helped build a coalition of single and partnered people and of LGBT- and straight-identified people who would permanently transform family benefits programs in the airline industry.

Meeting the Mainstream LGBT Rights Movement in San Francisco

In the mid-1990s, flight attendant activists were looking for a means to reinvent the movement. Militant, grassroots union mobilization had energized the rank and file in the 1970s and had provided a venue to build alliances with the women's, gay, and lesbian liberation movements. But after debilitating setbacks in failed strikes at Continental, TWA, and Eastern in the 1980s, the costs of mass mobilization seemed to far outweigh its benefits. Although those costs were most pronounced at the carriers subjected to the harshest managerial tactics during financialization, even such successful airlines as United, American, and Northwest were demanding concessions from flight attendants as industry average wage rates tumbled. On the eve of the domestic partner benefits campaign, for example, United Airlines flight attendants were starting at today's equivalent of $28,000 per year, roughly 45 percent less than they had made at the peak of the upsurge in the early 1980s.[5]

As downward pressure on wages intensified, a collective bargaining process that had once invigorated flight attendants became arduous. Aiming to reverse the decline in real wages, leaders of the Association of Flight Attendants (AFA) at United slogged through six months of tense negotiations in the second half of 1995, finally delivering a tentative agreement to their members the following February. Angry that the proposed contract gave management new scheduling flexibility for international flights, front-line flight attendants voted the agreement down[6] and circulated a series of underground newspapers that blamed the AFA negotiating committee for a weak, inept performance at the bargaining table.[7] Rank-and-file agitation proved insufficient to jumpstart negotiations, however, and contract talks remained stalled for a year after the failed ratification vote. Meanwhile, United reported gangbusters earnings: shares outpaced a red-hot "dot com" economy as they tripled in value between 1994 and 1997, and the company reported a $1.3 billion profit for 1997 alone.[8] Facing disgruntled, cynical members who were struggling to balance the high cost of living with falling wages at a profitable employer, activists who remained committed to the flight attendant union movement looked for a solution to the problem of rank-and-file discontent.

That solution walked up to union activists in May 1997. On a spring afternoon, United Airlines flight attendants Stan Kiino and Beth Skrondal were painting picket signs in the garage of the apartment building where they both lived in San Francisco's Pacific Heights neighborhood. The co-chairs of their union's communication and education committee, Kiino and Skrondal were brainstorming about ways to counteract disappointing flight attendant turnouts at rallies after a year of failed negotiations. Painting and talking in a sea of tagboard and stencils, the two barely noticed Jeff Sheehy walking up the alley. Sheehy, the president of the Harvey Milk Democratic Club, the LGBT caucus of the local Democratic Party, approached Kiino and Skrondal and asked for help.[9] In November 1996, Sheehy told the flight attendants, local activists had scored a notable victory for LGBT workplace rights. After Congress dealt the national LGBT movement a watershed blow by passing the Defense of Marriage Act on the same day that it defeated an LGBT workplace civil rights bill called the Employment Non-discrimination Act, Sheehy and his peers persuaded the San Francisco Board of Supervisors to ratify an ordinance requiring all firms doing business with the city to offer domestic partner benefits for unmarried same- and opposite-sex couples.

Three months later, however, United Airlines put Sheehy's victory in jeopardy when it filed suit on behalf of twenty-six airlines against the San Francisco law,[10] aiming to persuade a judge to either exempt some companies from providing the benefits or to overturn the entire ordinance. Sheehy asked Kiino and Skrondal to join him in building a linkage between flight attendants and LGBT activists, since United's intransigence at the bargaining table and in the partner benefits lawsuit made both groups into targets of the airline's political, economic, and legal apparatus. The goal, Sheehy argued, would be to isolate United, publicly shaming the airline so that firms in other industries would be afraid to add their names and financial resources to the lawsuit. Kiino beamed with excitement as he remembered that first back-alley conversation. "Jeff started talking about civil disobedience, saying, 'Now remember, the police and mayor are your friends.' I just stared at him in disbelief, as we had never done anything like that before!"[11]

Jeff Sheehy came to that conversation with a well-developed political play-book because domestic partner benefits advocacy was already a centerpiece of the policy agenda of mainstream institutions such as the Human Rights Campaign (HRC), the largest LGBT political action committee and a major donor to the Democratic Party, which Sheehy helped lead. The HRC turned to the private sector and to activism at major corporations precisely because of stinging setbacks in public venues. Given their immense economic resources and widely distrib-uted, confrontational antigay message, pro-family activists had rolled back LGBT rights at the ballot box. From Anita Bryant's "save our children" cam-paign, which invalidated municipal gay rights ordinances in the mid-1970s, to the anti-same-sex marriage amendments that helped turn out conservative voters after 1990, the LGBT movement faced daunting setbacks in popular referen-dums as evangelical Christians and their allies politicized so-called social issues such as feminism, abortion, and homosexuality. Pro-business and pro-family activists then leveraged social issues to build a mass movement against LGBT people, women of color, welfare recipients, and other marginalized groups.[12]

After 1990, private corporations provided the shield that LGBT activists needed from popular referendums during the upsurge of organizing around social issues. Since corporations have never been democratic institutions, and since deregulation, financialization, and the other neoliberal reforms made them even less democratic, activists could pigeonhole health coverage and termination protection for LGBT employees through corporate boards of di-rectors while dodging backlash from the right at the polls. Thus, although LGBT-led initiatives for same-sex marriage rights and nondiscrimination laws often failed in the 1990s, activists made Equal Employment Opportunity policies and domestic partner benefits the norm in the Fortune 500 by mid-decade. Mainstream LGBT activists had indeed found a new route to prove that gay is good, even if that meant abandoning the ballot box and building alliances with British Petroleum, Chase Manhattan, and American Express. LGBT institutions enjoyed such success in winning resources from major cor-porations that, in 1997, HRC president Elizabeth Birch announced, "The truth is it's corporate America that has been the unlikely hero in the movement for equality for gay and lesbian Americans."[13] In her comments, Birch named and endorsed the increasingly widespread gay-corporate alliance of the 1990s.

Flight Attendant Unionism Challenges Mainstream LGBT Activism

While many flight attendants sympathized with the HRC's overarching com-mitment to lesbian and gay rights, Birch's pro-business rhetoric revealed a potential barrier to a coalition between flight attendant unionists and the domestic partner benefits campaign in San Francisco. After all, the gay-corporate alliance of the 1990s was helping legitimate the pro-family, pro-work political consensus that flight attendants had spent three decades contesting. Advocacy for domestic partner benefits accomplished this in two important ways. First, private benefits for hardworking employees and their domesticated partners became a substitute for medical and retirement benefits for everyone.[14] At the same time as some companies spent money on extending domestic partner benefits, they aggressively lobbied to cut corporate taxes and to eliminate the public housing, education, and health programs that corporate taxes paid for. Second, domestic partner benefits remade LGBT identity and community to comply with corporate cost cutting.[15] In the age of domestic partner benefits, the LGBT person could access health and retirement coverage through productive employment, through a company-supported domestic relationship, or through both domesticity and hard work. Through LGBT institutions' détente with the Fortune 500, the LGBT person became everything that the poor, racialized, and feminized targets of pro-work politics were assumed not to be: gainfully employed in the private sector and in a responsible, committed, domesticated relationship.[16]

By constituting LGBT identity in sexual and racial regulation, the gay-corporate alliance abetted the transition to a neoliberal economy. In her incisive book *Against the Romance of Community,* Miranda Joseph theorizes the relationship between mainstream LGBT identity and the post-1970 economy. Joseph argues that in the age of the gay-corporate alliance, ideas about LGBT community supplement the capitalist system.[17] Whereas the notion of community is often invoked to describe a time of horizontal power relations before the development of the free market, Joseph insists that liberal capitalist modernity is made from oppressive communal discourses.[18] Rather than a space outside capitalism, community is an idea that facilitates the workings of the free market, filling in for what capitalism lacks. The political and cultural changes of the 1970s and 1980s helped make the LGBT community perform the work for capitalism that Joseph references.[19] Aggressive anti-unionism and a pro-work political culture made critiques of corporate power less common and less legible in all populations, including among LGBT people. Meanwhile, pro-family organizing coupled with homophobic scapegoating in the wake of the AIDS crisis convinced many gay leaders that they should turn away from the sexual complexity among LGBT people, pushing kink, bondage, sex parties, and polyamory to the margins of the movement by 1990. Who remained most visible, then, were middle-class, monogamous, domesticated LGBT people who complied with the renewed cultural commitment to the family ethic and the work ethic. Once it appeared that domesticity and hard work were the raw materials that produced the LGBT community, corporations and pro-work policymakers could leverage LGBT people and culture to validate the family values economy.

At its core, Joseph's argument is about political mobilization even more than it is about political economy. When community supplements capital—in this case by figuring gays to be domesticated, partnered, and hardworking—LGBT people are cut off from those who might otherwise be allies. Indeed, as they elevated same-sex domesticity, 1990s bids for domestic partner benefits lost relevance to single people, to working mothers, to nonromantic roommates, and to a host of other alternative families that, like same-sex couples, also needed companies to broaden the scope of their benefits programs. In an age when the nuclear family was a waning social form, and when gays and straights alike were broadening the definition of domesticity, the gay-corporate alliance made domestic partner benefits seem like an economic resource for the families of the past and not for the families of the future.

Unfolding in a far different historical context, the dispute between the city of San Francisco and United Airlines provided an opening to widen the coalition around employment benefits. Not only had family always been broadly defined in San Francisco, where single people, friends, and lovers headed up a variety of households, but United Airlines had long been home to a flight attendant movement dedicated to the economic needs of the unpartnered. Those histories intersected in the personal lives and political commitments of the flight attendants most involved in the domestic partner benefits campaign. Beth Skrondal, for example, refocused her activism around the benefits dispute soon after Jeff Sheehy approached her in that afternoon in Pacific Heights. Like 51 percent of her colleagues at United, Skrondal identified not as married, divorced, or partnered but as single.[20] A longtime San Franciscan who had lived in Haight-Ashbury during the counterculture of the late 1960s, Skrondal bucked demographic trends for young white women and stayed single, spending the 1970s in Miami as a flight attendant and union activist at National Airlines. Post-deregulation industry consolidation carried Skrondal from Florida back to California, and by 1990 she was flying for United Airlines and living on her own in an apartment in San Francisco's leafy Pacific Heights neighborhood.

Despite a passion for the labor movement and for social justice, Skrondal was at first reluctant to get involved with the partner benefits campaign when Jeff Sheehy and Stan Kiino followed up with her about the exchange in the garage. Skrondal reflected:

I remember Stan telling me, "Okay, we have to go over to the community church over in the Castro because there is a big domestic
partnership meeting there tonight." And I said, "Stan, I am not gay.
I will fight for domestic partnerships, but I do not want to go to this
meeting."[21]

Skrondal went on to say that although she had always actively supported
feminist and gay rights causes, she was at first uninterested in the partner
benefits campaign because it seemed irrelevant for—or perhaps even counter
to—the issue she had always most cared about: the economic and political
position of single people. Over a career when marriage, motherhood, homosexuality, and abortion had all been politicized social issues in her workplace,
Skrondal often felt adrift in her own social location as a single woman who
was the head of a household of one. With gay identity and domestic partnership so tightly interwoven in mainstream LGBT activist discourse, the domestic partner benefits campaign seemed to Skrondal like another demand
for resources that she would not have the privilege to access.

Skrondal soon changed her thinking on domestic partner benefits at
United. Obliging Kiino and going to the citywide meeting in the Castro that
May night, Skrondal saw a room full of labor, LGBT, and AIDS activists
testifying about the life-and-death importance of family benefits, expressing
anger, fear, and despair about the United Airlines lawsuit. Moved by activists'
political analysis and personal narratives, Skrondal joined the movement. As
a single person, Skrondal felt at least somewhat welcome because her fellow
activist, Stan Kiino, had also spent the majority of his adult life single, in his
case as a single gay man. A twenty-seven-year veteran of Pan Am and United,
Kiino lived by himself in the same Pacific Heights apartment complex as
Skrondal. He arranged his flight schedule around five- or six-day trips to the
South Pacific, maximizing days off to commute to care for and live with his
ninety-year-old mother in the Central Valley town of Hanford, California.
The son of Japanese immigrant parents, Kiino grew up in the 1960s without
the expectation and valorization of nuclear, single-generation domesticity
common to his white suburban counterparts and has never lived in that traditional arrangement.

As race and immigrant status helped Kiino frame his relationship to his
mother, he highlighted a host of alternative family relationships cultivated
during his airline career, dependencies that have enabled material and emotional sustenance outside domesticated, partnered realms. Kiino was particularly pointed, for example, when narrating the mutual support networks that
grew out of the AIDS crisis. In his early thirties, Kiino had spent a decade

flying for Pan Am when AIDS upended the lives of gay flight attendants, their coworkers, and their friends. The skills and rhythms of flight attendants' working lives, Kiino argued, made them critically important caregivers for friends, lovers, and acquaintances when the agents of traditional family—the state, parents, and spouses—were either unable or unwilling to provide compassion and care. Kiino reflected:

> AIDS was devastating. There are only a few men from my fifty-person training class at Pan Am still left alive. And that is true for a lot of airlines' flight attendant groups. . . . A lot of us weren't involved in any organization, but we spent all our time trying to help friends. As a flight attendant, I am used to sleeping in different situations because of layovers and jet lag. So I was the one who was flexible enough to stay over at people's houses because they needed help with their illness during the night. There was this era—where you just had to get used to it. You didn't know who was next to die.[22]

Kiino argued that friends with AIDS could count on flight attendants because they were used to sleeping away from home, because they expected to wake up and help people during normal sleeping hours, and because they regularly and calmly handled blood, vomit, and feces—the physical products of many AIDS-related illnesses—as part of the first-responder qualifications of their professional lives. Even more importantly, union wages, work rules, and personal leave benefits allowed Kiino the schedule flexibility and financial stability to take time off work during his friends' darkest hours, a practice that would have been much more difficult had Kiino worked one of the many low-wage, non-union jobs in the service sector. In Kiino's relationships to lost coworkers and friends, to his current peers aloft, to the union movement, and to his mother, kinship has been practiced much more broadly than the domesticated, partnered version espoused by the gay-corporate alliance.

In some ways, Beth Skrondal's and Stan Kiino's lives were hallmarks of the family values economy. Both were single adults who worked full time, who juggled responsibilities for family and work, and who could not fall back on the wages of a husband breadwinner or the unwaged labor of a domesticated wife. During three decades of activism, however, both had rejected the family ethic and the work ethic that were the bedrocks of the family values economy, staying single and building a union that demanded more money and less work. For Skrondal and Kiino, winning new medical and retirement benefits for some of their coupled friends would represent much more than a victory for coupled people. Challenging United Airlines' intransigence would constitute one more stop on a long journey of labor, feminist, and gay activism. Thus, even though neither Skrondal nor Kiino stood to gain any economic resources from a partner benefits victory, both led the charge to build a new connection to an LGBT movement that could help flight attendants win economic resources from airlines that, in the age of deregulation and financialization, had been shrinking rather than expanding corporate benefits.

United against United: Sexuality and Labor in the Streets of San Francisco

Beth Skrondal and Stan Kiino's practices of kinship were a deeply threatening prospect for the airlines and for other major corporations. If employees imagined families that crossed the boundaries of the household, of generations, of blood relations, and of legible intimacy, they could be inspired to make expensive new claims for flexible hours, for better pay, and for broader benefits programs. Skrondal and Kiino's kinship ties, in other words, threatened the commitment to both the family ethic and the work ethic that had driven the pro-business activist movement since 1970. Therefore, despite the fact that firms in other industries were extending domestic partner benefits to help build the gay-corporate alliance, United Airlines launched a vigorous countermovement against LGBT activists in San Francisco. United's intervention centered on a federal lawsuit it filed in conjunction with the Air Transport Association, the management lobbying group for the major passenger airlines. Reiterating big business's support for pro-work politics, the suit argued that withholding domestic partner benefits was necessary to protect the jobs of hardworking American families. Domestic partner benefits, United's attorneys insisted, are an expensive entitlement program for people who choose to live outside the nuclear family. Other interest groups, from environmentalists to product safety advocates to women's and minority rights groups, had won similar entitlements in the 1960s and 1970s. Their victories, as pro-business activists had previously argued, placed an economic burden on corporations, a burden that in turn meant fewer jobs for ordinary workers who were not part of such special interest groups. Reducing that economic burden—in this case by continuing to withhold domestic partner benefits—would be necessary to foster the corporate job creation that would restore the middle class.

United's case against domestic partner benefits rested on three pro-work legal claims. The first involved the dormant Commerce Clause of the U.S. Constitution. Since the Commerce Clause gives states the right to regulate business only within their boundaries, courts have long recognized a corresponding and inverse—though unwritten—*dormant* logic that prevents states or municipalities from governing companies operating outside their physical jurisdiction. United argued that the city of San Francisco not only regulated business extraterritorially with the partner benefits ordinance—requiring new employee compensation in Boston and Brussels and Beijing— but also, by requiring expensive new family benefits, placed an undue burden on United from which competitors would be exempt.[23] In the view of the airline's legal team, the San Francisco ordinance would give American, Delta, and other carriers a labor cost advantage over United, one that would jeopardize the jobs of all United employees.

In addition to their claim about interstate commerce, United made a second argument rooted in federal labor law. The airline proposed that the San Francisco ordinance violated the "minimum labor standards" principle of the Railway Labor Act because it would tip the balance of power in the labor-management relationship toward the union. The RLA mandated that all such realignments must occur in government-regulated negotiations: in formal collective bargaining, in mediation, in arbitration, or in a legal strike. Street-level gay activism, United insisted, was none of the above. Furthermore, the airline argued that activists such as Jeff Sheehy were imposing obligations on United that were inconsistent with the domain of collective bargaining offered by the RLA. LGBT issues, in other words, were beyond the scope of labor-management relations and thus out of bounds either in street-level protest or at the negotiating table. Through its RLA claim, United aimed to insulate the workplace from the LGBT rights movement, a move that would protect jobs and workers from grassroots activists' anticorporate agenda.[24]

The airlines rounded out their objections to the domestic partner ordinance by alleging that the law violated the Airline Deregulation Act (ADA) of 1978. Echoing the claims of 1970s pro-deregulation activists, United told the court that the ADA was primarily intended to promote free market competition, in which the laws of supply and demand would solely determine prices. Lower fares would stimulate consumer demand, generating new business that would promote economic growth and create jobs for the middle class. Mandating domestic partner benefits would constrain United's pricing flexibility by requiring higher airfares to offset the cost of health insurance for unmarried couples. The airlines made this argument in multiple contexts in the 1990s. Delta Airlines, for example, told a different federal circuit court in 1997 that all state civil rights laws violate the ADA because they generate undue pricing constraints.[25] For United and its peers, civil rights advances such as the San Francisco benefits ordinance would push the airline back to the high-price, low-growth model of the 1970s, in which the political gains of a feminist and gay minority came at the expense of all hardworking families.

In United's economic and cultural argument to the federal district court lay the root of flight attendants' interest in the partner benefits campaign. Even though the HRC's focus on domesticity and hard work did not resonate with the origins of the flight attendant union movement in women's, gay, and lesbian liberation, the terms of the airline's case were familiar—and offensive—to many on the front lines. For twenty years, the discourse of traditional family values had been a mechanism to devalue flight attendant labor and to pit racialized and feminized workers against the middle class. Flight attendants, for example, came into the 1970s making 20 percent less than their next-lowest-paid colleagues, a disparity rooted in managers' and male union leaders' assumptions that stewardesses were not breadwinners.[26] That same assumption helped single out flight attendants for disproportionately harsh treatment during the major strikes of the 1980s. Now, as executives tried to rebuff LGBT activists in San Francisco, they once again insisted that traditional family values—in this case heterosexual marriage—would be necessary for full economic citizenship in the airlines. In a workplace where over 50 percent of the population was single and where many people were in same-sex relationships, that insistence saved the company a huge amount of money, since fewer than half of United's twenty thousand flight attendants were eligible for any family benefits.

Given those historical inequities, flight attendants—both leaders such as Skrondal and Kiino and a broad swath of the rank and file—joined the domestic partner benefits movement in force. By doing so, flight attendants connected their ongoing campaign for a new union contract to the increasingly visible dispute for domestic partner benefits. On June 20, 1997, for example, AFA members assembled and marched in the San Francisco LGBT Pride festival, an annual happening that brought a million visitors to the Bay Area from across the globe, making it a centerpiece of both the city's cultural life and United's summer profit-making strategy. Activists donned screaming chartreuse T-shirts with jagged black letters that formed the word CHAOS. The shirts signaled AFA's trademark "Create Havoc Around Our System" strike strategy, which featured quick, unpredictable, hit-and-run work stoppages that guaranteed maximum operational disruption while reducing the chance of a lockout like that at TWA in 1986. Threatening to disrupt passengers'—and Pridegoers'—flight schedules, unionists passed out ten thousand leaflets that asked, "Is United really gay friendly?" and directed the audience to call the airline to demand a fair contract for flight attendants and domestic partner benefits for all employees.[27]

As they put the squeeze on a major corporation with a parade float, flight attendants challenged the political economic transformation of Pride festivals in the 1990s. As the millennium approached, gatherings that once served as hubs for socializing and political organizing had become bully pulpits for companies aiming to make money on the LGBT niche market. Beginning in the middle of the decade, communications firms including Witeck and Combs published a series of widely cited studies that identified the LGBT niche—and especially same-sex couples—as lucrative and particularly brand loyal. Corporations, especially those in the travel, real estate, and entertainment industries chasing dual-income couples with no children, used Pride festivals to cultivate the LGBT niche. Icelandair managers, for example, raffled off free trips to Europe at Pride in Seattle, Minneapolis, and New York, collecting contact information and demographic data from the LGBT community in the process.[28] Flight attendants' CHAOS T-shirts and strike-threatening leaflets interrupted this seemingly natural convergence between the airlines, gay travelers, and niche marketing. The campaign did so by offering a vivid challenge to corporate power that moved demands for full LGBT citizenship away from claims about domesticity and consumption and back toward Pride festivals' historic legacy of active political defiance.

The domestic partner benefits campaign used similarly colorful tactics when it took its cause beyond the Pride festival and into the streets of San Francisco. In the process, leaders helped deepen ties between front-line flight attendants and the LGBT movement. Three weeks after Pride, on July 10, 1997, the coalition staged the first in a series of civil disobedience–centered mass protests in downtown San Francisco, demonstrations demanding both a flight attendant contract settlement and domestic partner benefits for everyone at United. Leaders were particularly strategic in choosing United's Geary Street City Ticket Office as a target of economic intervention. Before the Internet became the airlines' primary customer service interface, city ticket offices provided face-to-face support for carriers' highest-paying customers. Frequent flyers from Wells Fargo, Cisco Systems, AOL, or other profitable United accounts could walk from their financial district offices to make reservations, change seats, and confirm upgrades at the ticket office, thereby avoiding long airport lines while building personalized business relationships with local United sales agents that the discount carriers could never provide. A throng of chanting, CHAOS T-shirt-wearing, picket-sign-waving flight attendants and scores of LGBT allies with bright rainbow flags quickly interrupted United's sophisticated and stylish customer service experience. "The whole thing was like theater," Jeff Sheehy recalled:

> First we assemble, march, and chant. Then we send in the United
> frequent flyers, who cut up their frequent flyer cards in the office in

front of the press. Then, at a given moment, those who volunteer to do civil disobedience block the doors and shut the office down. They arrest us and we go to jail.[29]

Sheehy described events that were choreographed as media spectacles for still photography and video feed. Plastic shards of cut-up frequent flyer cards were tossed through the air as police pushed through rainbow flag pickets to hand-cuff demonstrators blocking United's doors.

Despite flight attendants' readiness to draw on three decades of grassroots activist experience in direct action protests, activists faced a major tactical problem. Flight attendant union leaders quickly informed the partner benefits coalition that the Railway Labor Act severely constricts what flight attendants and other unionized groups may do and say during conflicts with employers. In particular, the RLA prevents union members from engaging in strikes, boycotts, sickouts, or any other act that could have a negative financial impact on an employer without prior approval from the federal agency that administers the law. Since flight attendants had no right to domestic partner benefits in their union contract, they had no legal basis to convince the agency that union members deserved to conduct acts of civil disobedience against United.

The HRC stepped in to solve this problem. Whereas the RLA would likely have allowed United to fire flight attendants and sue their union if rank-and-file activists took part in economic sanctions, labor law had no jurisdiction over the HRC or any other non-employee political group. Therefore, the HRC immediately called for a global consumer boycott of United Airlines and used publicity for the boycott to announce mass protests where flight attendants would picket on public sidewalks but would avoid participating in civil disobedience.[30] That role was left to local activists such as Sheehy and the HRC's press operation. Using the HRC as a shield for union activism helped protect flight attendants from being held liable for the economic consequences of the boycott, a fate that met pilots for American Airlines during the same period. In February 1999, when pilot activists called a sickout without federal approval to protest outsourcing of flight crew jobs, a judge fined the pilots' union $10 million for violating labor law, the largest penalty ever levied against a union in the airline industry.[31] As they hoisted the rainbow flag in front of the United ticket office, LGBT activists opened a new space for flight attendants to intervene in airline economics, a space the Railway Labor Act had previously foreclosed. Most importantly, new alliance partners made protest spaces much more fun and energizing than they had been during the earlier, stand-alone phase of the flight attendant contract dispute. Activists struggled to get fifty flight attendants to spend their day off at airport pickets, but organizers estimate that at least four hundred people showed up to march in the July 10 demonstration.[32]

Spectacles like the ticket office occupation helped activists transform LGBT identity in the streets of San Francisco. Every domestic partner benefits protest was awash in rainbow flags, the most widely recognized symbol for the mainstream LGBT community of the 1990s. Those flags, however, flew alongside union picket signs, next to throngs of indignant, chanting protesters, and amid acts of civil disobedience where policed dragged limp protesters across the pavement into paddy wagons. In the commotion of a passionate, angry crowd, the rainbow flag and the LGBT community became signs of political dissent. Even the HRC, which had been the architect of the gay-corporate alliance, was dedicating staff time and legal resources to an explicitly anticorporate practice, opening a space for flight attendants to put new economic pressure on United without fear of reprisal. The practice of active defiance moved the coalition away from the two categories that were otherwise dominant in mainstream LGBT politics: domesticity and hard work. In the 1990s, the family ethic and the work ethic were supposed to make up for the economic resources that twenty years of anti-union and antiwelfare policy initiatives had taken away. The San Francisco activists refused to make that trade-off and instead demanded new and affordable health and retirement benefits to meet the needs of a growing diversity of kinship practices. Because of that refusal, mainstream LGBT community and identity—at least for the duration of the San Francisco campaign—presented a new challenge to the family values economy.

"Are You Sitting Down?"

As the domestic partner benefits coalition protests turned heads in San Francisco, the contractual standoff between United and its flight attendants jumped back into the headlines with a rare development in collective bargaining in the airlines in the 1990s: a settlement. Only four days after the mass demonstration in front of the Geary Street Ticket Office, AFA reached a tentative agreement with United Airlines management.[33] While there is no documentary proof that direct action protests pushed management to make a contract offer—although local activists swear that United's labor relations department called AFA Local Council 11 president Liz Loeffler asking what it would take to "call her dogs off" immediately following the protest—it is clear that the San Francisco campaign turned the heat up on United by putting the flight attendant labor issues in the national spotlight.[34] Despite members' embrace of the news that eighteen months of negotiations had finally brought a deal, the accord was bittersweet for AFA members. On the one hand, the contract provided lucrative work rule improvements, rules that were better than those the flight attendants had won at the apex of the flight attendant union movement in the late 1970s. All layovers exceeding thirteen hours, for example, were required to take place in four-star hotels in the destination city's downtown, allowing flight attendants physical and mental outlets at museums, theaters, and river walks and preventing them from being cooped up in boring, isolated, expensive airport motels.

On the other hand, the contract came with an unusual duration and pay system that benefited management by forfeiting long-term real wage growth. The contract would last an unprecedented ten years, the longest ever under the Railway Labor Act. Wage increases were partially paid in lump sum bonuses that upped some employees' tax liability, and additional pay hikes granted after the first five years would come only via a binding arbitration system that denied flight attendants the right to strike. Though the agreement would make United flight attendants the highest paid of any U.S. airline, starting wages—of roughly $28,000 in 2015 dollars per year—were still approximately 35 percent lower in real-dollar terms than they were in 1976.[35] Since the 1970s, front-line flight attendants had insisted that robust real-dollar wage increases were the primary means to remedy the sexist legacy of the family wage system. Although the new contract would provide some of the work rules that flight attendants had long coveted, it would do little to remedy those historical disparities.

Mulling the virtues and the significant shortcomings of the pact, union leaders faced a difficult choice. If they endorsed the tentative agreement and the rank and file approved it in a referendum, they would strip the domestic partner benefits campaign of a potent resource: the threat of a flight attendant strike. Hundreds of flight attendants had massed in downtown San Francisco not just because they cared about LGBT issues but also because they wanted a raise. Coalition leaflets demanding both domestic partner benefits and a fair contract convinced both LGBT- and straight-identified flight attendants that joining the partner benefits campaign would further their economic self-interest. But if flight attendants ratified the contractual accord, a move that would lock in management's subpar wage offer and remove flight attendants' right to strike, the partner benefits coalition would lose its point of leverage on flight attendant wages and working conditions.

Although the partner benefits protests were invigorating the flight attendant union movement, AFA leaders remained wary of the broader political economic context surrounding labor disputes in the 1980s and 1990s. Strikes

had come with devastating consequences for even the most disciplined, politicized flight attendant unions and had jeopardized the very existence of the
Union of Flight Attendants Local 1 at Continental and the Independent Federation of Flight Attendants at TWA. In both of those cases, flight attendants
had staged defensive actions against management efforts to cut pay and benefits in half. In this case, however, management had agreed to industry-leading wages and work rule enhancements. Modest and incremental though the
improvements were, and despite their failure to offset the drastic setbacks of
the 1980s, union leaders recognized the immense strategic risk of forgoing a
pact and shifting to a militant, direct action approach like the one in San
Francisco. AFA therefore endorsed the tentative agreement and sent it to
rank-and-file United flight attendants for ratification. Members approved the
deal, but by an extremely narrow 51 percent to 49 percent margin.[36] Flight
attendants clearly understood the stakes of militant union activism in the
1990s and were deeply divided about how to move forward in an era when
other feminized service trades paid even less than airline work.

Although the AFA contract settlement changed the terms of the debate
for the San Francisco campaign, denying it the blaring color and imminent
strike threat of CHAOS, United flight attendants remained key players in a
movement directed against their employer. Major political and legal develop-
ments kept United Airlines activists in the news as the campaign moved
through its second year. On December 15, 1998, days before San Franciscans
would descend en masse on the United terminal at SFO to travel for the
holidays, the city's Board of Supervisors officially endorsed the campaign's
consumer boycott.[37] With the dramatic beaux arts façade of City Hall tower-
ing in the background, city leaders urged the public to support LGBT rights
by avoiding United, pledging that no city employee would be allowed to fly
the airline on city business. Officials made the simple claim that, regardless
of what the dormant Commerce Clause or the Airline Deregulation Act im-
plied, companies would not be allowed to classify and compensate employees
based on race, gender, or sexual orientation in San Francisco. Though the
HRC's familiar equal-sign logo adorned the podium from which city supervisors delivered their comments, the city's endorsement of the boycott drew
on a vastly different history of economic activism than the HRC's gay-corporate alliance. Since the early days of AFL craft unionism in the late nineteenth century, labor activists had used their economic and political
organizing power to sever relations between city governments and hotels that
locked out striking employees, builders that worked non-union, or contrac-
tors that violated public agreements.[38] Suddenly, an HRC that had focused
on persuading companies to voluntarily extend same-sex benefits was bor-

rowing from unions' long-standing push for compulsory, government-stan-
dardized regulation of pay, benefits, and working conditions.

In addition to the support from city government, the campaign got a
major boost from the legal system. On May 28, 1999, Ninth Circuit judge
Claudia Wilken lifted the temporary restraining order that had exempted
United from providing the benefits required by the San Francisco domestic
partner benefits ordinance. Wilken tossed out United's professed right to dis-
criminate, insisting that neither constitutional interstate commerce law nor
labor or regulatory policy allowed the airline to continue withholding domestic partner benefits. The decision validated activists' overall premise in the
dispute, that the LGBT movement should be able to influence the way a company does business even if that intervention would change the terms and
conditions of private employment contracts and increase companies' labor
costs. The dismissal of United's labor and regulatory case was, however, accompanied by an expansive caveat. Wilken exempted United from changing
its pension or medical benefit programs, arguing that the federal Employee
Retirement Income Security Act (ERISA) superseded the San Francisco ordinance. ERISA prevented firms from raiding employees' pension funds to sub-
sidize other business transactions. Given strict language that prohibited
outside groups from unilaterally changing pension benefits, Wilken found
that ERISA prevented municipal governments from amending benefits eligibility. Therefore, any court-ordered change to medical insurance or retirement
benefits would have to come from a new ERISA case that would have to make
its own, arduous way through the legal process.[39] Nevertheless, and much
more importantly, save for the avowedly conservative Salvation Army, no other
employers signed on to the lawsuit. Activists had thus achieved their strategic
goal of painting United Airlines as an obstinate outlier rather than the spear-
head of a new corporate movement against domestic partner benefits.

Refusing to allow the legal system to set the terms of debate for the campaign, activists continued to plan vivid, direct action protests to capture the
attention of United Airlines and the media. In July 1999, for example, activists learned that the American Center for Law and Justice, a conservative
think tank founded by family values stalwart Pat Robertson, had joined
United in suing San Francisco to block the domestic partner benefits ordinance.[40] Robertson was a close friend and confidant of fellow televangelist
Jerry Falwell, who had recently condemned Tinky Winky, the purple, alien-
like cartoon star of the British children's show *The Teletubbies*. Falwell
claimed that Tinky Winky was "gay"—presumably because of an antenna
that Falwell thought resembled a pink triangle and because of a purse-like
bag the "male" cartoon character carried as an accessory. Activists lampooned

United's alleged legal tryst with reactionaries Robertson and Falwell, recruiting local AIDS quilt designer and founder Gilbert Baker to create life-size Tinky Winky costumes that demonstrators wore while blocking the doors of United's city ticket office, getting arrested in front of an amused press. In a similar case of direct action, protesters piled suitcases in front of the same property, each adorned with the details of a discrimination lawsuit United had lost. "Get Rid of Your Tired Old Baggage," rainbow flag–clad picket signs shouted. The event mobilized a double entendre, figuring United's antifeminism, homophobia, and racism as outmoded and retrograde while poking fun at public frustration at United's propensity to lose passengers' luggage.[41]

United managers opted not to wait for the next legal plot twist or protest march to reveal their next move in the domestic partner benefits dispute. Instead, on July 31, 1999, just three weeks after the Tinky Winky protest, the airline shocked the industry and floored activists by capitulating to the San Francisco campaign's demands. The carrier announced that, effective immediately, it would offer full domestic partner benefits to the same-sex partners of all United employees worldwide. Two days later, American Airlines, freed from fear of the conservative reprisal that had met firms such as Walt Disney that had been first to offer domestic partner benefits in other industries, followed United's lead. US Airways joined the group a month later, and all carriers, even socially conservative Delta and cash-strapped TWA, had followed the pattern by April 2001.[42]

"We have changed the world," San Francisco's city supervisor Mark Leno trumpeted at a mass victory rally at San Francisco City Hall the day after United's announcement, projecting a euphoria common among those who worked on the domestic partner benefits movement.[43] Every one of the dozen campaign participants interviewed for this book spoke of phone calls that began with "Are you sitting down?" when news broke of the about-face, as if people would faint at the idea that activists could have an impact on a corporation in the 1990s. Just when it seemed as if caveats always invalidated good news for working people in the 1990s—flight attendants won a new contract, but it drags on for ten years, and flight attendants finally get a raise, but it adds up to less than flight attendants made thirty years ago—the domestic partner benefits story seemed to have few caveats. Even though activists lost the ERISA decision, for example, United would offer full medical and pension benefits to all eligible parties. In an age when neoliberal reforms seemed inevitable and uncontestable, flight attendants and their friends forced the world's largest airline to change the way it did business.

Despite the euphoria, and despite the lack of caveats like those coming from traditional collective bargaining, the victory had some notable short-comings. For example, United allotted the benefits as narrowly as possible, taking advantage of the HRC's focus on same-sex couples to decide who could use the new resources and who could not. Though all domesticated lovers of San Francisco–based employees could sign up for the program, a move United made so it could comply with the broad scope of the city ordinance, only same-sex couples could access domestic partner benefits in the one hundred fifty other cities where United employees were stationed. And since both domesticity and partnership were required to access the new benefits, alternative forms of family among friends, relatives, and neighbors, those ever more common among working people like flight attendants, remained squarely ineligible for the new resources. Radical feminist, gay liberationist, and queer critiques of marriage, monogamy, and domesticity were thus muted in a final settlement that privileged a same-sex version of traditional family values.

Even more critically for the future of the flight attendant movement, the neoliberal reforms that continued to intensify in the late 1990s and early 2000s put new strain on all family benefits programs. During the economic upheaval of the 9/11 crisis, which came just two years after the partner benefits decision, the airlines cannibalized the benefits that activists had just won. Invoking bankruptcy law to abrogate collective bargaining agreements, just as Frank Lorenzo did at Continental Airlines in 1983, managers at United, Delta, Northwest, and other airlines used the power of the courts to eliminate many forms of compensation. For example, family health insurance that had been free for employees at United Airlines before 9/11 now required hefty monthly premium contributions. Unable to balance insurance payments against a new round of pay cuts that lowered hourly wages by at least 10 percent, many flight attendants canceled the domestic partner benefits that they had signed up for after the 1999 victory.[44] As benefit givebacks pushed the lovers of some United employees to remain uninsured in an austere effort to make ends meet, LGBT leaders were forced to confront the broader political economic context of their activism. In an era when the family values of domesticity and hard work had become organizing principles of society, and as the gay-corporate alliance continued to endorse those values, corporations would tightly constrain the LGBT workplace movement, refusing to provide affordable benefits for the vast majority of straight- and gay-identified employees even as they marketed to the LGBT niche.

Conclusion: Against the Romance
of Middle-Class Families

To understand the sadness that followed the domestic partner benefits mobilization as evidence of its futility or its failure would miss the immense significance of the campaign at United Airlines. What is perhaps most striking about the domestic partner benefits movement was the way that it departed from the dominant discourse about trade union and LGBT politics in the 1990s. There were many echoes of feminist, queer, and unionist pasts on the picket lines in San Francisco. There was the echo of radical feminism, in which flight attendants' participation in the women's liberation movement helped challenge the airlines' control of flight attendants' bodies, households, and desires. There was the echo of the 1980s flight attendant strikes, when people at Continental, TWA, and Eastern risked and sacrificed their jobs to prove that a flight attendant is a breadwinner. And there was the echo of ACT-UP, a movement that challenged the Fortune 500 with politically pointed, visually compelling, and emotionally charged street protests.

Much less audible in the streets of San Francisco, however, was the widespread tendency of the past two decades to frame the struggle for economic justice as a bid to defend hardworking middle-class American families. In trade union advocacy for "working families," in the new upsurge of LGBT "marriage equality" activism in the 2010s, and in President Barack Obama's defense of progressive taxation and economic stimulus, the values of middle-class families are often presented with innocent trappings, as the things that give people solace, comfort, and stability in a disorienting economy. Front-line employees such as flight attendants remind us, however, that the family values of the middle class have been the primary means to justify—rather than to challenge—corporate efforts to eliminate pensions, cancel insurance, and cut wages. Hard work, self-restraint, and deferred gratification were all that Carl Icahn offered employees when he locked them out of TWA in 1986, and all that United Airlines offered flight attendants when it abrogated their benefits after 9/11.

Flight attendants Beth Skrondal and Stan Kiino help us envision an alternative to middle-class family values for working people. Their activism in San Francisco illustrates that queer and feminist legacies, those that openly indicted middle-class values, might tell us how to navigate an austere economy and inspire people to challenge four decades of rapidly increasing social stratification. After all, most jobs created in the past forty years require what flight attending and other feminized service jobs have always had: long commutes to work, toil at all hours of the day, the blurring of physical and emotional labor, and a tightrope walk to balance work with loved ones' emotional and economic needs. Family benefits—medical insurance, retirement beneficiary eligibility, and bereavement and emergency leave—are crucially important resources to relieve the stress that comes with working in a neoliberal economy. But for those benefits to be accessible to all working people, and especially to the single women who have faced the biggest challenge in the post-1970 economy,[45] they must be uncoupled from traditional family values. Only when they extend to workers like Beth Skrondal and Stan Kiino will family benefits become an effective solution for working people's economic problems. To make employment benefits work, then, labor activists must move nontraditional families from the margins of political practice—where they are squarely placed in both the pro-family movement and the HRC's gay-corporate alliance—to the center of demands for a fair economy.

AFA activists' political and economic success demonstrates that workplace-based trade unionism and the broader movement for queer, feminist, and racial justice depend on each other to be effective on the neoliberal landscape. Although traditional collective bargaining had become a demoralizing process in the 1990s, the domestic partner benefits campaign—especially when it joined AIDS activists dressed up as Tinky Winky—inspired flight attendants and brought them to the streets of San Francisco en masse. Flight attendants' presence, however, forced the domestic partner benefits movement to grapple with the right to organize, the right to strike, and the need for a living wage, issues that the gay-corporate alliance wholly ignored in most other venues. As the 1990s gave way to the 2000s, and as the September 11 attacks triggered the deepest and longest economic crisis in the history of the airline industry, the coalition between unions and broader social justice movements would become even more crucial to front-line flight attendants. Important though they would be, those coalitions were ever harder to maintain as material resources vanished. Union leaders would struggle to strike a balance between the bread-and-butter economic needs of their members and the commitment to social justice that grew out of the liberation movements of the 1970s.

THE EXPENSE OF JUSTICE

*Family Values and the Corporate Mergers and
Acquisitions Business in the Twenty-First Century*

W ith the domestic partner benefits victory at United Airlines, flight attendant activists had helped prove that unions could still be agents of social change at the end of the twentieth century. Theatrical protests and nonviolent civil disobedience interrupted managerial efforts to roll back previous decades' gains and won new resources for flight attendants that were impressive even by 1970s standards. Despite a sharp drop-off in real wages, the flight attendant profession continued to offer better pay and benefits than retail work, the hospitality industry, and most other sectors of the booming service economy. A headline-making strike victory at American Airlines over the 1993 Thanksgiving weekend and subsequent near-walkouts at Alaska, Midwest Express, and other carriers reveal unions' enduring contribution to wage and benefit premiums. Perhaps even more importantly, flight attendant jobs were available to a far wider swath of the workforce in the late 1990s than they were in the 1970s. As the major U.S. carriers spanned the globe in a booming technology economy, they sought candidates with a broad array of linguistic and cultural skills. In the process, people of Asian, African, and Latin American descent found new access to a unionized trade that had once been restricted to young, white, U.S.-born women.

Successful though activists often were, the overall posture of the flight attendant union movement was defensive as the millennium approached. As airfares continued to fall in a deregulated marketplace, and as the aggressive anti-union tactics that emerged during financialization became standard across the industry, flight attendant unions struggled to protect their members' share of a shrinking pool of economic resources. Activists at individual airlines worked to block management demands for cutbacks, fraying the solidarity that had bound flight attendants across carriers in the 1970s. Unions found it increasingly difficult to maintain long-standing feminist commitments to social justice in an age when economic scarcity pitted flight attendant groups against one another.

Nowhere were these emerging tensions more apparent or more destructive than at American Airlines in 2001. Shortly before Christmas 2000, American bought its once-formidable competitor Trans World Airlines off a bankruptcy court auction block. Soon after the purchase, the Executive Board of the American group's flight attendant union, the Association of Professional Flight Attendants (APFA), sent shockwaves through the industry when it voted to deny occupational seniority protection to TWA flight attendants who would join American as a result of the acquisition. Without credit for their years of service, and because airline employees are laid off in reverse order of seniority, former TWA flight attendants would be the first grounded if American downsized. After the APFA vote, a TWA flight attendant who had been flying since the 1960s would be laid off before a new hire at American, a policy that could force older women onto a job market where they would face significant age and sex discrimination. By making it far easier for American Airlines to eliminate older women's jobs, the seniority vote seemed not only to contradict the flight attendant union movement's long-standing commitment to lifetime employment and a family wage for workingwomen, but also to transgress decades of collaboration between American and TWA flight attendants. Like their peers at American, TWA flight attendants had organized at the nexus of the labor movement and of women's, gay, and lesbian liberation in the 1970s, and had certified their union, the Independent Federation of Flight Attendants (IFFA), just a month before APFA in 1977.

With TWA flight attendants' careers in jeopardy, flight attendants across the industry struggled to understand why the leaders of APFA voted for a policy that would allow American Airlines to ground the former members of IFFA. This chapter addresses this question as it unpacks the challenges facing the flight attendant union movement in the early twenty-first century. Particularly useful for answering flight attendants' troubling question is the work of Chantal Mouffe, a political theorist who has helped explain how businesses and governments built a consensus around neoliberal reforms after 1970. Describing what she calls the constitutive role of "the political,"[1] Mouffe argues that "political practice cannot be envisaged as simply representing the interests of preconstituted identities, but as constituting those identities themselves in a precarious and always vulnerable terrain."[2] For Mouffe, political mobilization does not simply translate the preexisting interests of political actors. Instead, it produces new subject positions with new interests. In the 1970s flight attendants' case, activism at the confluence of a still-powerful labor movement, of women's, gay, and lesbian liberationism, and of a highly mobile profession helped constitute a new political subject, one committed to labor feminism. Demanding more money and less time at work, this new subject challenged the ideology of domesticity and the devaluation of women's labor that was a consequence of domesticity. For the activist flight attendants of the 1970s, defending their basic economic self-interest would uphold a broader, principled commitment to social justice because a raise for a flight attendant was often a raise for single women, for unmarried parents, for same-sex couples, and for other people in the margins of traditional family.

By the late 1990s, the context of flight attendant political mobilization had shifted drastically. Whereas the flight attendants of the 1970s were part of a broad-based social movement that aimed to enlarge the definition of family and to challenge the devaluation of "women's work," by the 1990s a new consensus had emerged among policymakers around pro-family, pro-work politics. As a consequence of that consensus, union density plummeted and much of the feminist and LGBT activist movement retreated into mainstream political organizations that have often facilitated rather than contested the process of neoliberalization. Lacking the support of a wider social justice movement, unions such as APFA shifted their focus away from the daunting task of winning new resources for their members and toward a more manageable bid to protect their members' slice of an ever-shrinking economic pie. In this strategic decision a new political subject emerged. These new activists remained committed to the movement's long-standing goal of protecting the economic self-interest of flight attendants. But they would do so at the expense of justice, forfeiting the broader project of transforming social relations that had come out of the women's liberation movement. For TWA flight attendants, the shift to defensive activism came with a devastating cost. During the economic crisis that followed the attacks of September 11, 2001, the new American Airlines eliminated nearly 20 percent of its flight attendant workforce. Since they were first on the layoff list, all forty-three hundred former TWA flight attendants were grounded, and many would never get their jobs back.

In an era when the pro-family, pro-work cultural consensus seemed natural, inevitable, and uncontestable, one might assume that flight attendants' pressing need to defend their economic self-interest would have rendered the 1970s generation's social justice agenda an anachronism. In the airline industry, however, family values would have a harder time assuaging the tensions that came in the wake of neoliberal reforms. Flight attendant unions had, after all, spent thirty years identifying and contesting pro-family, pro-work ideology. As a consequence of that history, labor feminism remained central to the debate, vying for position against a narrower, defensive agenda in a painful political conflict that would reveal the stakes of trade unionism in the twenty-first century. The struggle between flight attendants for TWA and American Airlines demonstrates that cultural ideas about gender, family, and work would play a pivotal role in the debate over neoliberal reforms and that there would be no way to challenge downward economic redistribution without making those values the central focus of union activism.

Family Affair: Selling the American-TWA Merger with Family

Although TWA and American Airlines flight attendants had built similar unions at similar airlines in the mid-1970s, their employers followed diverging paths through deregulation and financialization. By 1995, TWA was the weakest surviving major airline. TWA's daunting financial problems were in part a result of Carl Icahn's 1986 leveraged buyout of the company (see Chapter 4). Unable to make the interest payments on the junk bonds that Icahn used to buy the company, TWA filed for bankruptcy in 1992 and then again in 1995, cutting unionized workers' wages in both cases.[3] The most painful blow to the company's long-term financial viability came in January 1995, when it defaulted on a $200 million loan that Icahn had made to facilitate TWA's emergence from its first bankruptcy. As a penalty for the default, Icahn forced TWA to allow him to become a ticket broker for the airline, a deal that would let him buy TWA tickets at a 45 percent discount and resell them for personal gain.[4] As a consequence of the Icahn brokerage, TWA's once-profitable transcontinental and transatlantic routes incurred heavy losses. Therefore, despite record industry earnings during the global technology boom, TWA lost $348 million in 1999.[5]

American, meanwhile, soared through deregulation. Leveraging a strong balance sheet in the early 1980s, American edged Braniff out of its Dallas hub and TWA out of Chicago, gaining a robust east-west route network with relatively little competition. The resulting profits provided the capital necessary for American to buy assets from competitors that were struggling with the transition to a deregulated marketplace. In 1991, for example, American acquired Eastern Airlines' Latin American routes after that carrier collapsed and then bought TWA's lucrative London Heathrow hub as the company scrambled for a means to repay its mounting debts. American hoped to build on its earlier successes in the acquisitions business when it engineered another large transaction involving TWA during the year 2000. In this case, American would purchase the remaining assets of the troubled airline in an effort to secure a second midwestern hub. Lucrative though American's Chicago O'Hare operation had been, it was choked with traffic during the economic boom of the late 1990s and ran constant air traffic control delays as a result of overcrowding. After the TWA buyout, American hoped to refocus O'Hare on the local Chicago business market and divert east-west connecting traffic through TWA's hub at Lambert field in Saint Louis.

The network synergies that resulted from the buyout would both augment the new company's finances and produce bitter tensions between American and TWA's flight attendant groups. Since American had flourished after deregulation, it hired crew members throughout the era and thus had a relatively young and junior workforce. Although these flight attendants faced the downward pressure on wages and work rules that affected workers across the industry, the American group was used to good news at work in the 1990s: a route network that grew across Latin America, Europe, and Asia and offered ample opportunities for lucrative long-haul flying. TWA, meanwhile, had withered. Many TWA flight attendants left the airline amid the unrest of the Icahn buyout, the 1986 strike, and the bankruptcies of the 1990s. Those who remained were mostly 1960s and 1970s veterans whose age provided a significant impediment to starting over in a new profession or at the bottom of another airline's seniority list.

Well aware of the strife that could result from combining two employee groups with wide disparities in seniority, compensation, and workplace culture, American Airlines managers looked for a tool to relieve the tension. They found that resource in a familiar category in the twenty-first-century political economy: family. Drawing on the logic of the family values economy—that domestic relationships can make up for economic insecurity—American retold the history of TWA as a family affair. "Family Ties, Shared Success," announced the bold masthead of a special TWA merger edition of American's employee newspaper the *Flagship News*. A glossy photograph captured a father and daughter embracing in front of the tail of a TWA DC-9. Both were wearing navy blue uniforms, though the elder's sported the interlocking gold globes of TWA while the young woman's bore American's iconic eagle. The text offered the pair's family history as an interpretive device for the merger, telling a story of frugality, hard work, delayed gratification, interdependence, and perseverance.

"When I was newly married to Scott, my husband of 15 years, I needed a good, full-time job. My dad prompted me to check out American Airlines." Now McAllister, her father, who went through a buyout in 1986 as an employee of Ozark Airlines that was bought by TWA, will be joining his daughter at American. . . . "You have to be doing things right to be where American is right now."[6]

Rather than duck the history of TWA's difficulties, the article used a family's story to manage their meaning. "We worked hard to make things go here at TWA and we're sorry they didn't work out, but now we just need to work together for American," reflected another TWA employee quoted later in the text.

As it inserted TWA's journey through deregulation into the framework of family, the article was able to reference the bitter pain of the airline's past while abstracting that pain from its political and economic context. The collapse of TWA, after all, was anything but a tale of the thrift, mutuality, and personal responsibility that the image of family invokes. Instead, greed, betrayal, and irresponsibility shaped TWA's turbulent path through the 1980s. For example, rather than prove their fidelity to the members of the TWA family, the airline's pilots and machinists crossed flight attendants' picket lines in 1986 and collaborated with Icahn to save their own careers. Meanwhile, as a result of the Icahn debt, the airline jettisoned valuable assets that employees had fostered for generations and used the proceeds to make interest payments to wealthy private investors who had no connection to TWA.[7] In the process, the Icahn deal became an emblem for a 1980s Wall Street culture that remade the U.S. economy around short-term economic gain and immediate gratification, the presumed antitheses of family values. But by packaging the merger with the emotional and cultural commitments that bind husband to wife and father to daughter, the *Flagship News* was able to hide these historical contradictions.

Even more important than the story's ability to contain the antagonisms of the past was its effort to manage the meaning of the present. The father and the husband, two of the social roles at the center of the *Flagship News* story, are imagined to provide safety and security for daughters and wives. Vulnerability, however, would define both TWA and American flight attendants' role in the new relationship they formed during the 2001 buyout. Since the tie-up would happen during the airline's third bankruptcy, TWA's employees were particularly vulnerable because the federal court system would wield the authority to impose another round of cuts to pay, benefits, and work rules. Although they had less to fear than the TWA group, American employees were also working in an anxiety-ridden industry where real wages continued to fall and where unionized firms faced intensifying low-cost competition both at home and abroad. Thus, instead of being a loving new familial connection like a marriage or a birth, the merger would force American and TWA flight attendants into a relationship that both groups had legitimate reasons to fear. Despite the efforts of management and of the *Flagship News,* it was those qualms that would determine American and TWA flight attendants' connection as they came together in 2001.

Coming Down with the Subcontracting Flu

American Airlines managers couched the TWA merger in a compelling narrative about family as part of an effort to thwart the political unrest that had come to define airline mergers. Corporate tie-ups had always raised the ire of airline workers, since changes to merged carriers' route systems often forced pilots, flight attendants, and ground crews to move away from domicile cities where they had lived for decades. After two decades of neoliberal reforms, employees had even greater reason for apprehension about the change that mergers would bring. In the case of the late 1990s, corporate restructuring was particularly ominous to workers because of the prevalence of a new managerial technology in the airline industry: subcontracting.

The roots of subcontracting lie in the revolution in aircraft technology that occurred the 1960s. In a rush to modernize and standardize fleets around jets, large airlines retired the planes that had been most efficient for serving the smaller cities on their networks: fifty-seat propeller planes such as the Convair 340 and Martin 404. Since they were unable to profitably serve such towns with expensive new jet aircraft, big carriers depended on local service airlines to fly puddle jumpers between outlying communities and major cities. A passenger originating in Appleton, Wisconsin, and bound for Seattle, for example, could board a North Central Airlines propeller-driven Convair, ride it to Minneapolis, and then transfer to a Northwest Airlines Boeing 707 for the rest of the trip. In the 1970s and 1980s, large airlines began to formalize their relationships with smaller companies, each carrier signing agreements with multiple regional airlines to carry their brands and feed their hubs. United Airlines, for example, hired Aspen Airways and Air Wisconsin to help it serve smaller cities. Both airlines remained separate companies but operated under the name United Express. Pre-1990 regional airline flying certainly siphoned some flight attendant jobs away from established lines. But since most aircraft were small propeller planes staffed by a single flight attendant, and since jumbo jets connecting the largest cities dispatched with a crew as large as eighteen, the majority of job creation remained at the major airlines.

Things changed in 1995. Canadian and Brazilian aircraft manufacturers jumped into the lucrative, dot-com boom in the U.S. domestic market by introducing a new generation of airplanes bringing the comfort and speed of jet propulsion to regional carriers. Hailed to deliver jet-set sophistication to small-town air travelers who had been forced to put up with tiny, bouncy, buzzing propeller planes, the major airlines ordered hundreds of the new jets for their regional partners. But instead of using these "regional jets" to modernize existing small-town routes, the major airlines deployed the new planes to lower their labor costs.[8] Rather than replace medium-sized jets coming up for retirement at the major airlines, managers stopped ordering such aircraft and transferred the flying to regional jet operators, who paid their crews far less than the majors.

The meteoric rise of the subcontracting system put employees on the defensive because it compounded the downward pressure on compensation that had defined airline labor relations since the early 1980s. The growth of subcontracting is indeed hard to overstate. By the summer of 2013, regional affiliates operated the statistical majority of large airlines' flights at almost every hub in the United States. For example, 69.9 percent of United's departures at its giant Chicago O'Hare hub were subcontracted. That means that 69.9 percent of "United" flights at Chicago were actually flown by airlines called Republic or Shuttle America or GoJet or SkyWest—names that most passengers would never recognize. Things were no different at American, where subcontractors ran 66.5 percent of departures at Chicago in 2013, or at Delta, where 67.8 percent of trips were subcontracted at Detroit.[9] The growing gap between the image and substance of airlines—in which airlines became "brands" offering sales, marketing, paint schemes, and interior design while shirking commitments to the people who sold tickets, who cleaned, catered, fueled, and flew airplanes, and who provided in-flight safety—disturbed workplace activists. Recognizing these vast operational changes, the flight attendant union movement began to ask a troubling question. If management could transfer the *majority* of operations to subcontractors, what would stop them from transferring *all* of the flying?

Responding to widespread fears that subcontracting would allow management to turn major airlines into brand identities with no employees, American Airlines workers made headlines as they confronted their employer about the practice. In the summer of 1998, an American pilot doing research on the company's SEC filings discovered that American had become the majority stockholder of Reno Air, a West Coast upstart with a growing presence in northern California and Nevada.[10] While the impetus for investing in Reno Air seemed innocent to some, since the partnership would provide American new access to the geographic epicenter of the dot-com boom, American's quiet stockpiling of Reno Air shares spawned workplace rumors that the airline planned to acquire Reno and operate it as a subcontractor. Though some Reno Air staff were unionized—flight attendants had voted in the Teamsters, and cockpit crews had joined the Air Line Pilots Association—the carrier was a low-cost progeny of deregulation and paid far less than American. Buying Reno Air and running it as a separate entity could allow American to fly big MD-80 jets on core routes with cheap, subcontracted crews.[11]

Aiming to interrupt this potentially damaging expansion of the subcontracting system, American's pilots took drastic action. In a striking tactical departure from the buttoned-down business unionism that had long dominated pilot politics, thousands of crew members stayed in bed in a grassroots-organized "sickout" on the weekend of February 10, 1999. Vanished pilots forced American to cancel nine hundred flights and spend nearly $50 million reaccommodating stranded passengers.[12] The immediate consequences of the aviators' mystery illness followed familiar post-deregulation plot lines. Management lawyers rushed from American's Dallas headquarters to the U.S. District Court for the Northern District of Texas in Wichita Falls to seek an injunction forcing pilots back to work. With an unflagging bravado, Judge Joe Kendall's decision bore down on "radical elements" among the pilots who caused a "ridiculous" and "outrageous" job action:

> When you realize this dispute is about the pilots wanting more money retroactively for flying the same airplanes to the same places merely because American bought a small airline many have never heard of, and you have been sleeping on the floor with your kids for a couple of days in some airport 1500 miles from home, it is hard to see the pilots as being mistreated. . . . But what a Federal Judge can do, and what I will do, is make people pay for what they break. So if the activity and consequent damages continue, all the assets of the Union, including their strike war chest, will be capable of safely being stored in the overhead bin of a Piper Cub.[13]

Pitting the injured, consuming nuclear family against greedy union bureaucrats, Judge Kendall served pilots with a temporary restraining order against the sickout, held individual union leaders in contempt of court for organizing the stoppage, and awarded American Airlines $10 million in damages to cover the cost of the unrest. Though the appellate courts tempered this Texas judge's stinging language, they upheld his punitive actions, eventually enforcing the largest damages award ever leveled against an airline union.[14]

While a court-orchestrated slap-down of union activism in the late 1990s is unsurprising, the American–Reno Air controversy stands out for the both inspiring and troubling new information it provides about labor solidarity amid the family values economy. On the one hand, the possibility of new austerity inspired vigorous labor activism. American publicly admitted that most of the pilots who came down with the subcontracting flu were not grizzled, senior jumbo-jet captains skipping posh layovers in Rio and Rome but young, newly hired domestic pilots.[15] These junior crew members often lived in crowded airport "crash pads" with other new pilots and flight attendants sitting on call for predawn check-ins and grueling all-nighters. Challenging the inevitability of a new round of work speedups and defying provisions in labor law that make it much easier to fire a junior employee than a senior one, young employees risked a decade of training and apprenticeship to participate in the action.

On the other hand, as new bonds solidified between junior American Airlines pilots, new tensions emerged between employees across firms. Rather than fellow workers struggling to make it in a lean world, union activists at American figured Reno Air employees to be their economic adversaries, strangers at the gate threatening to cheapen pilot and flight attendant labor. This widening rift between unionized groups was most evident in American pilots' and flight attendants' refusal to negotiate a seniority integration deal for incoming Reno Air employees. By the spring of 1999, it had become clear that American management had backed off any intent to subcontract to Reno Air and instead was taking concrete steps to subsume all inherited flying under existing American Airlines union contracts. Nevertheless, labor leaders insisted that opening American's contracts to rearrange seniority lists to accommodate newcomers from Reno Air aided and abetted management's insidious commitment to subcontracting. In the process, long-standing union procedures guaranteeing workers fair and equitable seniority credit during corporate mergers were tossed out. Instead of granting Reno Air employees recognition for their years of labor aloft, pilot and flight attendant leaders argued that Reno Air employees should be placed at the bottom of the American roster: any other formula would be a "voluntary reduction"—and therefore violation—of original American employees' seniority.[16] American's activists insisted that managers could use mergers and acquisitions as means to navigate a deregulated industry but that front-line employees should not have to take on the waylaid groups of workers created out of such connections.

Management, Unions, and the Practice of Confiscation

Although union leaders at American extended an olive branch to Reno Air flight attendants by going to the bargaining table and negotiating a small cash bonus for the lost seniority—workers got between $500 and $6,000, depending on how long they had been with Reno[17]—the unilateral action forcing newcomers to the bottom of the seniority list revealed something disturbing about labor activism as the millennium approached. As a consequence of the vast economic changes that had taken place since 1970, trade unionism was in some cases shifting from a generative practice to a confiscatory one. In the mid-1970s, the flight attendant union movement's victories at American and TWA made the pie bigger for all working people. If American flight attendants won improved duty rigs in contract talks, for example, TWA flight attendants would mobilize for those same rigs. If American flight attendants got a pension bump, then American ticket agents would get the same bump. By making the pie bigger, labor activists generated economic resources for colleagues in other trades and for their peers at other airlines. But in a deregulated and financialized industry, and as subcontractors took over more flying every week, those resources were vanishing. As the flying disappeared, union leaders at American Airlines recognized that one way to defend what they had so passionately fought for in the 1970s was to divide the pie differently, making their own slice as large as possible even if that made other employees' slices smaller. Subcontracting made activists less and less able to secure the resources necessary to allow flight attendants to be breadwinners, so some activists aimed to remedy the situation by confiscating those resources from other workers.

The new, defensive flight attendant unionism became the central dilemma of the American-TWA buyout in early 2001, a deal that was transforming the relationship between flight attendants, their colleagues at other airlines, and managers as the final details came together. Though American higher-ups, for example, cracked down on pilot activists in court after the Reno Air subcontracting flu, executives openly acknowledged that the labor movement had scored an advance during that fight. Recognizing the economic impact of the sickout, American managers admitted that they would have to respect pilots' and flight attendants' increasingly militant efforts to defend their seniority rights. American's vice president of employee relations, Jeff Brundage, told a Senate panel:

As you well know, there was a very difficult occurrence in another acquisition by American [the Reno Air deal], and we had learned our lessons. We had learned our lessons that we would have to go out of our way to inform our employees that we understood what their contracts said. . . . There was no circumstance under which we would make the TWA asset acquisition if [legal protections for TWA crews' seniority] were named because of the very tension they would have created with our own employees.[18]

Brundage clearly recognized that management had made a mistake in failing to adequately anticipate, acknowledge, and respect union contracts during airline consolidation. But to make up for that disregard, Brundage argued that American's legal department must strip job security protections from incoming employees' contracts, a move that would provide new protection for American employees against the incoming group from TWA. Brundage ceded no economic ground to the labor movement, offering no relief from the pay, benefit, and work rule givebacks that were the root cause of the dispute over subcontracting. Instead, he promised to shield his own employees by providing seniority protection during the industry's ongoing race to the bottom.

Brundage's promise—one that paradoxically transformed airline management from an architect of anti-unionism into a guarantor of unionized employees' contractual rights—guided American Airlines executives as they made their bid for TWA. American managers designed a unique set of stipulations for TWA in advance of the sale, requirements that would help American's employees protect themselves as economic resources continued to vanish. Most striking was a provision that forced TWA to file for bankruptcy before the deal closed. Rather than a simple reaction to TWA's debt load, the TWA bankruptcy plan was hatched by managers at American to take advantage of Section 1113 of the U.S. Bankruptcy Code, which allows companies to reject all or part of debt-generating contracts. American's leadership team identified two cases where Section 1113 would be necessary for a successful merger. First, they filed a motion against Carl Icahn's ticketing brokerage, which would protect the new company from Icahn's ongoing effort to divert resources from TWA's most valuable assets. Second and more troubling, American managers made an 1113 motion against the "Standard Labor Protective Provisions" (LPPs) in all collective bargaining agreements between TWA and its unionized workers.[19]

LPPs began to appear in airline union contracts during the push for deregulation in the 1970s. The provisions provided a safety net for employees when airlines reorganized during mergers, guaranteeing severance pay for those laid off, reimbursement for moving expenses during forced transfers, and a "fair and equitable" integration of union seniority lists. LPPs were originally enforced by the government, beginning in railroad labor relations in 1939, and first appeared in the airline industry with the proposed merger of United and Western Airlines in 1950. Government regulators sharpened and clarified LPPs in subsequent decades and standardized them after a particularly toxic labor dispute during the 1972 merger of Pittsburgh-based Allegheny Airlines and Ithaca-based Mohawk Airlines. The federal government then applied these "Allegheny-Mohawk" or "Standard" LPPs during airline mergers in the subsequent decade.[20] After the Airline Deregulation Act eliminated the federal agency that enforced LPPs, airline unions bargained with management and wrote Allegheny-Mohawk provisions directly into labor contracts. Though contractual language provided an important layer of insulation for workers, it left them newly vulnerable to the bankruptcy process because a single Section 1113 petition by management could invalidate workers' only protection during industry consolidation.

By the middle of the 1990s, three worrying trends faced flight attendants during airline consolidation. First, confiscatory practices such as the subcontracting system put new economic pressure on unions and shrank the size of the pie that workers would divide among themselves. Second, to avoid engaging unions on substantive reforms that would mitigate falling wages, airline managers pitted employee groups against one another, offering to favor their own employees as they redistributed an ever-shrinking pool of resources. Finally, the transition to a deregulated airline industry eliminated government-backed Labor Protective Provisions, which left all workers newly vulnerable to unilateral action by both unions and corporations. As American Airlines managers completed the transaction and acquired bankrupt TWA, all three trends would haunt the new relationship between two flight attendant groups that had been close allies for three decades.

"What Are the Chances We Could Get Away with It?"

The convergence of upwardly redistributive political economic reforms in the airline industry had immediate repercussions for the American-TWA buyout. Amid widespread, legitimate fear that layoffs would follow the acquisition, rank-and-file American flight attendants deluged APFA headquarters with phone calls when the news hit the papers in December 2000. Worried that the incoming TWA group would displace American Airlines flight attendants, many callers demanded that APFA defend their jobs by denying seniority protection to TWA crews just as the union had done in the Reno Air deal. Copies of the TWA flight attendant seniority list—some circulated online by grassroots activists and others distributed by APFA itself—blew through the flight attendant ranks. Union members recoiled at TWA flight attendants' seniority, a group with a disproportionate number of veteran workers when compared with American Airlines. Since 25 percent of TWA flight attendants had begun flying before 1970, and sixteen hundred people had been working for more than twenty-five years, American flight attendants knew that if the airline shrank, thousands of APFA members would lose their jobs.[21]

Management stoked American flight attendants' fears. A February 2001 flight attendant meeting at JFK Airport, for example, was "all but out of control" after the base manager held up a copy of the TWA flight attendant seniority list, emphasizing the immense seniority of the new group.[22] Susan French, chairwoman of APFA's merger and acquisition committee, described a rapidly deteriorating situation in a letter to John Ward, the president of the union:

> As you well know, our committee has been inundated with calls and letters from our membership. We have received well over 1000 telephone calls and emails. It has become quite clear to the M&A committee that the issue of the TWA seniority integration is a political bombshell with land mines everywhere one treads. At the same time, our research and investigation is leading us ever closer to the conclusion that stapling 4,000 TWA flight attendants to the bottom of our seniority list may be the most inappropriate move we can make, although it is exactly what our members want and expect.[23]

Facing a wave of unrest, and working to remain faithful to their union's long-standing identity as a proactive, member-driven organization that defends the economic self-interest of front-line workers, APFA struggled to craft an effective response to the TWA buyout. In the process, APFA leaders and members hardened their position against the TWA group as they began to consider the possibility of withholding credit for TWA flight attendants' years of service by "stapling" them to the bottom of the APFA seniority list, a move that would leave the most senior TWA flight attendant below everyone from American. As she delivered a barrage of questions to APFA general counsel Steve Moldof, French pointed to a worsening political situation:

> We'd like to know . . . the value, if any, of APFA becoming more involved in the [TWA] bankruptcy process. For example, can we endeavor to undo American's promise to offer the TWA flight attendants jobs? . . . It is abundantly clear that 99.9% of our members want TWA flight attendants to go to the bottom of the seniority list, and

that is exactly what they expect our union to do. Aside from the fundamental fairness issues raised by this position, what are the chances we could get away with it?[24]

Although the law was French's explicit premise, ethical questions shaped her query. Raising the "fundamental fairness" of a strategy that would help American Airlines "break its promise" to the TWA group, French struggled with the moral implications of an APFA decision to take a more punitive stance against TWA workers than management. In her framing of the seniority denial as an intervention to "get away with," trade unionism became a nefarious practice that would transgress—rather than reinforce—long-standing solidarity among rank-and-file flight attendants.

As they struggled to find an effective means to defend themselves during industry consolidation, APFA leaders understood that they would have to make a historic decision. They could, on the one hand, honor the long-standing alliance between APFA and IFFA and offer full credit for TWA flight attendants' years of service when they joined the merged airline. If they did so, however, union activists would have to be ready to ground thousands of their own colleagues at American Airlines. And perhaps more importantly, union leaders would have to override a groundswell of activism from members who—out of fear—were demanding that APFA staple TWA flight attendants to the bottom of the seniority list. American Airlines flight attendants had formed APFA and decertified the Transport Workers Union in 1977 precisely because male higher-ups had made union policy for four decades without effectively consulting an all-woman membership. If the Executive Board forced through a protective policy for TWA flight attendants, they would do so against the will of the majority of the rank and file, which would violate the democratic principles that had always been the foundation of APFA.

On the other hand, the union could defend its members' self-interest by stapling TWA flight attendants to the bottom of the seniority list. Doing so would make APFA members virtually immune to layoff even if American dropped routes and subcontracted more flights, because all forty-three hundred TWA flight attendants would have to leave the property before the first APFA member was grounded. This defensive move would, however, severely undermine the political economic agenda that had been the bedrock of both APFA and IFFA. Work rules were the central goal of 1970s labor feminist flight attendant unionism because they provided a consistent, dependable monthly wage that allowed every flight attendant to be a breadwinner for her family for her entire career. But if APFA went through with the seniority stapling, an arbitrary event late in a flight attendant's career, one that would take place with little notice and in a deeply inhospitable labor market for older women, it could end a flight attendant's ability to provide for her family. If they lost their seniority, TWA flight attendants could be cast into the vast uncertainty of the family values economy, where they would be forced to strike a precarious balance between work and family as they cobbled together multiple low-wage service jobs.

On the night before the APFA Executive Board began formally debating the seniority stapling, veteran American Airlines flight attendant activist Tommie Hutto-Blake scribbled an impassioned message to her colleagues on the stationery pad from her hotel room in Euless, Texas. Hutto-Blake paper-clipped the note to an article from a 1976 volume of the *American Civil Liberties Review* titled "Stewardesses: From Sex Objects to Women's Rights Activists." The essay included images from sexually exploitative airline marketing campaigns and chronicled union activists' effort to challenge the industry's inequitable employment practices. The author of the article was Kathleen Heenen, a TWA flight attendant and founding member of IFFA and an activist in Stewardesses for Women's Rights, the umbrella organization for feminist flight attendants from all airlines in the early 1970s. Hutto-Blake reminded her peers that flight attendants' previous victories were possible only because of an overtly feminist coalition of American and TWA workers.

> The TWA and American Airlines flight attendants have a shared history in our current struggle with Corporate America. Reflecting on this history will assist us in our current decisions. I urge the governing body to read and reflect on Heenen's article *before* making one of the toughest decisions of your career as a union advocate.[25]

Although she knew that potential layoffs and subcontracting made APFA leaders' decision much harder than those facing activists in the 1970s, Hutto-Blake insisted that the long-standing political economic agenda of the flight attendant union movement should guide the union's approach to seniority. For Hutto-Blake, the cross-airline solidarity that had turned flight attending from low-wage "women's work" into a means to provide for a family was far more important than APFA members' short-term economic self-interest.

Founding APFA member Patt Gibbs was even more pointed in her response. In a letter to President John Ward, Gibbs challenged the assumption that APFA had ever been a tool to represent flight attendants' preexisting interests. Instead, Gibbs argued, 1970s labor feminists had built the movement around their own principled commitment to social justice, a commitment that was sometimes unpopular with the rank and file. Gibbs told Ward:

Sometimes [my politics] caused me to lose an election for Union office, but my principles were more important than any election. I am
sure you remember hearing flight attendants say that the company
didn't like me because I was gay, or militant, or different looking, or
mean, but so what.[26]

Gibbs reminded Ward that since the airlines had limited hiring to women
who fit squarely within the boundaries of traditional white femininity, most
early-1970s flight attendants were indifferent to—or ambivalent about—the
labor movement and women's liberation. Although militant trade unionism
and radical feminism were peripheral to most flight attendants' lives, Gibbs
and her activist friends understood that all flight attendants would benefit
from the wage increases, the work rule improvements, and the family benefits
that the 1970s radicals were demanding. For Gibbs, union leadership was
never about simply representing what ordinary flight attendants wanted when
they came to work for the airlines. Instead, core activists would draw on the
leftist political projects of the 1970s to generate a new and far more ambitious
set of interests among the membership. Through this constitutive role of the
political, a marginal practice such as women's liberation ended up heavily
influencing all flight attendant unions' agendas in the 1970s.

The question for the APFA Executive Board was how Gibbs's observations
about the 1970s should inform the practice of trade union democracy in an age
when pro-family, pro-work values had remade the economy. Gibbs was abundantly clear that Ward and the rest of the APFA leadership team should be
willing to make an unpopular decision to preserve the core principles of the
movement, even if that decision cost them their elected offices. But as APFA
leaders came together in a hotel adjacent to the sprawling Dallas–Fort Worth
International Airport in late March 2001, most activists lacked Gibbs's resolve.
Twenty-first-century flight attendants understood that in a deregulated, financialized industry, managers were far more willing to pursue an aggressively anti-
union strategy than they were in Gibbs's day. The question for leaders, then, was
how to preserve a space for democratic union practice amid these harsh new
challenges.

"A Gross Injustice?": Implementing the March 22 Protocol

With the rise of the family values economy, lifetime employment—which
had been the defining feature of the U.S. industrial economy and the postwar
middle class—was vanishing. After thirty years of anti-union jurisprudence,
and with the growth of anti-union consulting firms that sold a broad array of

products to help break promises between companies and workers, job security and retirement benefits could evaporate quickly and without warning. Though employers and not unions had designed these products, labor leaders were, in an increasing number of cases, able to take advantage of anti-union technologies as they adopted a defensive position against other workers. Therefore, although there had been a robust debate about the moral and strategic implications of the TWA flight attendant seniority stapling in the weeks leading up to the Executive Board meeting, the recent history of anti-unionism overwhelmed that debate once APFA leaders sat down in Dallas.

On March 22, 2001, with no dissenting votes, the Executive Board of the Association of Professional Flight Attendants ratified a protocol that would staple the TWA flight attendants to the bottom of the merged company's seniority list.[27] That road map promised new security and mobility for the original American group, calling for "protections against furlough" and "preservation of the bidding seniority of the American Airlines flight attendants." To purchase these privileges, the document demanded "non-credit for bidding seniority for TWA years of service in the event TWA flight attendants transfer from the fenced St. Louis and JFK bases."[28] Members of the TWA group would receive credit for their years of labor aloft only if they stayed in their original bases in Saint Louis and New York and only during the months it took to finalize the operational merger. Once the deal was complete, the original American group would "preserve their seniority" by confiscating the seniority of all TWA flight attendants in all bases.[29]

News of the March 22 protocol rattled flight attendants when it appeared on the APFA website and on the union's HotLine phone network. Though airline seniority list mergers had always been contentious—accusations of internal wrongdoing, calls for union leaders to resign, rank-and-file lawsuits against labor leadership, and grassroots movements to relinquish union membership had plagued consolidation for decades[30]—no flight attendant union had ever jettisoned *all* newcomers' seniority on a wholesale basis. Flight attendants had always gotten *something* for their years of service, even if that something was a small cash payment as in the Reno Air deal.[31]

Given the unprecedented nature of the March 22 protocol, reactions by the affected parties varied widely. TWA flight attendants were, of course, devastated. Two years before the merger, TWA flight attendants had voted to leave the Independent Federation of Flight Attendants and join the International Association of Machinists and Aerospace Workers (IAM). Well aware that the airline's financial crisis had jeopardized all TWA flight attendants' careers, rank-and-file activists had opted to join forces with a union with deeper pockets and a larger legal staff than small, independent IFFA. The tie-up had been tumultuous from the start, and TWA flight attendants had widely criticized their IAM leadership for a tepid and bungled response to the American deal, especially after the union voluntarily waived its contractual LPPs to grease the skids for a merger it insisted was the only means to save TWA union jobs.[32] Nevertheless, Robert Roach, the general vice president of the IAM, vigorously responded to the March 22 protocol. In a letter to APFA, Roach blustered:

> Without even giving [TWA flight attendants] the benefit of a phone call, you announced on your "hotline" that in effect the APFA Board of Directors had voted unanimously to unfairly represent and prejudice TWA flight attendants represented by this organization. Be advised that if APFA goes forward with its announced plan to discriminate against TWA flight attendants . . . and place them at the bottom of the American Airlines' seniority list, we will take all legal measures available . . . to prevent this gross injustice.[33]

While management was well aware of—and soon willing to stoke—the interunion conflagration that Roach's rebuke signaled, American's labor relations department responded to the March 22 protocol as if nothing had happened. After all, every other airline merger had resulted in some sort of seniority negotiation process, and management knew that it would have to share the cost of hiring a neutral arbitrator to oversee such meetings. Robin Dotson, American's managing director of employee relations, sent a brief and straightforward note to APFA nearly a month after the March 22 protocol, announcing the company's readiness to begin a negotiation process despite the protocol's apparent refusal of refereed meetings. Dotson told APFA:

> In accordance with our commitment to the International Association of Machinists and Aerospace Workers ("IAM"), we are currently in the process of choosing a neutral facilitator to meet with APFA and the IAM to discuss the seniority integration of TWA flight attendants. Please let me know as soon as possible when the APFA Merger & Acquisition Committee will be available in the next month for this meeting.[34]

Two days later, on April 20, 2001, Dotson confirmed to both the IAM and APFA that American intended to hire Richard Kasher, a widely respected negotiations specialist who had bartered a seniority accord in the extremely contentious Pan Am–National Airlines merger of 1980,[35] to mediate seniority talks between the American and TWA flight attendants.[36] Over the coming days, Dotson, Roach, and Kasher coordinated their schedules and tentatively scheduled a summit meeting for late May in Philadelphia.[37]

Logistical preparations for seniority negotiations ground to a halt on April 23, 2001, when APFA president John Ward sent a terse yet revealing letter to Robin Dotson. Ward reflected:

> I have received your letters of April 18th and 20th.
>
> As you know, APFA is not a party to any agreement reached between American Airlines and the IAM to retain a facilitator for the purpose of discussing the seniority integration of the TWA flight attendants.
>
> As previously communicated, APFA intends to negotiate an Integration Agreement with the Company which is consistent with the guidelines set forth by the APFA Board of Directors on March 22nd, 2001.[38]

Ward's note to Dotson informed company higher-ups of APFA's intent to scuttle the Philadelphia meetings by refusing to participate, insisting that APFA would not be a party to seniority talks between TWA flight attendants and American management, and that the final postmerger seniority list should be determined only in a private, unrefereed meeting between Ward and American's labor relations department.

APFA never directly communicated with TWA flight attendants even as the union announced its intention to boycott the Philadelphia meeting. The only time Ward addressed the TWA group was in a half-page response to Roach's public censure of the March 22 protocol. Ward told TWA flight attendants and the IAM:

> The resolution adopted by the APFA Board of Directors represented its considered judgment as to how best to proceed with regard to the TWA transaction, consistent with its legal responsibilities. Rest assured that our Board gave careful attention to your presentations and the difficult issues presented. Contrary to the comments in your March 23rd letter, APFA has not taken steps to displace anyone, including TWA flight attendants who may become American flight attendants in the future, or to otherwise harm any flight attendants, and has not engaged in any "anti-labor activities."
>
> APFA has a long and proud history of providing outstanding representation to the American flight attendants and of joining with

and supporting flight attendants and others who are employed by air
carriers and other entities. . . . We look forward to continuing that
course in the days ahead and to lending support and deriving support from our fellow labor unionists in the difficult times that lie
ahead for us all.[39]

Though Ward broadly and philosophically engaged Roach's charge that
APFA was preparing to violate labor's timeless adage that "an injury to one is
an injury to all," he never made any reference—in this letter or in any other
public venue—to the logistics of the seniority merge process or to plans for
the neutral facilitation in Philadelphia. Instead, he left the merger at arm's
length, referring to TWA employees as "flight attendants who may become
American flight attendants in the future," even though the American Airlines
Board of Directors had already approved the TWA purchase agreement and
the closing was just fifteen days away.

Ward's radio silence toward TWA flight attendants' pleas for a pre-merger
seniority summit reveals the legal foundations of APFA's confiscatory strategy. American flight attendant leaders offered a new and strictly literalist
interpretation of airline labor law, one that would exempt them from even
discussing, much less arbitrating, the seniority issue with the TWA group or
their IAM union leadership. APFA avoided seniority negotiations by placing
TWA flight attendants in a troublesome legal time bind created by silences
in the Railway Labor Act, the 1926 law governing labor relations on the railroads and airlines. APFA understood that in the letter of the RLA, there was
no requirement for a union seniority summit during airline consolidation,
even though one had taken place in every airline merger before the American-
TWA affair.[40] The summit process was never written into the RLA because it
was instead part of the government-guaranteed system of Labor Protective
Provisions. But as TWA flight attendants were painfully aware, LPPs had
stopped being enforced in the decade after deregulation.

Absent any legal or regulatory framework for seniority mergers, APFA
simply made one up. Union leaders wagered that they could bypass the pre-
merger summit process, going directly to American management and submit-
ting a combined seniority list designed entirely by APFA with no input from
TWA flight attendants. American managers would keep the document, set it
aside while they prepared to merge the two companies, and then begin to
honor it once the operational merger occurred. APFA activists thus emulated
a non-union model of labor relations in which all personnel policy changes are
made behind closed doors without input from front-line employees.

Though writing TWA flight attendants out of the seniority integration would appear to have been a glaring lack of due process, especially because TWA crews would soon become APFA members and pay APFA dues, labor policymakers had given the nod to similar practices in other industries. In a 1988 merger of Riser Foods and Rini-Rego Warehouse, two outfits in the grocery industry from suburban Cleveland, the National Labor Relations Board argued that *time* decides whether or not unions could make deals with management that would negatively impact the seniority and working conditions of future members.[41] The board found that *prior* to the operational merger, *prior* to the moment the incumbent union begins representing the new members, the incumbent union can make any agreement it wants with management, even if that agreement would treat incoming members harshly. The company could then enforce this agreement *after* the operational merger. If it turns out that the agreement discriminates against incoming members, the board ruled that newcomers have no right to sue their new union because the agreement was made *before* they were members of that union.[42]

Herein lies the time bind. Since airline consolidation creates immense logistical challenges, combining vastly different schedules, facilities, training procedures, and aircraft fleets, most mergers involve an interim period in which two airlines are financially linked but operationally separate. For the American-TWA deal, between April 10, 2001 (the date the sale closed) and July 2, 2003 (when the government officially certified that the two companies had become a single airline operation), TWA flight attendants would continue to work TWA airplanes, follow TWA procedures, and remain members of their old union, the IAM. At the same time, American flight attendants would fly American airplanes, follow American procedures, and stay in their pre-merger APFA bargaining unit. APFA would begin representing *both* groups only after the government officially ruled that the operational merger had occurred. The problem for TWA flight attendants was that in the Riser–Rini-Rego case, the board found that workers are legally entitled to equitable treatment from only their *current* union. APFA would thus be exempt from the duty to provide TWA flight attendants a fair and equitable seniority agreement because it did not represent the group at the moment it submitted the seniority list to American. Without being members of APFA, TWA flight attendants lacked a legal procedural basis to interrupt—or even weigh in on—that agreement even though they would be subject to its dictates once they began to fly for the merged company in July 2003.

The December 17 Accords: Dispossession and Inclusion in the 9/11 Era

The American-TWA merger spiraled from a dispute to a crisis with the events of September 11, 2001, violence that took place a mere six months after APFA ratified the March 22 protocol and before it signed a final seniority deal with management. The attacks on the World Trade Center, on the Pentagon, and on four United and American Airlines jetliners unleashed the worst economic upheaval in the history of U.S. aviation. The economic hemorrhaging was made much worse the following year by the run-up to the second war with Iraq. International air travel to and from the United States fell off 32 percent between November 2002—the beginning of the Bush administration's final push for invasion—and the declaration of victory the following May.[43] With international travel in free-fall and the subcontracting system continuing to transfer flying away from big companies like TWA and American, all of the major airlines announced plans to seek deep economic concessions from all employees and to lay off thousands of flight attendants.

The situation was particularly intractable at American Airlines, where flight attendants had spent a year bogged down in a bargaining dispute with management. Six months before the 9/11 attacks, and while American was still turning solid profits, then-president Tommie Hutto-Blake warned all APFA members of a twofold crisis threatening the very survival of APFA. First, Hutto-Blake raised the possibility that management was preparing to force a flight attendant strike in an effort to break the union. "Management is not serious about concluding negotiations with a contract that the APFA membership could endorse," Hutto-Blake's "All-Call" recorded message told the rank and file. Second, management's new relationship with TWA could be a powerful new weapon in this union-busting strategy. American could bait an APFA strike and then force employees from TWA—which American would own by April 2001—to permanently replace flight attendants on APFA picket lines. Conversely, American could subcontract lucrative international flying to TWA, eliminating the jobs of APFA members without the hassle of a strike and lockout.[44]

The threatening tenor of negotiations provided deep incentives for APFA to pursue a strike-averting deal with American. The problem, of course, was that APFA had few cards to play at the bargaining table. The union had virtually no ability to credibly threaten a strike because rank-and-file members were desperate to protect their jobs amid downsizing rumors, skyrocketing unemployment, and anxieties about strikebreaking and subcontracting. Meanwhile, save for a successful public employee strike in Minnesota in October 2001, the intense nationalism and antiradicalism of the immediate post-9/11 era meant that strikes had all but vanished as a form of legitimate dissent, especially in the airline industry, which was the center of post-9/11 political and cultural anxieties.

American flight attendants did, of course, have one point of leverage they could use to bring order to the situation. APFA would make the final determination on the order of the new, combined American-TWA flight attendant seniority list. The quicker APFA resolved the seniority dilemma and provided the company with a new roster, the faster American could complete the costly interim period of the merger, proving to skittish investors that the two companies had become a single, efficient entity. Furthermore, the position of TWA flight attendants on the seniority list—whether credited for date of hire or stapled to the bottom—would deeply impact labor costs at the new airline. Since the TWA flight attendants were an older, senior group, their pay and vacation outlays would be much higher than those for junior people hired by American in the late 1990s.[45] If APFA stapled them to the bottom of the seniority list and made the TWA group the first in line for post-9/11 layoffs, American would score new cost competitiveness by being able to eliminate expensive, senior flight attendants at a moment when contracts forced United, Northwest, Continental, and other unionized carriers to restrict layoffs to lower-wage new hires.

This ominous political and economic context—of unprecedented financial turmoil in the airline industry, of APFA's pressing desire to provide economic security for members by locking in a new contract, and of the potential labor cost savings of stapling TWA flight attendants to the bottom of the American seniority list—shaped a pact between APFA and American that sealed TWA flight attendants' fate. On December 17, 2001, APFA president John Ward convened a meeting with the employee relations department of American Airlines, generating and signing two documents that would transform the tripartite relationship between American flight attendants, TWA flight attendants, and American Airlines. The first of these covenants was a concession by the company. In a letter titled "Agreement Prohibiting the Leveraging of TWA-LLC against the APFA," American made a legally binding promise to refrain from using former TWA flight attendants as subcontractors or replacement workers in the broader contract dispute between APFA and the company. The agreement stipulated that once the federal government officially gave APFA the right to represent incoming TWA flight attendants, American would recognize former TWA employees as under the jurisdiction of the APFA contract and refrain from subcontracting to TWA. Furthermore, if APFA struck American Airlines as a result of failed contract negotiations, the airline would immediately shut the TWA operation down, making it impossible to retain TWA flight attendants as permanent replacement workers.[46]

The second agreement between Ward and American managers was a quid pro quo for the first. In "Agreement on Seniority Integration and Related Matters between American Airlines, Inc., and Association of Professional Flight Attendants Representing the Flight Attendants of American Airlines, Inc.," the company and the union agreed that all incoming TWA flight attendants would receive a classification seniority date of April 10, 2001, the date American's purchase of TWA closed. Though the company complied with standard industry practices and agreed to honor TWA crews' seniority for pay and vacation purposes, the accord meant that every TWA flight attendant—even one who had worked her first trip on a piston-driven Lockheed Constellation in 1957—would have just six months of seniority to protect her job in a rapidly downsizing industry, less seniority than all nineteen thousand flight attendants originally hired by American.[47]

In an era when deregulation and financialization had thrown daunting hurdles in front of so many working people, American Airlines flight attendants won security and inclusion with the December 17 accords. When Ward signed the paperwork, APFA members were newly protected from the subcontracting system, sheltered from permanent replacement on the picket line, and cushioned from the mass furloughs impacting all other airline employees. The same pen strokes abandoned TWA flight attendants, exempting them from any remaining spoils of working for a powerful company like American. The interdependence between the December 17 documents' illuminates the inequitable contours of the twenty-first-century economy, one in which a few working people gain mobility by upholding the upward redistribution of wealth, power, and resources that define the family values economy.

Despite the watershed that the December 17 accords delivered to TWA flight attendants, the agreement by no means mitigated the broader austerity facing APFA members. Though the pact removed the immediate threat of a lockout or wholesale subcontracting, the subsequent truce between APFA and management that the December 17 accords helped enable what became the most inequitable and unpopular contract settlement in American flight attendants' history. That deal, solidified as caustic negotiations drew to a close in April 2002, rolled back most of the gains that American and TWA flight attendants had won in the late 1970s. APFA activists certainly took some consolation in preserving flight attendants' defined benefit pension plan, retirement benefits that were stripped from peers at Delta, Northwest, United, and other major carriers, but they nonetheless reeled as total flight attendant compensation was slashed by another 30 percent. The most notable of the concessionary contracts' many consequences was the dramatic speedup of flight attendant work, which came in the form of longer shifts, shorter layovers, fewer days off, less vacation and sick time, and smaller crews on every aircraft.[48]

Work speedups also meant that about 20 percent of American flight attendants would, at least temporarily, lose their jobs, a burden borne almost entirely by older women who began their careers at TWA. Mass layoffs began on November 1, 2002, when 420 flight attendants—all former TWA—were ordered to turn in their badges and flight manuals and leave American Airlines. The furlough process gradually but steadily worked its way through the entire TWA flight attendant population: all 1990s hires were gone by New Year's Day 2003, and only 1960s veterans were left by the end of the summer. Each new announcement meant that an older, more experienced group was faced with unemployment. When 259 TWA flight attendants got their pink slips on May 1, 2003, for example, they averaged 49.6 years old, with every furloughed flight attendant over age 40, and 42 percent of the group over 50. By the time the furlough process drew to a close at the end of the year, 3,394 TWA flight attendants were on long-term layoff from American Airlines, 1,500 of whom would never get their jobs back. The furloughed group averaged 51 years old, with 58 percent of those on layoff over 50. If TWA flight attendants had gotten full seniority credit during the merger, 3,085 of these flight attendants would have kept their jobs. The furloughed group would have averaged 36.8 years old, with just 12.3 percent of those in unemployment lines over 50, if date-of-hire seniority had been extended to TWA flight attendants, as it was in most other airline mergers.[49] These realities were most stark at Saint Louis, the airport where the majority of TWA crews were based. As the Saint Louis operation was depopulated in rounds of TWA layoffs, the airline brought in 900 original American hires as replacements, literally swapping out TWA bodies for American bodies and even forcibly transferring new American recruits from their Los Angeles and Miami stations to cover vanished TWA flight attendants' work. The process was complete on July 2, 2003, when the last TWA flight attendant turned in her wings, grounded in what had become perhaps the bitterest inter-union conflict in the history of the U.S. airline industry.

Labor Feminist Legacies and the Push for McCaskill-Bond

APFA's narrow commitment to the economic self-interest of its members helped make the American-TWA merger an immense setback for the flight attendant union movement. The grounding of former TWA workers buttressed the airlines' power over all flight attendants, regardless of which company they worked for. After the seniority denial, managers at every airline could use the threat of a merger and subsequent seniority loss to intimidate union members into taking further wage, benefit, and work rule concessions. Meanwhile, employers proved that they could ground a group of older women workers while avoiding legal sanction for age and sex discrimination. The TWA seniority stapling showed that management could roll back the watershed progress that 1970s flight attendant activists had made in eliminating airlines' discriminatory recruitment and retention programs.

Despite the blow that the seniority crisis dealt to the movement as a whole, the American-TWA merger would not eliminate labor feminist flight attendant mobilization. Instead, flight attendants from across the industry leveraged the ideas and the infrastructure that they had built during three decades of activism to challenge TWA workers' grounding. Flight attendants recognized that the political successes of the feminist and antiracist movements of the 1960s and 1970s could provide an opportunity to contest the seniority denial. Although the rise of pro-family, pro-work politics in the late 1970s reversed most of their unions' political economic advances, flight attendants knew that many previous legal gains had been institutionalized. After Title VII banned sex discrimination in the workplace, after corporate Equal Employment Opportunity statements formally welcomed female job applicants, and as corporate diversity rhetoric touted the value of women in the workplace, blatant sex discrimination had been cast outside the boundary of legitimate business practice by the year 2000. Though there was no consensus about the pay and benefits that a woman deserved on the job, most of the public and many employers agreed that a worker should not be fired simply because of her age or sex.[50] Therefore, TWA flight attendants appealed directly to public officials, insisting that the government reinforce its commitment to equal opportunity at work by banning seniority denials like the one that took place during the merger.

Flight attendants began to countermobilize in TWA's former hometown of Saint Louis, where thousands of workers' personal lives were in crisis after the mass layoff. Twenty-two-year veteran TWA flight attendant Roger Graham describes the political and emotional context of a new initiative he and his colleagues formed:

I was at home one night. I was with another flight attendant who was going through a difficult personal time because of the [postmerger] layoff and this really pissed me off. And I went into the bedroom and I told my partner how much this angered me. We had no money—

but we decided to go down to Dallas and picket our own union for doing nothing to get us back.[51]

Graham and a dozen other displaced flight attendants decided to travel to the Dallas headquarters of APFA, setting up picket lines in front of their new union and demanding that the organization invalidate the December 17 accord and renegotiate a fairer seniority integration agreement. Only forty people showed up, but since they had all spent precious time and money on the trip, they cultivated a new network of dedicated activists who would focus on finding new opportunities to challenge the seniority stripping.

Well aware the APFA would not reverse the seniority stapling, and seeing an opportunity to link the mass layoff to broader principles of fairness and equality that remained dominant after the 1960s, Graham and his colleagues shifted their focus toward electoral politics. During the summer of 2006, polls showed that the Senate race in the state of Missouri was in a dead heat. Incumbent Republican Jim Talent faced a vigorous challenge from upstart Democrat Claire McCaskill in a year that was swinging toward the Democrats nationally. TWA flight attendants learned that Talent would debate McCaskill on public television in the Saint Louis suburb of Clayton, Missouri. The activists who met at the Dallas protest contacted both Senate campaigns, telling Talent and McCaskill that they would deliver the votes of all twelve thousand displaced TWA employees in Missouri to whichever campaign came up with a better plan to remedy the mass layoff. Activists obtained ten seats for TWA workers in the small television studio and submitted a question about the layoff that the moderator promised to ask during the debate. Meanwhile, ninety additional TWA flight attendants rallied with bullhorns and signs outside the venue, drawing attention to their cause despite a driving rain and forty-knot winds.[52]

Though both candidates paid lip service to the injustice of the TWA affair on camera, only McCaskill was versed enough in labor and employment policy to sketch a means to not only overturn the layoffs but also prevent the situation from recurring at another employer. A week later, Roger Graham—who had taken the lead on the Missouri Senate strategy—met with McCaskill to review and finalize her legislative commitment to flight attendants.[53] Her intervention proved acceptable to Graham and the other leaders, who publicly promised to deliver the votes while posing for a media photo-shoot with McCaskill holding a model of a TWA Boeing 767.[54] McCaskill's pledge paid off politically: she upset Talent in the November general election, beating the incumbent by forty thousand votes as a deeply energized former TWA workforce turned out en masse to support her.

McCaskill quickly delivered on her promise to Graham's cohort in two ways. First, she called APFA leaders and American Airlines managers into a meeting, persuading the union and management to draw up an extension of "recall rights" for furloughed TWA flight attendants. Under the then-current APFA contract, grounded flight attendants would be first in line for new openings for five years after layoff. Since many TWA flight attendants had been grounded in mid-2002, those "recall rights" began expiring in 2007. The McCaskill deal moved those recall rights back to seven years, allowing the industry twenty-four additional months to recover from the 9/11 slump. The extension, however, would cover only the twelve hundred TWA flight attendants still on the recall list in December 2007, allowing American to permanently dump the fifteen hundred who had already passed the five-year mark. Many TWA flight attendants—especially veterans who had fought Carl Icahn and won the recall of every single striker during the 1986 lockout—scoffed at the deal, insisting that it violated the basic principle of the labor movement that an injury to one is an injury to all.[55]

McCaskill's other initiative drew much broader support among the TWA group and was far more historically significant. Joining forces with Missouri's other senator, Republican Kit Bond, McCaskill aimed to write key components of the Allegheny-Mohawk Labor Protective Provisions back into federal law. McCaskill's bill would restore the sections of Allegheny-Mohawk that guaranteed workers "fair and equitable" seniority credit during mergers and acquisitions. By pulling this particular language out of Allegheny-Mohawk, TWA activists and McCaskill were able to insert seniority policy into the broader cultural consensus around "fairness" and "equity" while avoiding the political backlash that would inevitably follow a pro-worker government regulation during the neoliberal era. To build support for the bill in Congress, TWA activists joined forces with the legislative affairs department of the Association of Flight Attendants (AFA), another large flight attendant union that had spent decades lobbying for government seniority protection. Doing so gave the grounded TWA group the political and institutional support of flight attendants from United, US Airways, Alaska, and twenty other airlines. Since the bill was vulnerable to veto by openly anti-union president George W. Bush, the coalition of AFA and TWA activists slid the McCaskill-Bond legislation into the Consolidated Appropriations Act of 2008, an omnibus bill with bipartisan support in Congress. The strategic move guaranteed McCaskill-Bond's amendment easy passage.[56] Though all flight attendants would continue to face the daunting challenge of working in a deregulated, financialized industry, TWA activists successfully stripped management of its ability to use the merger process to wield age and sex as means to divide and dispossess the flight attendant union movement.

Conclusion: The Challenge of Labor Feminism in the Twenty-First Century

Twelve years after the TWA buyout, and as the pain of losing their seniority still rankled former TWA flight attendants, American Airlines announced its next major strategic move as it worked to adapt to the permanent flux of a deregulated, financialized industry. On July 12, 2013, the shareholders of US Airways agreed to sell the company to American. US Airways had a strong presence in the growth markets of the U.S. Southeast and was itself an amalgamation of carriers that had chosen consolidation as a means to mitigate previous industry turmoil: Allegheny, America West, Mohawk, and PSA, among others. After the merger announcement, APFA once again had to decide how to integrate a new group of flight attendants into American Airlines. Unlike its decision in the TWA case, the union gave all former US Airways flight attendants credit for their previous years of service as they began their new jobs at American. Thanks to McCaskill-Bond, APFA was required to provide "fair and equitable" seniority protection to its new members. Senior US Airways flight attendants will continue to have first pick of lucrative international schedules once they join American and will have protection from layoff if the new company shrinks. Because of the law that TWA flight attendants helped write, APFA has been able to focus on the wage and work rule goals that unite all flight attendants rather than on the seniority issues that divide them. Even in an age when the labor movement is a third the size that it was in the 1970s, and even after feminist and gay activists' bold critiques of domesticity and family have faded from mainstream political debate, flight attendant union activism successfully protected the careers of tens of thousands of older workers who otherwise might have lost their seniority.

As McCaskill-Bond helped US Airways flight attendants keep their jobs, and as it allowed them to join their new colleagues at American as peers rather than subordinates, the flight attendant union movement proved that workers could still create political economic change in the twenty-first century. TWA flight attendants' perseverance discourages us from reading Chantal Mouffe's work in economic determinist terms—from assuming that a neoliberal economy inevitably produces defensive, ineffective unionism. TWA activists' ability to reorient the debate in a time of crisis is exactly why

Mouffe is hopeful about the political conflict that stems from democratic practice. For Mouffe, political debate—even when that debate is as caustic as it was in the wake of the TWA affair—is a positive, generative consequence inherent in the tension between liberty and equality that exists in every democracy.[57] There would have been no way to fully resolve the conflict between American Airlines' flight attendants' basic economic self-interest and a fair seniority deal for TWA workers. But it was political mobilization itself that opened a space for labor feminist flight attendants to act and allowed McCaskill-Bond to be the permanent, equitable consequence of the dispute.

The continued power of TWA flight attendants' insistence that every flight attendant deserves to be a breadwinner for her family for her entire career does not mean, however, that resurrecting 1970s-style labor feminism will save the flight attendant union movement. Though union contracts like those at United and American continue to allow some flight attendants to provide for their families, most new airline jobs are being created at discount airlines and subcontractors, where wages are low and work rules are scant. Meanwhile, thousands of other flight attendants who once worked for Eastern, Braniff, TWA, and other carriers have been displaced from the industry and are struggling to make ends meet with multiple, low-wage service jobs. Subcontracted flight attendants and other service employees have few of the resources that enabled 1970s activism; in many cases they lack union representation and the support of a broad-based social justice movement. Those workers, however, are living lives similar to those that 1970s activists politicized. They are waiting to marry, cohabitating with friends, having children while single, and using the household as a space to pool the economic resources of jobs that don't pay the bills. In an age when the domestic sphere has become a heavily leveraged place that mitigates economic uncertainty as much as it facilitates intimate relationships, the flight attendant union movement's long-standing critique of the family values economy is more relevant than ever. The question for activists, then, is how to make the movement's labor feminist past relevant to a new generation of workers who were never involved in the upsurge of the 1970s. I take up this question in the Epilogue.

EPILOGUE

The Future of the Flight Attendant Union Movement

On August 13, 2014, flight attendants for Virgin America voted to join the Transport Workers Union of America. With the representation election, activists brought collective bargaining to the industry's trendiest airline. Based in San Francisco, Virgin America is the carrier of choice for design-conscious tech workers. Travelers may relax in The Loft, Virgin's upbranded airport lounge, before they board their flight. Guests swivel in red minimalist modern armchairs, drinking mixologist-curated craft cocktails and eating canapés off of square plates. On the aircraft, passengers are greeted with white leather first-class seats, purple Plexiglas cabin dividers, and lavender mood lighting that provides a cool, calming glow. Onboard service comes from flight attendants who, at Virgin's behest, are young, racially and culturally diverse, and fashionable, and who are proud to work for a boutique airline that leads the industry's customer service rankings. As they joined the TWU, those hip young workers became the newest members of the flight attendant union movement.[1]

For demographic reasons, unionization would seem to be an unlikely political strategy for Virgin America flight attendants, who share little in common with the generation of activists who built the movement in the 1970s. The majority of the members of the new union's negotiating committee are black or Latino flight attendants who are under forty years old.[2] They work at the confluence of the technology and service industries, two of the least unionized parts of a private sector economy in which the overall union membership rate is falling through 8 percent. Unions reached their peak political and economic influence sixty years ago, when the bulk of their members were white men who worked in a manufacturing sector that largely excluded people of color and women. Since most Virgin America flight attendants were born after 1970, they grew up well after the peak of women's, gay, and lesbian liberation. Much of today's information about those movements comes from mainstream media that stereotype 1970s feminism as dowdy, humorless, and passé. Although previous activists' economic advances would undoubtedly impress many at Virgin America, the earlier generation of flight attendants often failed to address issues of race that are central concerns for many Virgin America flight attendants, focusing instead on a bid for a family wage that few of today's workers have ever expected to earn.

Despite the gulf between traditional trade unionism and the twenty-first-century service economy, Virgin America flight attendants face challenges at work that begin to explain their receptiveness to the union. Although they provide an indulgent experience for passengers, Virgin flight attendants live on a tight budget. Like crews at most of the carriers formed after deregulation, employees at Virgin start at $20 per flight hour.[3] Workers fly much more today than they did in the 1970s: duty periods regularly exceed twelve hours with as little as ten hours of rest between shifts. Even with the longer hours, however, it would be difficult for a Virgin flight attendant to earn more than $30,000 in the first year of flying. While wages have remained stagnant, rents have skyrocketed in Virgin's San Francisco base. The median price for a one-bedroom apartment in the city was $3,460 per month as of March 2015, a figure that exceeds most flight attendants' gross income.[4] Because of the scarcity and fear that resulted from the 2008 economic crisis, and the reduced effectiveness of unions after four decades of neoliberal reforms, younger people have rarely taken collective action at work to demand the economic resources they need. But regardless of their generation's unfamiliarity with trade unionism, the TWU's pledge to provide new resources to mitigate the high cost of living clearly resonated with the majority of Virgin America flight attendants.

Cultural parallels between the union upsurge of the 1970s and the careers of present-day flight attendants provide further explanation for the TWU vote. Flying for Virgin America gives young workers vast physical and social mobility. Like 1960s Pan Am, TWA, and United stewardesses, Virgin crews lay over in stately downtown hotels in booming global cities and interact with employees from cutting-edge firms in the leading sectors of the economy. Though city nights in New York, Los Angeles, and Chicago arouse a host of desires among flight attendants, small paychecks prevent them from fulfilling many of those desires. Furthermore, inadequate longevity pay and minimal retirement benefits discourage Virgin flight attendants from staying on the job long-term or from using their career to support a family. In an age when domesticity and marriage are celebrated on both the left and the right, a Virgin America flight attendant paycheck barely supports a single person. Therefore, many workers—by choice or by necessity—live far beyond the boundaries of the conventional household. Though the immediate cultural and economic dynamics of the twenty-first century shaped flight attendants' decision about the union, these conditions bore striking similarity to those that produced the flight attendant union movement in the 1970s.

Virgin America workers' decision to vote in the TWU exemplifies the rule and not the exception in twenty-first-century U.S. airline labor relations, as flight attendants at many carriers continue to authorize union representation. This final chapter of the book reflects on the future of the flight attendant union movement, explaining why crew members at companies such as Virgin America continue to organize even as the labor movement faces unprecedented challenges, and showing the relevance of their decision to workers in other industries. I demonstrate that highly exploitative labor has become the norm in the airline industry, both for customer service agents, flight attendants, and other lower-paid workers and for historically more privileged machinists and pilots. Many new airline jobs pay little more than minimum wage, are temporary and/or part time, and are highly mobile, forcing workers to move from city to city with little notice and few opportunities to return home to visit family. Thus, working for even the most successful carriers often places great stress on employees' families, requiring long blocks of time away from home and necessitating that each family member have at least one other job to supplement the small airline income.

Before 1970, the family wage system had temporarily alleviated many of the pressures that airline workers now face. In the heavily unionized manufacturing, construction, and transport industries, employers provided the wages and benefits necessary for one person to comfortably support an entire family. But because ideas about whiteness, manhood, and heterosexuality were used to justify the family wage and to decide who received it, the system excluded far more people than it benefited. As workers in a feminized trade, flight attendants were always on the margins of the family wage system, including during the brief period before 1985 when they reaped some of its benefits. Flight attendant unionism thus has been about the struggle to balance family and work without a family wage. Out of both necessity and political commitment, activists demanded economic resources for older women, for single and divorced parents, for households of one, and for people who cohabitated with friends and lovers. Now that the family wage has disap-

peared from nearly all sectors of the economy, flight attendants' previous
strategies are relevant to a wider audience and to a population far more diverse in terms of race and age than the young white women who led the
struggle in the 1970s. This chapter traces how new rank-and-file leaders are
transforming previous generations' arguments about sexuality and family to
help build a twenty-first-century workplace activist movement.

Family Values and the Rise of Casual Labor in the Twenty-First-Century Airline Industry

The struggle to balance low-wage jobs with family responsibilities is not
unique to Virgin America flight attendants, to the airline industry, or to the
neoliberal economy. Anxieties about domesticity have inflected debates
about U.S. labor policy for at least one hundred fifty years, especially during the period of rapid industrialization that followed the Civil War. A
century before flight attendants confronted the airlines about women's economic mobility, industrialization was transforming men's and women's social roles.[5] In the agrarian economy, women and men worked in close
proximity. When they moved into factory work, however, jobs physically
separated people from their kin. More time in anonymous, public, urban
spaces provided new sexual opportunities for both women and men. Meanwhile, by turning yeoman farmers into wage workers who were dependent
on their employers, and by providing women with paychecks that brought
economic independence, industrialization undermined traditional manhood.[6] As workers struggled to adapt to a changing relationship between
gender and power, the economy boomed at the turn of the twentieth century. Manufacturers pushed some workers to spend sixty or more hours on
the assembly line to meet growing demand and required others to travel far
from home to harvest the timber and minerals necessary to build industrial
products. These dynamics further strained domestic relationships for an
ever-wider swath of the U.S. population.

Sexuality played an explicit role in the public controversy that surrounded
industrialization. For example, as historian Colin Johnson demonstrates, the
widespread use of "casual labor" in the early twentieth century provided a
visible yet highly stigmatized alternative to the nuclear family. Johnson shows
that casual labor was an "intentionally vague term" that described the work
of "seasonal migrants and other transients whose relation to the wage labor
economy was distinguished primarily by its irregularity."[7] Employers hired
poor and often immigrant men to travel great distances to extract natural
resources for the manufacturing economy. After long stints in lumber camps,

in copper mines, or along the railroad, casual laborers would return to major cities to spend weeks or months waylaid between jobs. Lacking the time and money to support a family, these men lived in a homosocial world, passing their time on the streets and in saloons, relying on other men for emotional support, and finding regular erotic outlets only in homosexual sex or commercial sex work. Life on the road produced widely recognized social identities—the hobo, the tramp, and the bum—that were defined by an unwillingness to accept full-time work and a refusal to domesticate into a traditional nuclear family.[8] Though workers who found full-time, year-round jobs near their homes could form families that appeared to be more traditional than casual laborers' kinship networks, cultural anxieties about aberrant sexualities affected the many workers who spent seven days a week in the factory.

By the end of the nineteenth century, social reformers and employers were turning to a new remedy for the social dislocation that came with industrialization: the family wage. Instead of reducing wages to maximize profits, some companies increased pay to stabilize social relations, a move that they assumed would also increase productivity. The family wage system made industrial work far more predictable, guaranteeing full-time employment, a dependable year-round paycheck, and a sufficient income to save for retirement. To soothe the cultural anxieties that stemmed from the loss of family farms and the rise of unskilled labor, the family wage turned the workingman into a breadwinner, the leader of his own, independent, self-reliant family. Husbands' paychecks would tamp down workingwomen's independence, allowing them to reorganize their once-public lives around a new world of domesticity, caregiving, and motherhood.[9] The family wage would, in other words, help get men off the road and women out of the public sphere, reorganizing family life around domesticity. By its peak in the immediate post–World War II era, the family wage had brought the urban, industrialized economy in line with traditional heteropatriarchal values.

The family wage system heavily influenced the structure of airline work. Air transportation is highly unpredictable: macroeconomic cycles, seasonal demand spikes, and technological advances leave route networks in a constant state of flux. Operational irregularity makes the airlines ideally suited to the part-time, temporary, and contingent employment practices that had defined casual labor. But because the airline industry took off at the peak of the family wage system during the New Deal era, the work process was anything but casual. Union contracts with strict work rules provided workers with full-time year-round jobs, regular hours, a constant pay rate, and ample time off in an employee's home domicile city. With a family wage, a person could be both an airline worker and a dependable breadwinner for his or her family.

The economic benefits of the family wage were so robust that even flight attendants, who had been systematically denied access to the system, organized their movement around the basic principle of the family wage in the 1970s. The campaign for higher pay, stricter work rules, a better retirement, and more time off inspired a generation of rank-and-file flight attendants to get involved with their unions. When TWA flight attendant Janet Lhuillier described her union's victory in Chapter 2, for example, she focused her analysis on the core economic benefits of the family wage system: home ownership, time off for leisure, and enough money to pay for children's college education. Indeed, with slogans such as "We Are Breadwinners," flight attendants reinforced family wage ideology even as they openly critiqued its heteropatriarchal foundations. Conventional notions of domesticity influenced what activists wanted out of their careers and out of their unions even though such notions helped stigmatize flight attendants' families and devalue their labor.

Immediately after flight attendants' watershed gains, neoliberal reforms undermined the family wage system as the hegemonic model for the labor market. A family wage is an expensive commitment for an employer because high compensation rates, paid vacation, paid sick leave, and pension commitments all drive up labor costs. By 1980, large firms in Latin America and East Asia were making high-quality industrial products while paying unskilled workers far less and were thus able to undercut U.S. companies that were locked into the family wage. Therefore, and as Chapters 3 and 4 demonstrated, the political economic changes of the 1980s—deregulation and financialization—took direct aim at the family wage system and allowed companies to break their commitment to the family wage even as corporations and pro-business activists lauded traditional family values. With a new set of tools to trim compensation, airline managers reorganized the industry around a far more flexible model of employment, one that has begun to resemble casual labor in its economic and social dimensions.

Many new airline jobs are similar to casual labor because they are very low wage and part time. These practices are emerging not just among flight attendants, who had been subjected to poor compensation and short tenure before 1980, but also among the historically male-dominated labor groups that had always expected a family wage. Customer service agents, for example, were members of the International Association of Machinists at many carriers before deregulation and thus benefited from the union's commitment to the family wage system. Today at Delta Airlines, however, many employees begin their customer service careers in a non-union program called "ready reserve," where the starting wage is $9.07 per hour. Though they may fly for free on Delta flights, ready reserves have no other benefits: no health insurance, no sick pay, no vacation, and no retirement. Ready reserve is a part-time position, and workers rarely accrue more than twenty hours per week. Despite the short hours, they often work every day of the week because Delta schedules ready reserves to cover the morning or evening rushes but then sends people home during the slow midday periods. Frequent shifts make it particularly difficult to juggle a ready reserve position with other jobs, a balancing act that a maximum gross annual wage of just over $9,000 per year forces most ready reserves to perform. Indeed, since they bring home less than $200 a week and have no health insurance, most ready reserves must find at least one other full-time job to meet their families' needs, which in turn drastically reduces the amount of time available to spend with friends, children, and lovers.[10]

On the other hand, other airline jobs resemble casual labor because they require workers to spend long blocks of time on the road and outside the nuclear family. At Las Vegas–based Allegiant Airlines, for example, some pilots spend months away from home without a guaranteed break to visit friends or family. Every Allegiant pilot has a domicile city where trips begin and end and where his or her family would presumably live. But if demand for air travel temporarily moves away from that city, a pilot may be assigned to Allegiant's Virtual Domicile Base (VDB) program. In that case, the company pays for travel to a new city, which could be anywhere in the continental United States. The pilot then spends an entire schedule month in a motel near that airport and shares a rental car with one other worker. VDB pilots receive ten days off during the month, but there is no complimentary transportation home. Furthermore, pilots report that in some VDB cities, Allegiant has tended to schedule days off on the slowest days of the week— Tuesday and Saturday—and not in blocks of two or more days. Thus, even if a pilot paid to fly home, there would not be time to travel.[11]

Although some pilots choose the VDB base, often because it includes a roughly $700 per month tax-free per diem budget that a pilot can send home to family as a remittance, the vast majority are forced onto the assignment. Since seniority determines schedules, junior pilots may receive multiple VDB assignments in a row. Allegiant pays for transportation directly to the new VDB city but does not provide for a stop home on the way.[12] Therefore, some junior pilots go months at a time without a break to see their families. For VDB pilots, airline work has distinct parallels to early-twentieth-century casual labor. Itinerant groups of mostly male workers leave their loved ones and live on the road, flying long trips with short layovers and then sitting idle with other men in airport motels until Allegiant calls with the next assignment. Living far beyond the boundaries of domesticity and away from commitments to wives and children, the VDB pilots work in rhythms that transgress traditional family values.

In the vast uncertainty that Delta ready reserves and Allegiant VDB pilots face on the job, one begins to see why the discourse of family values resonates with so many workers in the twenty-first-century economy. As historian Bethany Moreton has shown in her highly original scholarship on Wal-Mart, family values provide both ideological and financial resources for people to adapt to a labor market that undermines domesticity. Describing the social role of the "Christian servant," for example, Moreton shows that evangelical Protestantism helps make low-wage labor compatible with traditional gender ideology. In one sense, Christ is a patriarch in evangelical thought, a spiritual leader who guides his followers. But he is also meek, one who rejects self-aggrandizing, decadent values and who serves his people. Emulating Christ as a servant, a man can be both the patriarch and a low-wage worker, someone who is a moral and political leader but not a breadwinner.[13] Meanwhile, a commitment to family values also provides financial security.[14] After the demise of the family wage, one job at Wal-Mart or one position at Delta Airlines on ready reserve could never support a family. Pooling the resources of five or six of those jobs, however, could. Therefore, as families struggle to live on jobs that provide four-figure annual incomes or require four-month sojourns away from home, marriage and domesticity can be key survival strategies.

Moreton's work is particularly important because it shows how cultural values have shaped white Protestants' relationship to the economy during the post-1970 period. It is less useful, however, for understanding how people of color, recent immigrants, feminists, queer people, and others cast outside the discourse of traditional family have navigated a changing economy. Flight attendants thus provide an important alternate account of lower-wage workers' response to neoliberal reforms. Activists have refused the trade-off at the core of the family values economy: that family values can replace the family wage. Flight attendants have focused instead on winning back the wages, benefits, and work rules that the airlines have taken away over the past thirty years. Therefore, although many individual flight attendants have supported the evangelical Christian movements that are the context for Moreton's work, the most distinct political trend among the flight attendant population as a whole over the past three decades has been an unwavering support for trade unionism.

The trend is consistent and unmistakable in all sectors of the airline business. Flight attendants at Spirit, Frontier, and other low-fare carriers have voted in unions. So have those at Envoy, Endeavor, Compass, PSA, and other firms that operate as subcontractors (see Chapter 6) for the major airlines.[15] At Southwest, a company that is famous for uninterrupted profitability and unmatched employee morale, flight attendants voted in the Transport Workers Union. The giant international carriers American and United, meanwhile, are also union shops. There are notable exceptions, of course. New York–based jetBlue, which is a large and relatively young airline recognized for top-notch customer service, has non-union flight attendants. There is an organizing drive under way, however, and since jetBlue pilots voted to unionize in April 2014,[16] followed shortly thereafter by pilots and flight attendants at Virgin America, the political momentum is clearly running in union activists' favor. Delta, which has fended off the labor movement in no fewer than six representation elections since World War II, remains the largest holdout.[17] The Atlanta-based carrier's willingness to pay wages that are competitive with unionized firms, and unions' historic weakness in Georgia, Florida, Louisiana, and other southern states where the majority of Delta flight attendants live, explains some of the challenge facing organizers. Nevertheless, the support for a non-union workplace among some Delta flight attendants does not reflect an industry-wide pattern.

Flight attendants at most carriers are joining a movement for social and economic change that bears a resemblance to the dynamic of the 1970s. The substance of today's flight attendant activism, however, is vastly different from the earlier upsurge. Though flight attendants at Virgin America, Frontier, and Compass are building their own unions just as Pan Am, Continental, and TWA activists did, the breadwinner wage and ironclad work rules that defined flight attendants' 1970s agenda will be unattainable for a new generation that works in a deregulated, financialized industry. Additionally, because of far greater age, gender, class, and racial diversity among today's flight attendants, newer activists do not necessarily share their predecessors' goals. Most 1970s flight attendants were young white women who lived in close proximity to the family wage system and for whom home ownership, college education, leisure time, and a secure retirement were realistic prospects. But because they face an economy that is defined by casual labor practices—the low-paid, part-time, temporary jobs that require constant moves—contemporary flight attendants may not see home ownership, kids' college, and a secure retirement as their most pressing needs. While they respond to a different set of urgencies, newer flight attendants are broadening the horizons of the movement, taking up new issues that were beyond the immediate concern of the white, middle-class workers who were the previous generation's majority.

The View from the Ninth Floor: Sexuality, Race, and Activism among Young Flight Attendants

Union representation is as important to many flight attendants today as it was to the activists of the 1970s. But as the culture and economics of the industry change, flight attendants are joining the movement for different reasons than they did forty years ago. Before deregulation, the airline industry was a place for privileged workers. Many jobs, including those of international flight attendants, required a college education and the ability to speak multiple languages, and most airline positions came with free health insurance, a pension, and a family wage. Because of those perks, and because the overwhelming majority of managers with the power to hire and fire were white, the airline industry remained overwhelmingly white until 1980. With the rise of casual labor practices, however, and as low-wage subcontractors employed an ever greater share of the workforce, airline workers have become a far less privileged group that includes many more workers of color. Growing diversity brings a new imperative for the flight attendant union movement. As the streets erupted in a bitter struggle over police violence and mass incarceration in 2015, activists demonstrated that dominant ideas about race and sexuality have drastically limited young Latino and black people's social and economic mobility. Racist and heteropatriarchal ideology presents young workers of color with immense challenges when they come to work for the airlines. Unions' intervention in the politics of race and sex is thus crucial for a new generation of flight attendants who are trying to turn their jobs into lifetime careers.

Few flight attendants better illustrate the stakes of the contemporary movement than Unwav Dante Harris, who is a young African American man and an activist in the Association of Flight Attendants (AFA) at United Airlines. Harris began doing union work in the early 2000s, when he was commuting into the airline's San Francisco crew base. Like many at United, Southwest, and Virgin America who fly to work to avoid the astronomical rents in the Bay Area, Harris lived in a distant city with lower housing costs—in his case, near Burbank in southern California. Despite the hassle of a three-hundred-mile commute to the union office on the airline's jammed Los Angeles–San Francisco shuttle, Harris began giving up precious days off to help build AFA soon after United hired him.[18]

Though he dedicated most of his early activism to the contractual rights of newly hired flight attendants, Harris argues that race was the motivating factor in his decision to join the movement. Explaining why he became an activist, Harris began the story of his political journey in a place where no United flight attendant would ever want to be: on the ninth floor of United's world headquarters in suburban Chicago. He first saw the ninth floor after being summoned there during the nine-week training program that all flight attendants must complete before they begin flying. A call to the ninth floor is usually the last experience a trainee has at United because the offices of human resources, labor relations, and corporate security—the groups that collaborate on employee interrogations and terminations—are immediately outside the elevator. As Harris's heart pounded that day, the elevator doors opened, and one of United's only African American training supervisors stood outside. Harris was unexpectedly confused, however, as she looked not stern but humiliated. During their brief interaction, the supervisor questioned Harris about his stylish and well-trimmed goatee:

> The black woman supervisor looks disgusted—like she has been put up to it by white managers. She says to me, "We just got to the point where we can have corn rows. Can you just wait until you get out to the line to wear the goatee?"

The supervisor quietly pushed Harris to tone down his look, presumably because when combined with his braids, his fit muscular frame, and his dark complexion, the goatee made Harris seem threatening to white passengers— or even to white employees. Harris indicated that he would comply with her request and then quickly removed himself from the situation, as he was so humiliated that he was starting to cry:

> There are only three times I have cried in my career as an adult and this was one of them. I was like, "Why do I have to shave when the white guys don't?" A white guy in the uniform manual has a goatee and it is in my face.

Harris was shaken as he witnessed one of the few African American women who had made it into airline management giving up her authority in front of a subordinate, an inversion of the corporate hierarchy to which a white manager would not be subjected. Speculating that white higher-ups had forced her to invent a racist dress code that clearly violated her own integrity, Harris watched as the supervisor contradicted United's employee appearance manual, which explicitly allowed men of all racial backgrounds to have facial hair. As Harris cried while riding the elevator back downstairs, he wanted to quit.

He of course refused that urge, recognizing that being a black flight attendant would have to be about learning to stand up to management strategically while remaining employed to fight another day.

As he describes a personal experience with overt racism, and as he cites that racism as a reason to build his union, Harris contradicts the story that major corporations tell about race and about unions in the twenty-first century. Employers often point to ambitious, successful young people of color like Dante Harris as evidence that companies value diversity and that corporate managers—rather than unions—are black and brown people's most important ally in the struggle against inequality. As sociologists Frank Dobbin and John Sutton have shown, after victories by the social movements of the 1960s and 1970s, companies have used a "profit framing" to insist that they value diversity.[19] Recognizing that they could no longer reserve managerial and front-line positions for white men, employers began to accommodate feminist and antiracist claims by arguing that a broader swath of social and cultural perspectives would help companies compete in a global economy that values difference and innovation. Recruiting a young black man for a profession made up mostly of white women would, according to profit framing, make United Airlines a more competitive corporation. United would thus be more interested in hiring and retaining Harris than it would in hiring and retaining a white flight attendant, which would make a union even less necessary for Harris than for his white coworkers.

Harris's experience at the company tells a far different story. From his first days on the job, Harris was forced to respond to explicit and inequitable treatment from both managers and coworkers. When he was called to the ninth floor of corporate headquarters, for example, Harris was already in the middle of another contentious situation while completing flight attendant training. During the program, recruits live with colleagues in hotel-like suites on a campus next to United Airlines' world headquarters. Shortly after classes began, rumors circulated that Harris's suite mates—both of whom were nineteen-year-old gay white men—were regularly having sex in the bedroom that the airline had provided them. United's corporate sexual harassment program strictly forbade sexual relations on company property. Flight attendants could have sex in their layover hotel rooms while off duty but not while sharing space with other recruits at the conference center. If United could prove that a trainee violated the no-sex policy, that person would be fired immediately.

Harris purposely avoided feeding the rumor mill about his suite mates to protect his own career and was thus disturbed to be pulled out of emergency procedures training—in which flight attendants face grueling drills for in-flight fires, bomb threats, and postcrash evacuations—and summoned to the ninth floor. Harris described how the ensuing investigation pitted him against managers and flight attendants.

> They said, "Mr. Harris, come upstairs now." They put me in a room with the other three trainees accused of sexual harassment and left us there. They didn't question us. They just let me sit there with the accused. They made it look like I was the accuser. They put me by myself then and threatened to fire me if I didn't talk. . . . They were all fired, and no one talked to me for the last three weeks of training, calling me homophobic and a gay hater. They told us all we couldn't talk—so I couldn't talk about the questioning and . . . I didn't say anything. . . . They shamed my parents when they came for my flight attendant graduation, saying I was homophobic. . . . All of the others involved were white.

In the days after the interrogation and firings, Harris's white colleagues seemed not to consider that he was also in the process of being singled out and threatened because of his sexuality. Instead, because he was a young black man who sometimes wore hip-hop gear when he was off duty, they figured him to be hypermasculine and homophobic, the source of gay white men's oppression rather than another young person who—given the goatee intervention—was also navigating the airlines' sexual repression. When managers left Harris in an interrogation room and pressed him to testify against his peers, and when his coworkers shamed an African American family who was proud of their son for winning access to a career at an esteemed company with few black employees, Harris faced the same barriers as a flight attendant that other young black men were facing across the economy and society. Corporate diversity discourse would not protect Harris from that treatment.

Worried that his job was in jeopardy after the tumult in the training center, Harris turned to the AFA for support and began an activist career that would quickly carry him to the top of the union. The child of labor activists, Harris recognized that in some cases, unions had opened doors for black workers in segregated industries. Harris grew up in New York City with a father and an uncle who were activists in the Amalgamated Transit Union, an organization that made headlines during the Cold War as a hotbed of black labor radicalism. As a child, Harris always wanted to be a union president, something that seemed honorable and achievable in a black New York labor family in the 1980s despite the growing power of the pro-business activist movement. Given that family past, Harris sought out mentors in AFA Council 11 in San Francisco when he reported for his first day on the line and began taking classes on bargaining and arbitration at the National Labor College while he flew. After he built up enough seniority to transfer to United's Los Angeles flight attendant base, Harris connected with local African American labor and political leaders, who helped him kick off his first campaign for his local's presidency in 2008. Harris lost that race, but he stayed in permanent campaign mode and eventually defeated the incumbent president during the next electoral cycle in 2011.

Harris's career as a flight attendant demonstrates that unions are particularly important because they can provide access to careers that had been systematically denied to African Americans. Activism, after all, brought black flight attendants to the airline industry. In 1959, after a pressure campaign from local leaders in New York, Margaret Grant became the first African American stewardess for a major airline when she joined TWA. Energized as the race barrier was broken in the revered airline industry, the Congress on Racial Equality staged a pro-TWA march through Harlem to publicize Grant's hire among African Americans.[20] Initial access to the industry, however, revealed new struggles for black flight attendants. In 1967, for example, Joanne Fletcher testified to civil rights investigators from the state of New York that she had encountered a pattern of systematic discrimination against dark-skinned black women. Fletcher was eventually hired by Eastern Airlines but had previously had applications accepted by multiple other carriers, only to be rejected after meeting company recruiters in person.[21] Thirty years after Fletcher's case, white people's implicit and explicit anxieties about black men's hairstyles, skin color, and masculinity would jeopardize Dante Harris's career. Like the earlier generation of black women, Harris turned to workplace activism to protect his job.

In an era when unions have faced daunting economic setbacks, Harris's career illuminates their relevance to a new generation of flight attendants. Labor activism has helped prevent the airlines from being another industry that is locked off to young African American men like Harris. The loss of the family wage, the loss of free health insurance, and the loss of a secure retirement are a disappointment to Dante Harris, as they are to his white colleagues. And in a deregulated, financialized industry, Harris's access to the comforts of middle-class life is fleeting, as it is for every flight attendant. Nevertheless, Harris owns a home and continues to build seniority after eighteen years in the business. For young African American men who face disproportionate discrimination in the labor market, the security of a union job like Harris's is rare and hugely important. Therefore, while focusing on middle-class white workers makes the loss of the family wage and the decline of union power the central narrative of the recent history of the airline industry, Harris's activism points to the unions' enduring strength. Harris's accomplishments begin to explain why young flight attendants at Virgin America, Frontier, and so many other airlines have bucked political economic trends and voted for union representation.

"Are You Getting Hustled?": The Airline Pension Crisis and the Politics of the Aging Body

During his career as a union leader, Dante Harris has confronted cultural assumptions about young workers' bodies and sexualities. Harris's success as an activist, however, does not mean that young people's issues are the only task for today's flight attendant leaders. Instead, the emergence of casual, low-wage employment practices has made aging workers' issues increasingly central to the movement's agenda. Before 1980, the family wage system kept the airline workforce relatively young. People worked through young adulthood and the middle years and then used their retirement benefits to leave the workforce as old age approached. But as affordable retirement benefits have vanished from the airlines and other industries, employees must continue to work, balancing long hours of labor against the physical process of aging. Working full time well into one's elder years presents a challenge because the culture and economy of the United States continue to privilege youth. Therefore, whereas the 1970s flight attendant upsurge was in part a response to the exploitation of young women's bodies, today's activists—some of whom walked the picket lines in the 1970s—are invigorating the movement as they confront the exploitation of aging bodies.

The airlines' ongoing effort to reduce their labor costs has been particularly hard on older flight attendants. The root cause of most senior workers' financial distress has been the termination of major carriers' defined benefit pension plans, programs that had been a key feature of the family wage system. Employees who worked full time for a whole career—which most companies defined as thirty years—would receive a fixed monthly payment after retirement. The amount of that payment was usually similar to a worker's monthly wage before retirement. Because they were guaranteed the benefit, and because most flight attendants spent their whole paychecks as providers for their families, pension beneficiaries rarely set aside extra money for retirement. After the crisis of September 11, 2001, and as they faced new competition from lower-cost upstarts like jetBlue and Frontier, most of the major carriers announced that they would terminate their defined benefit pension plans. The airlines planned to replace the benefits with defined contribution pension plans—which are often called 401(k)s—that are far cheaper for employers and transfer the risk of retirement savings away from the company and to workers.

Flight attendants at United, US Airways, Northwest, Delta, and other carriers that terminated their defined benefit pension plans had some protection. The Employee Retirement Income Security Act (ERISA), which Congress passed in 1974 to shield older workers at troubled firms, created an entity called the Pension Benefit Guarantee Corporation (PBGC), which would nationalize companies' pensions in the event of financial distress. While the PBGC would provide baseline pension coverage for employees, the amount the government would pay was capped, and any additional benefits won through collective bargaining would not be protected. Therefore, ERISA provided no insurance for many of the enhanced benefits that flight attendants had won during the upsurge of the 1970s. Furthermore, PBGC payments were of little help to flight attendants in the middle of their careers, those who had not worked long enough for full pension eligibility under the old system but who lacked enough future working years to build up their 401(k)s. As a result of the cutbacks facing middle- and full-seniority employees, two-thirds of flight attendants at United Airlines lost half of their expected retirement income during the pension termination process, a move that also dumped $23 billion of unfunded pension liabilities on taxpayers.[22]

The pension termination was a traumatic experience for workers who had thought that they could count on a secure retirement. Terry Sousoures, a San Francisco–based flight attendant for United Airlines, became emotionally elevated as she described her employer's actions in 2005. Sousoures was a veteran of labor unrest in the airline industry, having been fired from United in 1985 when she refused to cross the picket line in a coalition strike between pilots and flight attendants. After AFA helped her and other strikers win their jobs back, Sousoures became a lifelong union activist. Sousoures is a nuts-and-bolts trade unionist, someone who tends not to show her emotions and who is most comfortable in the minutiae of contract language and federal safety regulation. It was thus unnerving to see her lose her composure when the subject of pensions came up in our interview. Halfway through her technical explanation of ERISA pension regulation, Sousoures became visibly distraught: "Losing my pension is the worst feeling. I can't make up for what I lost. I feel like I can't grow old." Sousoures paused, falling silent. "I want to kick and scream and cry about it."[23]

Angered and motivated by the pain of coworkers like Terry Sousoures, flight attendants countermobilized against the pension termination. Senior flight attendants led the charge, since they were the primary targets of the cutbacks. Though some of these older women had helped build the movement forty years ago, their new campaign looked far different from 1970s flight attendant activism. During the sexual revolution, the airlines had made flight attendants' bodies a centerpiece of their public image. Selling young women's youth, attractiveness, and sexual availability, managers insisted that stewardessing should be a temporary, low-paid job for a girl who would eventually settle down and domesticate. Activists responded by refusing to bare their bodies for the airlines' exploitation and by insisting that they deserved a family wage, lifetime employment, and a secure retirement like all other airline workers. But forty years later, after the family wage and the retirement benefits have vanished, flight attendants' bodies have changed, as people are now forced to work well into their old age. The activists of the 2010s, therefore, have made the aging body a foundation of their politics, presenting it as an archive of exploitation and as the center of a demand for more resources.

Nowhere was the aging body more visible than in the activist work of a group of senior flight attendants from Los Angeles who called themselves the Stewardesses Stripped. Joining forces in 2005, the Stewardesses Stripped came together to publicize the pension termination and to demand economic relief for older workers. Activists soon became famous for a series of stewardess-themed pin-up girl calendars in which models appeared half-naked in sexually provocative poses. By including the word "stewardess" in the title of the calendars, the group referenced the sexual objectification that all older flight attendants confronted when they began their careers in the 1960s and 1970s. But instead of using young models who would look like stewardesses from the previous era, the older activists posed, baring the bodies of women in their fifties and sixties. The Stewardesses Stripped clearly had fun dressing up, just as many senior flight attendants did when they put on their Valentino or Pucci or Halston uniforms decades ago at the beginning of their careers. However, the group was also defiant, presenting the graying, sagging, and scarring that occurred over forty years on bodies that, because of the pension termination, faced having to work long into old age.

Humor, sexual innuendo, and anger work together in the text and image for each month. For the October 2007 page, for example, the caption reads, "Our retirement benefits are going up in smoke. It's time to sound the alarm!" and appears under the image of a burlesque-clad flight attendant in her fifties straddling a vintage hook-and-ladder fire truck.[24] "Are you getting hustled?" the caption for another month in 2007 asks. "Don't get caught behind the 8-ball," reads the text that frames an image of an older flight attendant in stilettos and panties splayed across a billiard table while suggestively stroking a pool cue. Making an even more historically salient reference, a different month's caption below a nearly nude, aging flight attendant in fishnets and a tiara asks, "Coffee, tea, or me without a pension?" The layout alludes to the 1968 pulp novel *Coffee, Tea, or Me*, which titillated audiences with an embellished account of the sexual exploits of a young, attractive stewardess.

The bold work of the Stewardesses Stripped caught the eye of the public. Flight attendants and other activists scrambled to buy the pin-up girl calendars, T-shirts, and other merchandise from the group's online store. The project also received its share of negative feedback; some critiques came from older flight attendants who had always presented themselves as genteel and lady-like and who saw the art as inappropriately risqué, while others came from those who saw humor as an insensitive response to the economic crisis. Responding to the positive and negative commentary, Georgia Nielsen, a forty-two-year veteran flight attendant for United Airlines before her retirement in 2002 and the official historian of the Association of Flight Attendants, argues that humorous, sexually explicit art leveled a pointed, indignant political protest:

> These women are angry. They know exploitation of their bodies and they have just turned it around! They are saying, "I am sixty and I have been violated. You have taken my clothes. You have taken what I need. You are putting me out here with promises made and not kept, and I am going to show you what this looks like."[25]

By condemning "promises made and not kept," Nielsen demonstrates that the Stewardesses Stripped took the domain of morality that had been a foundation of the family values economy and turned it against major employers. Corporations had used morality to justify the economic changes that took place during senior flight attendants' careers, arguing that deregulation and financialization would create new opportunities for hardworking American families. Commitment and personal responsibility were among the core values that employers had mobilized. But in this case, the airlines took a group of women who had been required to display their bodies for airline profits in the 1960s and 1970s and forcibly stripped them of their retirement, breaking the commitment that management had made to support these women in their old age. Arguing that activists were saying "you have taken my clothes" and "I am going to show you what this looks like," Nielsen frames the Stewardesses Stripped as a moral response to a corporate act of sexually inflected economic violence.

While the Stewardesses Stripped made political art to publicize older flight attendants' crisis, activists built new infrastructure to back up the protest. In 2004, for example, workers formed the first union for retired flight attendants, the Retiree Association of Flight Attendants (RAFA). Signing up one thousand members in the first locals in San Francisco and Los Angeles, the new union served two purposes.[26] First, it mobilized retirees to bolster their younger peers' activism, bringing the experience and energy of retired flight attendants to today's picket lines and contract disputes. Second, RAFA activists went to their state legislatures and to Washington to demand legislative protection for current and future retirees, working to block the courts and the airlines from making further cutbacks to flight attendants' remaining pension benefits and defending the Social Security system that all flight attendants depend on. Building a movement within and beyond the workplace around the interests of older workers, RAFA continues to charter new locals—opening London and Honolulu chapters in 2012 and canvassing Portland and Miami to connect retirees in 2013[27]—and to augment active flight attendants' grassroots activism with retiree ranks.

Retired flight attendants' activism reveals the complex role that age plays in the twenty-first-century labor market. Most of the new jobs created in the airline industry and in other sectors of the economy are far better suited to younger workers than they are to older ones. Low pay and scant benefits require people to work longer hours. Temporary and seasonal work compels people to move long distances to find new jobs. Jobs that force people to move frequently, to stay up late, to get up early, and to perform physically demanding labor without access to medical care favor a young body. But without sufficient pay to save for retirement and without the income that a defined benefit pension plan guarantees, many young workers are going to have to work until they are old, and in some cases very old, when they will inevitably need the paid sick leave and medical insurance that fewer and fewer jobs provide. Therefore, and as the Stewardesses Stripped insisted in an art project about their aging bodies, advocacy for aging workers must be a core of twenty-first-century workplace activism.

Conclusion: Toward a New Coalition Politics for Airline Unions

Recent flight attendant activism has engaged the airline workplace through a broad set of alliances. For Dante Harris, the African American labor and political establishment in Los Angeles provided the mentorship and grassroots organizing network that helped him become president of his Association of Flight Attendants local. Similarly, the Retiree Association of Flight Attendants supports the movement for economic security for all seniors, especially the campaign to defend Social Security, Medicare, and other social safety net programs for older people. For both Harris and the leaders of RAFA, trade unionism has been the foundation of a political practice that has overcome immense odds. Their success demonstrates that despite the hurdles that face today's contract negotiators, collective bargaining is a necessary component of the effort to contest the family values economy. But as

Harris and the RAFA activists also show, collective bargaining is no longer sufficient as the sole foundation of the struggle for economic justice; it must be complemented with coalition-based activism that engages the world outside the workplace and beyond the boundary of the airline industry.

Coalition building has allowed airline activists to make substantive advances in the twenty-first century. For example, there are a handful of Delta Airlines stations where ready reserve customer service agents make more than the standard wage of $9.07 per hour. In Oakland, California, workers start at $12.17.[28] The pay premium is the result of a local living-wage law that covers all workers at the airport.[29] Although unions were a driving force behind the ordinance, the campaign opted not to pursue traditional collective bargaining as an economic strategy. Most people on the front lines at the Oakland Airport are marginal workers: young people, elders, recent immigrants, women of color, and others who struggle with the constant unpredictability of a deregulated, financialized economy. Turnover is high in many airport positions, and because of their age, race, and documentation status, most employees feel insecure in the workplace.

Union leaders recognized that such vulnerability would make the contentious, time-consuming process of certifying a traditional union unworkable, especially at a company like Delta, where managers had thwarted organizing efforts by flight attendants, mechanics, and other more privileged workers. Thus, rather than base their effort solely at the airport, activists teamed up with religious leaders, immigrant rights groups, and racial justice organizations to engage workers in their neighborhoods, in their churches, and through grassroots social service agencies. Although an individual corporation was not the primary target of the campaign as it would have been in conventional collective bargaining, trade unionism heavily influenced the movement: the bid for a wage hike and better work rules—the standard topics in most contract talks—was at the core of rank-and-file organizers' effort to engage their coworkers on the job.[30]

The coalition in Oakland deepened the argument about family and work that flight attendants have been making since the 1970s. Jobs for those who serve food, empty the trash, and load baggage at the airport leave people with scant resources. The Oakland activists explicitly argued that ideas about race, immigration, and class have justified workers' precarity, making long hours and low wages seem natural and reconciling the contradiction between the American value of hard work and the clear failure of airport jobs to deliver the material rewards that work is imagined to provide.

Like the flight attendant union movement, the Oakland campaign also challenged employers' effort to use ideas about sexuality and family to rationalize the tenuousness that racism and anti-immigrant policies produce. Most low-wage airport jobs require what flight attending always has: commuting long distances to work, toil at all hours of the day, the blurring of physical and emotional labor, and a tightrope walk to balance work with loved ones' emotional and economic needs. Since the early 1970s, the ideology of domesticity has explained those stresses not as the result of falling real wages and a much longer workday, but as the consequence of families with the wrong values. Rejecting that moral explanation for poverty, flight attendants and the Oakland activists have shown that regardless of people's values, most twenty-first-century jobs require people to live far beyond the boundary of the heteropatriarchal nuclear family. Workplace-based social movements must thus explicitly engage the changing nature of marriage, domesticity, and kinship as they push for better pay, because these cultural categories have been the central venue for debates about economic change. To motivate people to organize at work, as flight attendants for Virgin America and other successful new airlines have, social activists must move the needs of today's flexible new families from the margin to the center of the bid for a fairer economy, just as they have in four decades of flight attendant activism.

METHODOLOGICAL APPENDIX

Researching Contemporary History

Since the early 1970s, neoliberal reforms have transformed the production of knowledge about political economy.[1] Deregulation, privatization, and other market-oriented policy changes have made it considerably more difficult to procure accurate information about big business.[2] As Chapter 4 argues, for example, financialization reduced the number of stakeholders with the power to influence airlines' operational practices. When Carl Icahn, Frank Lorenzo, Alfred Checci, and other Wall Street bankers staged hostile takeovers of major carriers in the 1980s, they bought off boards of directors, fired existing management teams, closed crew bases, and locked out unionized workers. As the new executives eliminated jobs, many employees—both in middle management and among the rank and file—were forced to leave the industry on short notice, which prevented them from continuing to intervene in airlines' affairs from the inside. Rapid staffing changes and an increasingly insulated corporate decision-making process have meant that there are far fewer informants with the access to privileged information that had previously been crucial for scholars who study economic and social change. To meet the challenge of a business environment that often obscures good data, this project uses an interdisciplinary methodology that has three parts: ethnography, archival research, and historical analysis of legal and legislative documents.

The most important factor in the research strategy for this book is my own lifelong connection to the airline industry. From the time that I was a small child, I had a strong interest in aviation. By the early 1980s, and with the support of patient parents, I was taking weekly trips to the airport in my hometown—Minneapolis–St. Paul International—to watch the planes take off and land. Those years were politically turbulent, and on more than one occasion I stood and watched throngs of angry Eastern Airlines flight attendants, pilots, and ground workers chanting, "EASTERN YES! LORENZO NO!" and selling buttons and T-shirts with Lorenzo's name circled and crossed out. The strikes at Eastern, TWA, Continental, and other carriers were on the television news with great regularity, and for an aviation-centered young person, they were the background of my childhood.

I eventually turned that interest into a career, and in September 1998, I was hired as a flight attendant for United Airlines, flying out of the Chicago, Boston, and San Francisco crew bases during a five-year career. I became a union activist soon after I joined the company, and in June 2001 I was elected council representative for Association of Flight Attendants Council 11 in San Francisco. Through my work as an internal organizer and grievance representative, I made connections to union leaders at most of the major and regional airlines. Many of those people had participated in the women's, gay, and lesbian liberation movements and had led the flight attendant upsurge of the 1970s. By the year 2000, those seasoned activists had become political and intellectual mentors for my younger generation of union leaders. After I left the airline industry, and once I began doing research for my Ph.D. dissertation in American studies, many of those mentors agreed to become informants for my work. The ethnographic component of the book is, therefore, not a random sample of flight attendants. Instead, I intentionally interviewed activists who had played pivotal roles in many of the industry's most transformative moments.

For the approximately thirty activists who were respondents for the project, I conducted what Mary Jo Maynes, Jennifer Pierce, and Barbara Laslett have theorized as "life history interviews."[3] Instead of using a detailed, standardized questionnaire for all participants and limiting interviews to oral historical accounts of particular organizing drives or strikes, I structured the interviews with open-ended questions that aimed to uncover information about each respondent's entire life course. Those questions included but were not limited to the following: What was your family life like as a child? Why did you become a flight attendant? Why did you get involved in political activism? How has your job and your activism shaped your relationship to your friends, lovers, and children? By asking these general questions, I let the flight attendants decide which events they thought were most important in their personal lives as well as in the history of the airline industry. The interviews were all relatively long; the shortest took place in a single two-hour sitting, and several stretched over multiple meetings on multiple days. I let all the activists choose the setting for their interviews, which allowed me to conduct ethnographic fieldwork at our meetings. One flight attendant, for example, cooked me dinner in the kitchen of the house that she had bought with one of the big raises of the late 1970s. Another took me to the Kansas City law firm where she had helped plan a strike. An activist who was not a flight attendant but who had worked with flight attendants in the gay liberation movement allowed me to conduct our entire interview where he worked: the engine repair shop at United Airlines' maintenance base in San Francisco. The visual and spatial context provided an interpretive tool that deepened my understanding of activists' descriptions of their own lives.

Every flight attendant I interviewed was passionate as she or he described the challenge of being an activist in a deregulated, financialized industry. But while those recollections provided detail and nuance that would never have been available in an archive or a newspaper, my respondents' emotional investment in the subject matter also suppressed information. All of the interviewees for the book had been dispossessed in some way, losing their careers, being forced to move away from family and friends, or being stripped of their pensions. Dispossession provoked visceral anger in these workers—anger at airline managers, at union leaders, and even at coworkers and friends who had different reactions to trauma. Because of this painful context, some activists used the interview process as a platform to "set the record straight"—and to advocate for their own version of deeply contested events. One person was highly transparent about the fact that she had prepared for the interview and had decided ahead of time which details about her union's past she would reveal and which she would hide. "For official purposes, you have to tell the version of the story you want to last," she told me as we began to talk.[4]

That flight attendant's strategic narration by no means invalidates her testimony. Instead, it provides an incitement to search for other "versions of the story" that might complement or contradict her analysis. Archives facilitated that search and thus became the book's second methodological foundation. A number of professionally curated collections have extensive holdings about the major airlines from the post-1970 period. The Tamiment Library Wagner Labor Archives at New York University, for example, possesses troves of information from the flight attendant unions at Pan Am, Eastern, Southern, TWA, and other major carriers. The Tamiment offers generous travel fellowships, and after winning one of those grants, I spent a month doing full-time research in its collection. In other cases, unions manage their own collections: the Association of Professional Flight Attendants at American Airlines employs a professional archivist at its Dallas headquarters to catalog its historical documents, and the Association of Flight Attendants houses much of its recent material in its local union offices. Both APFA and AFA were gracious in granting me access to those materials. APFA, for example, allowed me to spend a week working long days in its archive, using the scanner, the copier, and the coffeemaker even as activists were busy crafting an emergency response to their employer's economic crisis.

Although traditional collections with finding aids provided much of the data for this project, the airline industry's recent instability has limited the scope of those archives and has produced wide lacunae in their holdings. In 1997, for example, TWA flight attendants decided to change unions. After a long and often bitter disagreement over which union would better meet flight attendants' needs, the IAM, which became the victor in the dispute, stopped paying rent on the previous union's office. The landlord terminated the lease for nonpayment and dumped the contents of the office—including the union's archive—into a landfill.[5] Therefore, there is no professionally curated archival collection of the materials from TWA flight attendants' daunting and headline-making journey through the 1980s. Copies of some of those documents still exist in private collections, and the holdings of Mary Ellen Miller, Kaye Chandler, and Paula Mariedaughter were therefore crucial to the development of Chapter 4 of this book.

Like their trade union counterparts, the major carriers also have archives. Delta and American, for example, house their records in sprawling museums that celebrate these companies' role as innovators in global aviation. But after the contentious politics of the past four decades, and because employers have been reticent to share information that could benefit the push for labor, environmental, and safety regulation, the airlines provide only deeply restricted access to their materials. Delta Airlines, for example, granted me access to only documents dating from 1941 or earlier, which despite the prompt and charming response from the company's archivists, was wholly unhelpful to a scholar studying the post-1970 period.

Corporations undoubtedly restricted the flow of information as they broke commitments to cities, workers, and retirees. Nevertheless, the ensuing disputes left a dense paper trail. That trail, which exists in the courts, in congressional records, and in the media, provides the third methodological foundation for this book. By the early 1980s, changing managerial practices in the airline industry provoked a flurry of lawsuits between individual carriers, unions, former executives, shareholders, the Securities and Exchange Commission, consumer groups, and overseas governments. As those cases wove their way through federal district courts, the appellate courts, and even the U.S. Supreme Court, they produced reams of documentation. During the same period, and although Ronald Reagan's presidency is sometimes remembered as uncontested, Democrats—many of whom were still solidly pro-union and from self-identified working-class districts—held a majority in one or both houses of Congress. They assailed Reagan's antilabor agenda and convened congressional hearings on most of the period's airline disputes, which produced tens of thousands more pages of sworn testimony from managers, workers, union leaders, and regulators. Those materials, and the throng of *Wall Street Journal* reporters who meticulously covered one of the most tumultuous industries in one of the most tumultuous periods in the financial history of the United States, provide information that fills many of the gaps in archival collections and in individual workers' recollections of the period. Therefore, while scholars will probably never know exactly what Wall Street financiers said to their lawyers as they mobilized against airline unions, documents from the courts, Congress, the SEC, and the media provide a fairly clear picture of how money and power flowed through their enterprises.

The wealth of information about the ongoing crisis in the airline industry reveals that writing contemporary history—which this book most certainly is—can be a rigorous, methodical process even though it is contested. The history of the present comes with undeniable pressures. Most of the stakeholders described in this project are still alive and are deeply invested in the narrative that I have produced. Regardless of whether those stakeholders are elite airline CEOs or grassroots union organizers, they are staunch advocates for their own political positions and are committed to refuting their opponents' ideas. Nevertheless, as they made their arguments, corporate managers, union leaders, feminists, and queer activists delivered a wealth of information about the contemporary period. Although Carl Icahn, for example, left no formal archive of his involvement with Continental, TWA, and other airlines, he told his story to the public in vivid detail. Whether on the pages of *Cosmopolitan* magazine or on the witness stand in Congress, he admitted that he wanted to drastically reduce flight attendant wages and to enforce deeper cuts on flight attendants than on other airline workers. In Icahn's case, historians don't need to search the archives for a smoking gun, because he admitted both the motivation and the method for the crime. There is, of course, far more to Icahn's story than he presented on the pages of a fashion magazine, which is why I used ethnographic, archival, and legal and legislative research to offer a different framework for the contemporary period than that of Icahn and his Wall Street cohort. By using an interdisciplinary methodology, this book offers a thorough explanation for the history of the present while preserving the complexity of the period.

NOTES

ABBREVIATIONS

APFAA	Association of Professional Flight Attendants Archives
JL	Janet Lhuillier private collection
MEM	Mary Ellen Miller private collection
PM	Paula Mariedaughter private collection
TLWLA	Tamiment Library Wagner Labor Archives

INTRODUCTION

1. Narrative derived from Elizabeth Skrondal, personal interview, March 18, 2005.

2. "Strike Report: U.S. Airlines under the Railway Labor Act" (Washington, DC: Department of Labor Bureau of Labor Statistics, 2007), 1–2.

3. Eric Klinenberg, *Going Solo: The Extraordinary Rise and Surprising Appeal of Living Alone* (New York: Penguin, 2013), 5.

4. Wendy Wang, Kim Parker, and Paul Taylor, "Breadwinner Moms," Pew Research Social and Demographic Trends, May 29, 2013, available at http://www.pewsocialtrends.org/2013/05/29/breadwinner-moms/, accessed June 2, 2013.

5. David Leonhardt, "The North-South Divide on Two-Parent Families," *New York Times,* June 11, 2015, A3.

6. For a thorough analysis of the relationship between falling real wages and the reorganization of family life in global cities, see Saskia Sassen, "Economic Restructuring in the American City," *Annual Reviews of Sociology* 16 (1990): 465–490.

7. Wage data for all airline trades from Trans World Airlines, *Average Annual Wage Data from the Big 5 Airlines,* date omitted but current to 1972, Tamiment Library Wagner Labor Archives, New York University (hereafter cited as TLWLA).

8. Kathleen M. Barry, *Femininity in Flight: A History of Flight Attendants* (Durham, NC: Duke University Press, 2007), 15–16.

9. McGuire v. Trans World Airlines, Inc., 535 F. Supp. 1283, No. 70 Civ. 3947 (IBW), May 10, 1982, 10–16.

10. Ibid., 17–18.

11. Ibid., 19–23.

12. Ibid., 49–53.

13. Georgia Panter Nielsen, personal interview, August 18, 2006.

14. Barry, *Femininity in Flight*, 111–114.

15. For a discussion of the economic differences between stewardess retirement benefits and those of male airline workers, see William Lindner, Letter to Fredric Simpson, June 12, 1974, TLWLA. See also McGuire v. Trans World Airlines, Inc., 10–16.

16. For a particularly sharp analysis of how cultural ideas about femininity rendered stewardesses' labor invisible and in turn justified stewardesses' disproportionately low wages, see the analysis of emotional labor in Arlie Russell Hochschild, *The Managed Heart: Commercialization of Human Feeling* (Berkeley: University of California Press, 1983).

17. For a thorough analysis of the political economy of 1960s airline advertising, see Barry, *Femininity in Flight*, 176–179.

18. Ibid., 111–114.

19. Ibid., 169.

20. "Tentative Pact Reached at Continental Airlines," *New York Times,* December 16, 1980, B19. Wages converted from 1980 to 2012 dollars using the rate of inflation based on the Consumer Price Index.

21. For a thorough analysis of the relationship between the family wage, sexism, and the modern middle class, see Dorothy Sue Cobble, *The Other Women's Movement: Workplace Justice and Social Rights in Modern America* (Princeton, NJ: Princeton University Press, 2005).

22. Kim Phillips-Fein argues that big business's rise to power in the 1970s borrowed elements of its mass media and political strategy from the leftist social movements of the 1960s. Thus, she uses the term "pro-business activism" to describe business's new intervention in the 1970s. See Kim Phillips-Fein, *Invisible Hands: The Making of the Conservative Movement from the New Deal to Reagan* (New York: W. W. Norton, 2009), chap. 9.

23. For an especially apt use of neoliberalism as a historical category to contextualize deregulation, see the cogent discussion of "accumulation by dispossession" in David Harvey, *The New Imperialism* (Oxford: Oxford University Press, 2003), chap. 4.

24. For a summary of the political and economic context of the rise of evangelical Christian politics in the 1960s, see Lisa McGirr, *Suburban Warriors: The Origins of the New American Right* (Princeton, NJ: Princeton University Press, 2002), 217–261.

25. Bethany Moreton, *To Serve God and Wal-Mart: The Making of Christian Free Enterprise* (Cambridge, MA: Harvard University Press, 2009), 5.

26. Robert O. Self, *All in the Family: The Realignment of American Democracy since the 1960s* (New York: Hill and Wang, 2012), 17–46.

27. Data on pay cut proposal from "TWA/Ozark Proposed Merger and Its Effect," *Off the Line,* Summer 1986, 13, Mary Ellen Miller private collection.

28. Christopher Lasch, *A Haven in a Heartless World* (New York: Basic Books, 1977).

29. Association of Flight Attendants Employee Assistance Program, *Selected Results from a Survey of Flight Attendants' Post 9/11 Views about Their Jobs and Careers* (Washington, DC: Association of Flight Attendants, 2003).

30. Edward Epstein, "United Airlines Capitulates on Partners Issue: Full Benefits Worldwide for Gay, Lesbian Couples," *San Francisco Chronicle,* July 31, 1999, final ed., A1; see also Harriet Chiang, "American Adds Benefits for Domestic Partners: Airline Joins United in Offering Full Coverage," *San Francisco Chronicle,* August 6, 1999, final ed., A19.

31. For a detailed summary of the process that led to the rapid decline in union membership rates in the 1980s, see Jeremy Brecher, *Strike!* exp., rev., and updated ed. (New York: PM Press, 2014), 243–288.

32. Nicole Raeburn, *Changing Corporate America from the Inside Out: Lesbian and Gay Workplace Rights* (Minneapolis: University of Minnesota Press, 2004).

33. Lisa Duggan, *The Twilight of Equality? Neoliberalism, Cultural Politics, and the Attack on Democracy* (Boston: Beacon Press, 2003), 50.

34. Dean Spade, "What's Wrong with Trans Rights?" in *Transfeminist Perspectives in and beyond Transgender and Gender Studies,* ed. Anne Enke, 184–194 (Philadelphia: Temple University Press, 2012).

CHAPTER 1

1. For a thorough analysis of that history, see Kathleen Morgan Barry, *Femininity in Flight: A History of Flight Attendants* (Durham, NC: Duke University Press, 2007), 159, 165–173.

2. "Strike Report: U.S. Airlines under the Railway Labor Act" (Washington, DC: Department of Labor Bureau of Labor Statistics, 2007), 1–2.

3. Wage data for all airline trades from Trans World Airlines, *Average Annual Wage Data from the Big 5 Airlines,* date omitted but current to 1972, Tamiment Library Wagner Labor Archives, New York University (hereafter cited as TLWLA).

4. Anna Clark, *The Struggle for the Breeches: Gender and the Making of the British Working Class* (Berkeley: University of California Press, 1995), 198–215.

5. Ibid., 221–227.

6. For a thorough analysis of the labor strategies of airline ground crews, as well as wage data for ground service workers and machinists, see Liesl Miller Orenic, *On the Ground: Labor Struggle in the American Airline Industry* (Champaign-Urbana: University of Illinois Press, 2009), 135–143, 191–209.

7. Margot Canaday, *The Straight State: Sexuality and Citizenship in Twentieth-Century America* (Princeton, NJ: Princeton University Press, 2011), 142–152.

8. For a comprehensive analysis of the connections between Fordism, the suburban home mortgage, race, and sexuality, see Grace Kyungwon Hong, *The Ruptures of American Capital: Women of Color Feminism and the Culture of Immigrant Labor* (Minneapolis: University of Minnesota Press, 2006), 67–106.

9. Elaine Tyler May, *Homeward Bound: American Families in the Cold War Era* (New York: Basic Books, 1988), 6–9.

10. Kathy Lynch, personal interview, August 16, 2006.

11. Janet Lhuillier, personal interview, March 19, 2008.

12. Trans World Airlines, *Average Annual Wage Data from the Big 5 Airlines.*

13. Janet Lhuillier, personal interview, March 19, 2008.

14. Kaye Chandler, personal interview, August 6, 2008.

15. Trans World Airlines, Advertisement, *New York Times,* date unknown, Winter 1970–1971, Paula Mariedaughter private collection (hereafter cited as PM).

16. Paula Mariedaughter narrative based on Paula Mariedaughter, personal interview, June 24, 2008.

17. Trans World Airlines, photograph, date unknown, likely Winter 1969–1970, PM.

18. On the Stewardesses for Women's Rights, see Barry, *Femininity in Flight*, 174–210.

19. Mary Ellen Miller narrative based on Mary Ellen Miller, personal interview, March 19–20, 2008.

20. Barry, *Femininity in Flight*, 150–152.

21. The Air Transport Association quickly sued the EEOC for issuing this decision, blocking the EEOC from definitively denying that sex was a bona fide occupational qualification for the stewardess profession until 1968. See Barry, *Femininity in Flight*, 165–169.

22. Ibid., 169.

23. For a much more detailed analysis of gay men's place in the history of flight attendant labor, see Phil Tiemeyer, *Plane Queer: Labor, Sexuality, and AIDS in the History of Male Flight Attendants* (Berkeley: University of California Press, 2013), 60–80.

24. Ibid., 109–135.

25. McGuire v. Trans World Airlines, Inc., 535 F. Supp. 1283, No. 70 Civ. 3947 (IBW), May 10, 1982, 11.

26. Phil Tiemeyer, "Male Stewardesses: Male Flight Attendants as a Queer Miscarriage of Justice," *Genders—Online Edition* 45 (2007), available at http://www.genders.org/g45/g45_tiemeyer.html.

See also Phil Tiemeyer, "Manhood Up in the Air: Gender, Sexuality, and Corporate Culture in Twentieth Century America" (Ph.D. diss., University of Texas, Austin, 2007).

27. McGuire v. Trans World Airlines, Inc., 8.

28. Richard Wagner, personal interview conducted with Phil Tiemeyer, August 5, 2008.

29. Wage data from *Agreement between Trans World Airlines, Inc. and the Flight Attendants in the Service of Trans World Airlines, Inc. as Represented by The Transport Workers Union of America, AFL-CIO, Signed July 29, 1976* (New York, 1976), 9–12.

30. William Lindner, Letter to Fredric Simpson, June 12, 1974, TLWLA.

31. For a detailed history of the differences between flight attendant and purser pay and the relationship between those differentials and the Equal Pay Act, see McGuire v. Trans World Airlines, Inc., 10–16.

32. Ibid., 8.

33. William Brigham, Letter to TWA flight attendants, December 4, 1970, TLWLA.

34. William Brigham, Letter to all pursers, December 4, 1970, TLWLA.

35. Peggy McGuire, Letter to Buddy Ledger, July 29, 1974; Peggy McGuire, Letter to Matty Guinan, July 30, 1974, TLWLA.

36. William Lindner, Memorandum to all American Airlines local TWU presidents, April 18, 1975, TLWLA.

37. Transport Workers Union Local 552 Executive Board, Mailgram to American Airlines flight attendants, date missing, likely third week in June 1975, TLWLA.

38. William Lindner, Letter to all Air Transport Division representatives, July 9, 1975, TLWLA.

39. American Airlines, Letter to all American Airlines flight attendants, September 2, 1975, TLWLA.

40. Association of Flight Attendants, cover letter for tentative agreement, January 31, 1976, TLWLA.

41. Transport Workers Union Local 552, Flyer titled "Your New Contract Gains," May 1976, TLWLA.

42. Transport Workers Union Local 552, tentative agreement vote results, May 27, 1976, TLWLA.

43. Mike McGraw, "Tentative Agreement Averts TWA Strike," *Kansas City Star,* June 5, 1976, Mary Ellen Miller private collection (hereafter cited as MEM).

44. Negotiating committee data from Transport Workers Union, "TWA Strike Deadline Near; U.S. Mediators Press Talks," *TWU Express,* June 1976, 1, MEM.

45. Ernest Mitchell, Letter to Fredric Simpson, March 17, 1976, TLWLA.

46. *Business Week,* August 9, 1976, TLWLA.

47. Transport Workers Union, untitled tentative agreement summary, June 1976, New York, TLWLA.

48. Alice Hartmann, "Union Not Sure TWA Contract Will Pass," *Kansas City Star,* June 8, 1976, MEM.

49. Ernest Mitchell, Letter to TWA flight attendants, June 11, 1976, TLWLA.

50. Mary Ellen Miller, personal interview, March 19–20, 2008.

51. Arthur Teolis, Letter to TWA flight attendants, June 14, 1976, TLWLA.

52. Mike McGraw, "Tentative Agreement Averts TWA Strike," *Kansas City Star,* June 5, 1976, MEM.

53. Transport Workers Union Local 551 Executive Board, Letter to TWA flight attendants, June 7, 1976, TLWLA.

54. Transport Workers Union, Tentative agreement vote results, June 26, 1976, TLWLA.

55. Transport Workers Union Local 552 Executive Board, Letter to all TWA flight attendants, July 30, 1976, TLWLA.

56. Arthur Teolis, Letter to Ernest Mitchell, July 26, 1976, TLWLA.

57. Repps B. Hudson, "Convention Flights Threatened," *Kansas City Star,* date unknown, likely July 20–23, 1976, MEM.

58. Flight statistics from *The Official Airline Guide—North American Pocket Guide,* April 1, 1974, courtesy of www.departedflights.com, available at http://www.departed flights.com/MCI74p1.html.

59. Petition from Kansas City–based TWA flight attendants to TWU Local 551, June 21, 1976, TLWLA.

60. Flyer for Los Angeles flight attendant layovers, author unknown, exact date unknown, likely late July/early August 1976, TLWLA.

61. Judy Marsalis, Letter to Ernie Mitchell, July 26, 1976, TLWLA.

62. Petition from TWA flight attendants to Ernest Mitchell, approximately July 28, 1976, TLWLA.

63. Transport Workers Union Local 552 Executive Board, Letter to all TWA flight attendants, July 30, 1976, TLWLA.

64. Transport Workers Union, Tentative agreement vote results, August 20, 1976, TLWLA.

65. Wage data from *Agreement between Trans World Airlines, Inc. and the Flight Attendants in the Service of Trans World Airlines, Inc.,* pp. 9–12. All annual wage data presented here are based on an assumption that a flight attendant will be compensated for one thousand hours per year, which is the basic standard that many airlines use to evaluate the cost of "book rate" hourly wage rates in contracts. Individual flight attendants, however, may fly more or less than this number; thus it is a ballpark figure and not indicative of what every flight attendant took home. The one-thousand-hour pay figure remains constant throughout this book. Inflation data from the Consumer Price Index as calculated by the Bureau of Labor Statistics.

66. D. J. Crombie, Letter to all union leaders at TWA, July 26, 1976; Transport Workers Union Local 552 Executive Board, Letter to all TWA flight attendants, July 30, 1976, TLWLA.

67. Committee for an Equitable Contract, flyer, Dallas, Texas, Committee for an Equitable Contract, 1975, Archives of the Association of Professional Flight Attendants, Euless, Texas.

68. Robert Callahan, Letter to Eastern Airlines flight attendants, date unknown, likely early 1977, TLWLA.

CHAPTER 2

1. I take the concept of the second shift from Arlie Russell Hochschild and Anne Machung, *The Second Shift: Working Families and the Revolution at Home,* rev. ed. (New York: Penguin Books, 2012).

2. Dorothy Sue Cobble, *The Other Women's Movement: Workplace Justice and Social Rights in Modern America* (Princeton, NJ: Princeton University Press, 2004), 7–8.

3. Ibid., 139–143.

4. Ibid., 140.

5. Ibid., 140–142.

6. For a signature text by a labor historian and leader of the rank-and-file democracy movement, see Peter Rachleff, *Hard-Pressed in the Heartland: The Hormel Strike and the Future of the Labor Movement* (Cambridge, MA: South End Press, 1993).

7. For the broader historical context of the rank-and-file democracy movement, see Nelson Lichtenstein, *State of the Union: A Century of American Labor* (Princeton, NJ: Princeton University Press, 2002), chap. 6.

8. Janet Lhuillier, personal interview, March 19, 2008.

9. Gender data from Independent Federation of Flight Attendants (IFFA), "Peace and Goodwill, Bread and Freedom," June 1, 1986, Janet Lhuillier private collection (hereafter cited as JL).

10. Mary Ellen Miller, personal interview, March 19–20, 2008.

11. Ernest Mitchell, Letter to Arthur Teolis, October 21, 1976, Tamiment Library and Wagner Labor Archives, New York University (hereafter cited as TLWLA).

12. Arthur Teolis, Letter to all TWA flight attendants, October 22, 1976, TLWLA.

13. Matty Guinan, Letter to Victoria Frankovich, Arthur Teolis, and Jim Tuller, October 27, 1976, TLWLA.

14. Traces of these affinity groups appear in Transport Workers Union Air Transport Division archive Box 112, Folders 3 and 4, TLWLA. During the summer of 1975, for example, flyers from a group called the Committee for a Fair Contract appear and then vanish. By early 1976, the flyers had the slogan "How Much More Can You Take" and may have been from the same or other dissident groups, TLWLA.

15. Elizabeth Metrick, Letter to Patt Gibbs, August 27, 1976, TLWLA.

16. Tommie Hutto-Blake, "TWU President's Newsletter," March 17, 1977, TLWLA.

17. Tommie Hutto-Blake, Letter to Kathy Knoop, February 4, 1977, TLWLA.

18. Tommie Hutto-Blake, Letter to Barbara Feeser, March 7, 1977, TLWLA.

19. Transport Workers Union Local 551, Summary of election results, February 8, 1977, TLWLA.

20. Transport Workers Union Local 551, Summary of election results, March 22, 1977, TLWLA.

21. Association of Professional Flight Attendants, Untitled newsletter, April 1977, TLWLA.

22. Transport Workers Union Local 552, Summary of election results, May 3, 1977, TLWLA.

23. "National Mediation Board Elections for Flight Attendants" (Washington, DC: National Mediation Board, 1976), TLWLA.

24. Work rule data from Transport Workers Union Local 550, 1972 contract negotiations dossier, exact date unknown; data current to 1972, TLWLA.

25. Ibid.

26. Line guarantee parameters from *1996–2001, 2001–2006 Agreement between United Air Lines, Inc. and the Flight Attendants in the Service of United Air Lines, Inc. as Represented by The Association of Flight Attendants* (Chicago, 1996), 50.

27. "Continental Airlines Debtor-in-Possession Emergency Work Rules Highlights," in "Oversight Hearing on Effect of Bankruptcy Actions on the Stability of Labor-Management Relations and the Preservation of Labor Standards," Hearing before the Committee on Education and Labor, U.S. House of Representatives, October 5, 1983, 29.

28. Independent Union of Flight Attendants, Summary of opening contract proposal to Pan Am, December 1977, TLWLA.

29. Independent Union of Flight Attendants, Contract settlement summary, April 1979, TLWLA.

30. Independent Union of Flight Attendants, Contract settlement summary, June 1979, TLWLA.

31. Negotiations under the Railway Labor Act normally happen only after union contracts expire. APFA moved to speed up the bargaining process to get cash in flight attendants' hands as quickly as possible. See Association of Professional Flight Attendants, Letter to American Airlines flight attendants, July 27, 1977, Archives of the Association of Professional Flight Attendants, Euless, Texas (hereafter cited as APFAA).

32. Robert Crandall, Letter to American Airlines flight attendants, July 11, 1977, APFAA.

33. Work rules varied by carrier but reflected APFA's bargaining goals by the mid-1980s. Only Pan Am, for example, had a truly "four-tier" reserve system, but American and United implemented seniority-based multi-tier rotating systems. American eventually implemented a low-time "on availability" system for flight attendants who wanted to fly less. US Airways allowed reserves to "pass" on the reserve list to tailor their schedules to individual tastes for hours worked and layover destinations.

34. See, especially, David Montgommery, *The Fall of the House of Labor* (Cambridge: Cambridge University Press, 1987), chap. 5.

35. Strikes, nevertheless, did happen under the RLA; airline workers spent over twenty-two hundred days on strike in the 1970s. Airline management thus used a second strategy to improve its hand against unions during walkouts. Because the federal regulation of the airlines in 1933 explicitly banned new entrants from joining the marketplace, blocking banks and wealthy individuals from starting airlines to cherrypick TWA and its peers, the big carriers were immune to losing market share to upstarts during protracted strikes. All that the airlines needed to accomplish to weather labor unrest was find the money to keep paying bills when walkouts blocked them from selling tickets. To do this, airline management invented the "mutual aid pact" in 1958. The administrations of all the regulated airlines agreed to pony up cash to a general fund based on the size of their operations. If employees walked out, the struck airline would automatically be entitled to cash payments to cover lost revenue. Compensation was based on the solvency of the fund, and by the mid-1970s airlines could expect to recover 35 percent to 50 percent of their normal operating income in a no-strings-attached grant, making it much easier for management to sit back and wait for striking employees to run out of money. Data from "How Airlines Make Money by Not Flying: Facts about Inter-airline Strike Subsidies" (Washington, DC: Air Line Pilots Association, date unknown, approx. 1974), APFAA.

36. Background data on expedited negotiations from "Collective Bargaining in the Airline Industry, Report 546" (Washington, DC: U.S. Department of Labor Bureau of Labor Statistics, 1979), 4, APFAA.

37. "Record for 1977," *630 News*, March/April 1978, 3, Mary Ellen Miller private collection (hereafter cited as MEM).

38. "Text of Accelerated Negotiation Agreement," *630 News*, March/April 1978, 3, MEM.

39. "Company's Opening Proposals," *630 News*, March/April 1978, 4, MEM.

40. "IFFA's Opening Proposals," *630 News*, March/April 1978, 5, MEM.

41. "IFFA Negotiating Committee Members," *630 News*, March/April 1978, 8, MEM.

42. "New Contract Improvements," *630 News*, November/December, 1978, 1, MEM.

43. Mike McGraw, "Tentative Package Reached; Flight Attendants, TWA Settle on Early Agreement," *Kansas City Star*, July 14, 1978, MEM.

44. Contract negotiator and soon to be IFFA president Vicki Frankovich published an exhaustive, moment- to-moment analysis of contract talks in IFFA's newspaper, the *630 News*. That series of publications, plus e-mail contact with Frankovich herself, provides the basic timeline here. See Vicki Frankovich, "Never Have So Few; Spent So Much; Only to Lose the Good Will of So Many!" *630 News*, April 1983, 3, MEM.

45. Ibid., 3.

46. Ibid., 3–4.

47. Ibid., 4–5.

48. Kenneth M. Jennings, *Labor Relations at the New York Daily News: Peripheral Bargaining and the 1990 Strike* (Westport, CT: Praeger, 1993), 2.

49. Frankovich, "Never Have So Few," 5.

50. This sequence of events is described in Frankovich, "Never Have So Few" and then reconfirmed in e-mail correspondence between the author, Miller, and Frankovich on March 24 and 26, 2009.

51. Mary Ellen Miller, personal interview, March 19–20, 2008.

52. Frankovich, "Never Have So Few," 5.

53. Mary Ellen Miller, personal interview, March 19–20, 2008.

54. Ibid.

55. Data from pre-concessionary contract between General Motors and the United Automobile Workers in 1988 and adjusted for inflation. Data presented in Ruth Milkman, *Farewell to the Factory: Autoworkers in the Late Twentieth Century* (Berkeley: University of California Press, 1997), 25.

56. Flight Attendant wage data from *Agreement between Trans World Airlines, Inc. and the Flight Attendants in the Service of Trans World Airlines, Inc. as Represented by the Independent Federation of Flight Attendants, Signed April 12, 1983* (New York, 1983), 12.

57. Janet Lhuillier, personal interview, March 19, 2008.

58. Independent Federation of Flight Attendants (IFFA), "Peace and Goodwill."

59. Judith Stacey, *Unhitched: Love, Marriage, and Family Values from West Hollywood to Western China* (New York: New York University Press, 2011).

60. Elizabeth H. Pleck, *Not Just Roommates: Cohabitation after the Sexual Revolution* (Chicago: University of Chicago Press, 2012).

61. Wendy Wang, Kim Parker, and Paul Taylor, "Breadwinner Moms," Pew Research Social and Demographic Trends, May 29, 2013, available at http://www.pewsocialtrends.org/2013/05/29/breadwinner-moms/, accessed June 2, 2013. For popular references to the study, see, for example, Catherine Campbell, "U.S. Women on the Rise as Family Breadwinner," *New York Times*, May 29, 2013, B1.

62. Campbell, "U.S. Women."

CHAPTER 3

1. I borrow the concept of a pro-business activist movement from Kim Phillips-Fein, who argues that business interests were successful in creating political change in the 1970s in part by borrowing political strategies from the progressive social movements of the 1960s. Kim Phillips-Fein, *Invisible Hands: The Making of the Conservative Movement from the New Deal to Reagan* (New York: W. W. Norton, 2009), chap. 9.

2. Ibid., 214–221. See also Robert O. Self, *All in the Family: The Realignment of American Democracy since the 1960s* (New York: Hill and Wang, 2012), 302–303.

3. "Continental Airlines Debtor-in-Possession Emergency Work Rules Highlights," in "Oversight Hearing on Effect of Bankruptcy Actions on the Stability of Labor-Management Relations and the Preservation of Labor Standards," Hearing before the Committee on Education and Labor, U.S. House of Representatives, October 5, 1983, 29.

4. Calculated at one thousand hours per year, the Emergency Work Rules starting wage was exactly the same as the average TWA flight attendant total compensation from 1957. But since the TWA flight attendant workforce was junior in the 1950s, the difference between starting and average compensations was quite small. Also, without any rigs, overall compensation at Continental would have been even lower than it seemed in 1983. Thus the average 1957 and starting 1983 wage make a fair comparison. Wage data from Trans World Airlines, *Average Annual Wage Data from the Big 5 Airlines,* date omitted but current to 1972, Tamiment Library and Wagner Labor Archives, New York University (hereafter cited as TLWLA).

5. Nelson Lichtenstein, *State of the Union: A Century of American Labor,* rev. and exp. ed. (Princeton, NJ: Princeton University Press, 2013), 214–245.

6. Thomas K. McCraw, *Prophets of Regulation: Francis Adams, Louis D. Brandeis, James M. Landis, and Alfred E. Kahn* (Cambridge, MA: Belknap Press of the Harvard University Press, 1984), 237.

7. "Savings and Loan Policies in the 1970s and 1980s," Hearings before the Committee on Banking, Finance, and Urban Affairs, U.S. House of Representatives, October 1–3, 1990 (Washington, DC: U.S. Government Printing Office, 1990), 44.

8. Self, *All in the Family,* 248–275.

9. To understand how AEI and other conservative think tanks were selling a new political identity to solve the economic problems of the United States in the 1970s, see Jason M. Stahl, *Right Moves: The Conservative Think Tank in American Political Culture since 1945* (Chapel Hill: University of North Carolina Press, 2016).

10. Ibid.

11. Phillips-Fein, *Invisible Hands,* 215–216.

12. Stahl, *Right Moves.*

13. For a historical analysis of the foundations of airline regulation, see McCraw, *Prophets of Regulation,* chaps. 2 and 6.

14. For a summary of the functions of CAB regulation, see Lee James Van Scyoc, "Effects of the Airline Deregulation Act on Market Performance: Price, Capacity, and Profits" (Ph.D. diss., University of Nebraska, Lincoln, 1987).

15. Paul Ignatius, Testimony, "Regulatory Reform in Air Transportation," Hearings before the Subcommittee on Aviation of the Committee on Commerce, Science, and Transportation of the U.S. Senate, June 15, 1976, 1018.

16. Donald Nyrop, Testimony, "Regulatory Reform in Air Transportation," April 4, 1977, 1484–1490.

17. John W. Snow, "The Problem of Airline Regulation and the Ford Administration Proposal for Reform," in *Regulation of Passenger Fares and Competition among the Airlines,* ed. Paul W. MacAvoy and John W. Snow (Washington, DC: American Enterprise Institute, 1977), 31.

18. William T. Coleman, Testimony, "Regulatory Reform in Air Transportation," April 7, 1976, 229.

19. McCraw provides a thorough intellectual history and political genealogy of Alfred Kahn in *Prophets of Regulation,* chap. 6.

20. McCraw, *Prophets of Regulation,* 226. To understand the relationship between government regulation and Kahn's theory of marginal pricing, see Alfred E. Kahn, *The Economics of Regulation: Principles and Institutions,* rev. ed. (Cambridge, MA: MIT Press, 1988).

21. Kahn drew national attention for his success in using deregulation to bring down utility rates while leading the New York Public Service Commission. See McCraw, *Prophets of Regulation,* 243–256.

22. Senator Edward M. Kennedy, Testimony, "Regulatory Reform in Air Transportation," April 6, 1976, 170–172.

23. Ibid., 163.

24. United Airlines, *System Timetable, Effective April 27th, 1969* (Chicago: United Airlines, 1969), 59, available at http://www.timetableimages.com/ttimages/ua/ua69/ua69-30.jpg, accessed July 25, 2014.

25. Francis A. O'Connell, Prepared statement, "Regulatory Reform in Air Transportation," April 1976, 1271.

26. Kennedy, Testimony, "Regulatory Reform in Air Transportation," 163.

27. Snow, "Problem of Airline Regulation," 31.

28. Kennedy, Testimony, "Regulatory Reform in Air Transportation," 164.

29. Frank Lorenzo, Testimony, "Regulatory Reform in Air Transportation," April 12, 1976, 513.

30. Ibid., 514.

31. Ibid., 516.

32. Ibid., 514.

33. Ibid., 510.

34. David R. Graham and Daniel T. Kaplan, "Airline Deregulation Is Working," *Regulation,* May/June 1982, 32.

35. Independent Union of Flight Attendants, Newsletter for Pan Am flight attendants, June/July 1981, TLWLA.

36. Independent Union of Flight Attendants, Newsletter for Pan Am flight attendants, August/September 1981, TLWLA.

37. "Tentative Pact Reached at Continental Airlines," *New York Times,* December 16, 1980, B19.

38. Bill Sing, "TIA's Motion's Gaveled Down at Noisy Continental Meeting," *Los Angeles Times,* May 7, 1981.

39. "CAB Backs Texas Air on Its Bid for Continental," *New York Times,* March 3, 1981.

40. Sing, "TIA's Motion Gaveled Down."

41. Ibid.

42. Tim Waters, "Continental Airlines Chief Is Found Shot to Death," *Los Angeles Times,* August 10, 1981.

43. Ibid.

44. Bill Sing, "Continental: What Lorenzo Won?" *Los Angeles Times,* October 14, 1981.

45. Bill Sing, "Continental, Texas Air OK Financial Merger," *Los Angeles Times,* July 14, 1982.

46. Associated Press, "Troubled Continental Ending All U.S. Flights till Tuesday," *New York Times,* September 25, 1983.

47. "Continental Airlines Debtor-in-Possession Emergency Work Rules Highlights," 29.

48. "Continental Air to Keep 4,200 on Job," *New York Times,* September 26, 1983.

49. Thomas J. Lueck, "More Flights Cancelled in Strike at Continental," *New York Times,* October 4, 1983.

50. "Continental Resumes Talks with Pilots," *New York Times,* November 30, 1983.

51. Janet R. Jakobsen, "Sex + Freedom = Regulation: Why?" *Social Text* 23.3–4 (Fall/Winter 2005): 286.

52. Ibid., 292.

53. Kathi Weeks, *The Problem with Work: Feminism, Marxism, Antiwork Politics, and Postwork Imaginaries* (Durham, NC: Duke University Press, 2011), 54.

54. Ibid., 64.

55. Ibid.

56. Charles Murray, *Losing Ground: American Social Policy, 1950–1980* (New York: Basic Books, 1984), 219–236.

57. Ibid., 160.

58. Ibid., 160, 158.

59. Ibid., 228.

60. To understand the pressures of long hours and declining pay on middle-class and professional families, see, for example, Arlie Russell Hochschild, *The Time Bind: When Work Becomes Home and Home Becomes Work,* rev. ed. (New York: Holt Paperbacks, 2001). To understand the impact on poor families, see Sandra Morgen, Joan Acker, and Jill Weigt, *Stretched Thin: Poor Families, Welfare Work, and Welfare Reform* (Ithaca, NY: Cornell University Press, 2009).

CHAPTER 4

1. The sequence of events between Frankovich and Icahn were relayed in sworn testimony in front of the House Aviation Subcommittee during the November 21, 1985, proceedings for the hearing "Airline Mergers and Acquisitions: The Question of Labor Protection." Testimony reproduced in "TWA/Ozark Proposed Merger and Its Effect," *Off the Line,* Summer 1986, 13, Mary Ellen Miller private collection (hereafter cited as MEM).

2. For an interdisciplinary cultural analysis of financialization, see Randy Martin, *Financialization of Daily Life* (Philadelphia: Temple University Press, 2002); On the connections between the economic crisis of the 1970s and financialization, see Greta Krippner, *Capitalizing on Crisis: Political Origins of the Rise of Finance* (Cambridge, MA: Harvard University Press, 2012).

3. Karen Ho describes this process as "the shareholder value revolution." See Karen Z. Ho, *Liquidated: An Ethnography of Wall Street* (Durham, NC: Duke University Press, 2009), 123–129.

4. Ibid., 124–125.

5. Wall Street does not always react positively to news of layoffs. Amid fears that the economy is sliding toward recession, layoff news often causes share prices to decline. But

with the focus on efficiency and labor unit costs in the 1980s, austerity measures brought increased value for shareholders. See Ho, *Liquidated*, 1–2.

6. The details of the TWA flight 847 were extensively covered in the newspapers and news magazines during the period. All details in this account were widely reported, and all appear in William E. Smith, "Terror aboard Flight 847," *Time*, June 24, 2001.

7. Bryan Burrough, William Carley, John D. Williams, and Mark Zieman, "Texas Air Agrees to Purchase Trans World Airlines for $23 a Share in Cash, Debt, or $793.5 Million Total," *Wall Street Journal*, June 14, 1985, eastern ed., 1+.

8. For an analysis of the M&A boom, see Ho, *Liquidated*, 133–150.

9. "To Regulate Attempts to Acquire Control of Airlines," Hearing before the Subcommittee on Aviation of the Committee on Public Works and Transportation of the U.S. House of Representatives, June 6, 1985 (Washington, DC: U.S. Government Printing Office, 1986), 66.

10. "Continental Airlines Debtor-in-Possession Emergency Work Rules Highlights," in "Oversight Hearing on Effect of Bankruptcy Actions on the Stability of Labor-Management Relations and the Preservation of Labor Standards," Hearing before the Committee on Education and Labor, U.S. House of Representatives, October 5, 1983, 29.

11. Ibid.

12. To understand the historical roots of antibanking discourse, see Emily S. Rosenberg, *Financial Missionaries to the World: The Politics and Culture of Dollar Diplomacy* (Durham, NC: Duke University Press, 2004), chap. 2.

13. "To Regulate Attempts to Acquire Control of Airlines," 55.

14. Narrative from Drexel Burnham Lambert, "High Yield Bonds," April 24, 1985, white paper submitted as an appendix to "The Financing of Mergers and Acquisitions," Hearing before the Subcommittee on Domestic Monetary Policy, U.S. House of Representatives, May 3, 1985 (Washington, DC: U.S. Government Printing Office, 1985), 388.

15. Icahn's analysis from "Takeover Tactics and Public Policy," Hearing before the Subcommittee on Telecommunications, Consumer Protection, and Finance, U.S. House of Representatives, March 28, 1984 (Washington, DC: U.S. Government Printing Office, 1984), 184–185.

16. Ibid.

17. "To Regulate Attempts to Acquire Control of Airlines," 117.

18. All statistics from airline industry schedules are from *The Official Airline Guide*, the authoritative reference for airline schedules, as accessed through the widely referenced website www.departedflights.com. Aircraft and schedule information appears as presented by the airlines. Thus there may be some minor irregularities in the statistics I present because of the airlines' own imprecision. See *Official Airline Guide North American Pocket Guide Flight Schedules*, April 1, 1974, and *Official Airline Guide North American Desktop Edition*, November 15, 1979, available at http://www.departedflights.com/oagintro.html, accessed June 10–15, 2010.

19. My analysis of the strategic and economic decline of TWA rests on layering TWA's flight schedules from the 1970s over analysis of urbanization, financialization, and globalization in the work by Neil Smith, Saskia Sassen, and David Harvey on the 1970s. See especially Saskia Sassen, "Economic Restructuring in the American City," *Annual Reviews of Sociology* 16 (1990): 465–490, and David Harvey, *Spaces of Capital: Towards a Critical Geography* (Edinburgh, Scotland: Edinburgh University Press, 2001).

20. Financial details of the Braniff-American 727-200 deal from John Nance, *Splash of Colors: The Self-Destruction of Braniff International* (New York: William Morrow, 1984), 153–154.

21. *Official Airline Guide North American Edition,* February 15, 1985, available at http://www.departedflights.com/oagintro.html, accessed June 10–15, 2010.

22. John D. Williams, "Icahn's Group Plans to Make a Bid for TWA," *Wall Street Journal,* May 22, 1985, 1.

23. Teri Agins and Mark Zieman, "TWA Holder Icahn Tops Texas Air Bid with $24-a-Share Cash-Preferred Offer," *Wall Street Journal,* August 6, 1985, eastern ed., 1+.

24. William M. Carley, "Takeover Battle Nearly Ended in Secret Meeting, Aide to Icahn Says," *Wall Street Journal,* August 16, 1985, eastern ed., 1.

25. "Financing of Mergers and Acquisitions," 151.

26. Letter from Paul Volcker in "Issues Relating to High-Yield Securities (Junk Bonds)," Hearing before the Subcommittee on General Oversight and Investigations, U.S. House of Representatives, September 19, 1985 (Washington, DC: U.S. Government Printing Office, 1986), 8.

27. "Final Oversight Hearings on the Savings and Loan Industry in the 100th Congress," Hearings before the Committee on Banking, Housing, and Urban Affairs, U.S. Senate, August 2–3, 1988 (Washington, DC: U.S. Government Printing Office, 1988), 31.

28. Data for final Icahn transaction narrative from Daniel Hertzberg, "TWA Names Carl Icahn as Chairman but His Victory Is Seen as Bittersweet," *Wall Street Journal,* January 6, 1986, eastern ed., 1+.

29. Jeremy Brecher analyzes the relationship between the antiwar movement and the labor movement in *Strike!* rev. and updated ed. (Cambridge, MA: South End Press, 1999), chap. 7.

30. See the discussion of Kim Phillips-Fein's work in Chapter 3.

31. William M. Carley, "TWA Pilots Agree to Accept Pay Cuts of up to 20% if Icahn Acquires Airline," *Wall Street Journal,* July 3, 1985, eastern ed., 1.

32. See note 1.

33. Ibid.

34. "To Regulate Attempts to Acquire Control of Airlines," 127.

35. *Cosmopolitan* article excerpted in "Cosmo Glorifies Icahn," *Off the Line,* Spring 1988, 14, MEM.

36. "IFFA Negotiations and the Sale of TWA . . . A Chronology," *630 News,* Spring 1992, 5, MEM.

37. Data and narrative of permanent replacement worker hiring from "TWA/Ozark Proposed Merger," 13–14.

38. Ibid.

39. "IFFA Negotiations and the Sale of TWA."

40. IFFA, "Flight Attendant Union Asks Our Help in Fighting Back," flyer, July 1986, MEM.

41. "IFFA Negotiations and the Sale of TWA." See also National Mediation Board, "Strike Report: U.S. Airlines under the Railway Labor Act" (Washington, DC: National Mediation Board, 2007).

42. Mary Ellen Miller thoroughly discussed the coordination of the "sweeper flight" missions in her personal interview, March 20, 2008.

43. The category of "breadwinner" dominates every IFFA strike publication. See, for example, "Los Angeles Strike Photographs," *Off the Line,* March 1986, 13, MEM.

44. See, for example, "Marsha Smyser Agrees We Can Do It!" photograph, *Off the Line,* Spring 1989, 1, MEM.

45. Janet Lhuillier, untitled photograph, March 1986, Janet Lhuillier private collection.

46. Ibid.

47. IFFA, untitled photograph, *Off the Line,* exact date unknown, 1988, MEM.

48. To understand how conservatives approached the white working class through moral traditionalism, see the smart discussion of Richard Viguerie's activism in Kim Phillips-Fein, *Invisible Hands: The Making of the Conservative Movement from the New Deal to Reagan* (New York: W. W. Norton, 2009), 215–216.

49. For a particularly clear way that a deserving, procreative, heterosexual working class is pitted against a nonprocreative and nondomesticated elite in a labor/left publication, see Francine Cavanaugh, A. Mark Liiv, and Adams Wood, "Boom: The Sound of Eviction" (Whispered Media, 2001), DVD.

50. The McCain-Palin campaign's creation of "Joe the Plumber" and middle-class liberals' revulsion at Joe the Plumber provide a stark example of how both elite conservatives and liberals assume that white working-class people are drawn to reactionary cultural politics.

51. IFFA Negotiating Committee, "IFFAGram," April 8, 1986, 2–3, MEM.

52. IFFA Negotiating Committee, "IFFAGram," April 29, 1986, 1, MEM.

53. IFFA Negotiating Committee, "IFFAGram," May 2, 1986, 1, MEM.

54. IFFA Mailgram, May 18, 1986, MEM.

55. For a summary of Icahn's legal campaign and IFFA's defense against it, see "IFFA's Strike-Related Legal Action," *Off the Line,* October 1986, 1–3, MEM.

56. Trans World Airlines, Inc. v. The Independent Federation of Flight Attendants, 87-548, Supreme Court of the United States, 489 U.S. 426; 109 S. Ct. 1225; 103 L. Ed. 2d 456; 1989 U.S. LEXIS 1197; 57 U.S.L.W. 4283; 110 Lab. Cas. (CCH) P10, 946; 130 L.R.R.M. 2657, argued November 7, 1988, decided February 28, 1989, 3–4.

57. Dixie Daniels, personal interview, September 1, 2008.

58. For an analysis of the impact of financialization on pilots' personal and professional lives, see "Flying Cheap," *PBS Frontline,* Rick Young, dir., May 25, 2010.

59. The relationship between the rise of the service economy and the disappearance of the husband breadwinner is a key theme of Bethany Moreton's *To Serve God and Wal-Mart: The Making of Christian Free Enterprise* (Cambridge, MA: Harvard University Press, 2009), especially chap. 7.

60. Data for Icahn's 1987 privatization from William M. Carley and Teri Agins, "TWA Proposes $1.2 Billion Plan to Go Private," *Wall Street Journal,* July 23, 1987, eastern ed., 1+.

61. Data on light bulb bond affair from Linda Sandler, "TWA $300 Million Notes Secured in Part by Light Bulbs," *Wall Street Journal,* June 2, 1989, eastern ed., 1.

62. "Summary of TWA's New Demands," May 26, 1986, 1, MEM.

63. Charles Storch and Carol Jouzaitis, "United Execs Could Score Buyout Bonanza," *Chicago Tribune,* September 23, 1989, 1.

64. Charles Storch, "Bankers Bring Down United Buyout," *Chicago Tribune,* October 14, 1989, 9.

65. Narrative on the unwinding of the junk bond market from Drexel Burnham Lambert general counsel Richard J. Davis in "Leveraged Buyouts and Bankruptcy," Hearing before the Subcommittee on Economic and Commercial Law, U.S. House of Representatives, March 1, 1990 (Washington, DC: U.S. Government Printing Office, 1991), 122–125.

66. Federal Deposit Insurance Corporation, *History of the Eighties—Lessons for the Future* (Washington, DC: Federal Deposit Insurance Corporation, 2000), 187.

67. Flight Attendant wage data from *Agreement between Trans World Airlines, Inc. and the Flight Attendants in the Service of Trans World Airlines, Inc. as Represented by the Indepen-*

dent Federation of Flight Attendants, Signed April 12, 1983 (New York, 1983), 12, and *1996–2001, 2001–2006 Agreement between United Air Lines, Inc. and the Flight Attendants in the Service of United Air Lines, Inc. as Represented by The Association of Flight Attendants* (Chicago, 1996), 24.

CHAPTER 5

1. Jeremy Brecher provides a labor history of the 1980s that places the rapid decline in union membership rates in the context of public policy shifts and a changing political economy. See Jeremy Brecher, *Strike!* exp., rev., and updated ed. (New York: PM Press, 2014), 243–288.

2. Nicole Raeburn, *Changing Corporate America from the Inside Out: Lesbian and Gay Workplace Rights* (Minneapolis: University of Minnesota Press, 2004).

3. Kitty Krupat, "Out of Labor's Dark Age: Sexual Politics Comes to the Workplace," in *Out at Work: Building a Gay-Labor Alliance,* ed. Kitty Krupat and Patrick McCreery, 1–23 (Minneapolis: University of Minnesota Press, 2001).

4. Margot Canaday, *The Straight State: Sexuality and Citizenship in Twentieth-Century America* (Princeton, NJ: Princeton University Press, 2011), 137–173.

5. Flight attendant wage data from *Agreement between Trans World Airlines, Inc. and the Flight Attendants in the Service of Trans World Airlines, Inc. as Represented by the Independent Federation of Flight Attendants, Signed April 12, 1983* (New York, 1983), 12, and *1996–2001, 2001–2006 Agreement between United Air Lines, Inc. and the Flight Attendants in the Service of United Air Lines, Inc. as Represented by The Association of Flight Attendants* (Chicago, 1996), 24.

6. Association of Flight Attendants United Master Executive Council Negotiating Committee, Letter to the membership, April 9, 1996, Ed Sanford private collection.

7. The most widely circulated underground newspaper was called *The IBS,* a humorous reference to the "inflight briefing sheet," the document that provides technical data to flight attendants for each trip. See, for example, "Bend-o, Bend-o; Bend-o Come and I Wanna Contract," *The IBS* 3.2 (March/April 1997): 3, Beth Skrondal private collection.

8. James Ott, "United Remakes Itself for Global Competition," *Aviation Week and Space Technology* 147.1 (July 7, 1997): 54.

9. Stan Kiino, personal interview, November 20, 2004.

10. United filed the suit in tandem with the Air Transport Association of American (the national lobbying group for all of the airlines) and FedEx. But because United was by far the wealthiest entity with the deepest pockets—and because activists learned that it was United's management team that spearheaded the lawsuit—they chose to make United the target of the campaign.

11. Stan Kiino, personal interview, November 20, 2004.

12. To understand how conservative activists used social issues to gain control of political debate in the United States, see Donald T. Critchlow, *Phyllis Schlafly and Grassroots Conservatism: A Woman's Crusade* (Princeton, NJ: Princeton University Press, 2007). To understand how the category of "social issues" shrank from a broad catchall to a direct referent of homosexuality and abortion, see Bethany Moreton, *To Serve God and Wal-Mart: The Making of Christian Free Enterprise* (Cambridge, MA: Harvard University Press, 2009), 118–120.

13. Elizabeth Birch, "HRC Corporate Equality Index Coverage: HRC in the News" (Washington, DC: Human Rights Campaign, 1997), available at http://www.hrc.org/pressroom/cei%5Fnews.asp, accessed December 4, 2004.

212 NOTES TO CHAPTER 5

14. To make this argument about domestic partner benefits replacing the social safety net, I reference Janet Jakobsen's argument that neoliberal reforms have shifted the United States "away from the state and toward the family." See Janet R. Jakobsen, "Can Homosexuals End Western Civilization as We Know It?" in *Queer Globalizations: Citizenship and the Afterlife of Colonialism*, ed. Martin Manalansan IV and Arnaldo Cruz-Malave (New York: New York University Press, 2002), 56.

15. My argumentation about the transformation of LGBT identity in the age of neoliberalism is deeply informed by Lisa Duggan's analysis of *homonormativity* and Miranda Joseph's analysis of how the LGBT community operates as a *supplement*—in the Derridian sense—of capitalism. See Lisa Duggan, *The Twilight of Equality? Neoliberalism, Cultural Politics, and the Attack on Democracy* (Boston: Beacon Press, 2003), and Miranda Joseph, *Against the Romance of Community* (Minneapolis: University of Minnesota Press, 2002).

16. For analysis of the demonization of women of color as sexually aberrant and "dependent" on the state, and the use of this dependency as an excuse to roll back the welfare state in the 1990s, see Nancy Fraser and Linda Gordon, "A Genealogy of Dependency: Tracing a Keyword of the U.S. Welfare State," *Signs* 19.2 (Winter 1994): 314–319.

17. Joseph derives the concept of supplementarity from Derrida's work in *Of Grammatology*. See Joseph, *Against the Romance of Community*, 2–3.

18. Ibid., 3–13.

19. To understand the specific political economic function of communal discourses on the terrain of neoliberalism, see Joseph's discussion of production and performativity in ibid., 30–36.

20. Association of Flight Attendants Employee Assistance Program, *Selected Results from a Survey of Flight Attendants' Post 9/11 Views about Their Jobs and Careers* (Washington, DC: Association of Flight Attendants, 2003).

21. Narrative derived from Elizabeth Skrondal, personal interview, March 18, 2005.

22. Stan Kiino, personal interview, March 15, 2005.

23. Air Transport Association of America, Airline Industrial Relations Conference, and Federal Express Corporation v. City and County of San Francisco, San Francisco Human Rights Commission, and San Francisco Airport Commission, U.S. District Court for the Northern District of California, Case no. 97–1763 CW, 992 F. Supp. 1149; 1998 U.S. Dist. LEXIS 4837; 158 LRRM 2138; 76 Fair Employment Practice case (BNA) 1108; Employee Benefits case (BNA) 1116, 10–13.

24. Ibid., 35–36.

25. Ibid., 28–34.

26. Wage data for all airline trades from Trans World Airlines, *Average Annual Wage Data from the Big 5 Airlines,* date omitted but current to 1972, Tamiment Library Wagner Labor Archives, New York University.

27. Elizabeth Skrondal, personal interview, March 18, 2005; Stan Kiino, personal interview, March 15, 2005; Jeff Sheehy, personal interview, November 20, 2004.

28. On the political economy of corporate marketing at Pride, see Susan Craddock and Alex T. Urquhart, "Target(ing) HIV Prevention," in *Queer Twin Cities*, ed. The Twin Cities LGBT Oral History Project, 269–304 (Minneapolis: University of Minnesota Press, 2010). See also Bob Witeck and Wesley Combs, *Business Inside Out: Capturing Millions of Brand-Loyal Gay Consumers* (New York: Kaplan Publishing, 2006).

29. Beth Skrondal, Stan Kiino, and Jeff Sheehy extensively discussed the civil disobedience rallies in their interviews. See also Crispin Hollings, personal interview, November 19, 2004, and Ed Sanford and Loyd Scobee, personal interview, March 18, 2005.

30. On the HRC's role in the announcement and publicity for the boycott, see Jason B. Johnson, "S.F., Gay Rights Groups Support Boycott against United: Domestic Partner Rules Contested by Airline," *San Francisco Chronicle,* December 15, 1998, final ed., A25.

31. To understand management's Railway Labor Act case against American Airlines pilots, see American Airlines v. Allied Pilots Association, Order of Contempt, U.S. District Court for the Northern District of Texas, Wichita Falls Division, Case no. 7:99-CV-025-X. See also K. Fairbank, "Pilots Union Fined 45.5 Million for Sick-Out," *Philadelphia Inquirer,* April 16, 1999, C1.

32. Both Stan Kiino and Beth Skrondal described their elation at arriving at the Geary Street Ticket Office to see swarms of flight attendants lining up and at having to persuade police to shut down additional lanes of traffic to accommodate the size of the protest. Both claimed that police estimated four hundred attendees, and both said that previous rallies had garnered about fifty participants.

33. Association of Flight Attendants-CWA, "Directory of Media Releases," July 14, 1997, available at http://www.afacwa.org/default.asp?id=639, accessed March 8, 2010.

34. Stan Kiino, personal interview, November 20, 2004, and Kathy Lynch, personal interview, August 16, 2006. Kevin Lum discussed United's partner benefits overture, and then its silence, in detail with me in Kevin Lum, personal interview, November 21, 2004.

35. Wage data comparisons from *Agreement between Trans World Airlines, Inc. and the Flight Attendants in Service of Trans World Airlines, Inc. as represented by the Transport Workers of America, AFL-CIO, Signed July 29, 1976* (New York: Trans World Airlines, 1976) and *Agreement between the Flight Attendants in Service of United Airlines as Represented by the Association of Flight Attendants, AFL-CIO, and United Airlines, Inc.* (Chicago: United Airlines, 1997).

36. Details on the contract from *Agreement between the Flight Attendants in Service of United Airlines.*

37. Johnson, "S.F., Gay Rights Groups Support Boycott."

38. To understand how urban institutions helped shore up collective bargaining as a basis for U.S. unionism during the progressive era, see Bruno Ramirez, *When Workers Fight: The Politics of Industrial Relations in the Progressive Era, 1896–1916* (New York: Greenwood Press, 1978).

39. John Schmeltzer, "Some Partner Benefits Ordered in Airline Case," *Chicago Tribune,* May 28, 1999, Chicagoland final ed., 3; see also Edward Epstein, "Airline Keeps Leases for Now: United Wins Ruling in Battle with S.F. over Partners' Law," *San Francisco Chronicle,* August 29, 1998, final ed., A15.

40. Reynolds Holding, "S.F. Partners Law under Fire Again," *San Francisco Chronicle,* June 18, 1997, A14.

41. Sheehy and Kiino personal interviews.

42. Edward Epstein, "United Airlines Capitulates on Partners Issue: Full Benefits Worldwide for Gay, Lesbian Couples," *San Francisco Chronicle,* July 31, 1999, final ed., A1; see also Harriet Chiang, "American Adds Benefits for Domestic Partners: Airline Joins United in Offering Full Coverage," *San Francisco Chronicle,* August 6, 1999, final ed., A19.

43. Epstein, "United Airlines Capitulates."

44. Economic information on the concessions from the December 2001 informational "roadshows" on the concessions at the San Francisco Airport Marriott. The author was present at all road shows and operated trips under the new and old work rules.

45. Wendy Wang, Kim Parker, and Paul Taylor, "Breadwinner Moms," Pew Research Social and Demographic Trends," May 29, 2013, available at http://www.pewsocialtrends.org/2013/05/29/breadwinner-moms/, accessed June 2, 2013.

CHAPTER 6

1. Chantal Mouffe, *The Democratic Paradox* (London: Verso, 2000), 13.

2. Ibid., 99–100.

3. Michael J. McCarthy, "TWA Says It's in Talks with Icahn to Trade Airline Tickets for Debt," *Wall Street Journal,* January 12, 1995, eastern ed., A5.

4. TWA and affiliated parties filed dozens of lawsuits against Icahn over the Karabu venture. For legal background, see Trans World Airlines, Inc. v. Karabu Corp., U.S. Bankruptcy Court for the District of Delaware, Case no. 92-115, Adversary no. 96-40, 196 B.R. 711; 1996 Bankr. LEXIS 619; 29 Bankr. Ct. December 236, May 31, 1996.

5. "TWA/American Airline Workforce Integration," Hearing before the Committee on Health, Education, Labor, and Pensions, U.S. Senate, June 12, 2003, 34.

6. "Family Ties, Shared Success," *Flagship News* 57.3 (March/April 2001): 1+, housed at Association of Professional Flight Attendants Archives (hereafter cited as APFAA).

7. See Chapter 4 for a complete discussion of the ALPA picket crossover policy and the sale of TWA assets.

8. For a thorough, quantitative analysis of regional jet service in the United States, see Aleksandra Mozdzanowska, "Growth and Operating Patterns of Regional Jets in the United States," *Journal of Aircraft* 42.4 (July/August 2005): 858–864.

9. All data are from the published online schedules of United, American, and Delta Airlines from a peak day in the summer travel season—Thursday, June 20, 2013. The data are compiled by a user on the popular enthusiast website airliners.net and became the central data set for technical discussion of all airline operational strategies for the summer of 2013. All data are from American, Delta, and United's uploads to the Official Airline Guide, available at http://photos.airliners.net/aviation-forums/general_aviation/read.main/5750206/, accessed May 26, 2013.

10. This information came from a synopsis of the Reno Air affair by Holly Hageman, a former aide to American Airlines CEO Robert Crandall, which was posted on the official Allied Pilots Association Listserv. See Holly Hageman, "Dysfunctional Airline/Union Relations 101," Allied Pilots Association Listserv, February 8, 1999, APFAA.

11. Pilots' objections to Reno Air subcontracting are thoroughly summarized in Allied Pilots Association, "Special Report to the Membership," March 15, 1999, APFAA.

12. Jane Allen, Letter to American Airlines flight attendants, February 10, 1999, APFAA.

13. American Airlines v. Allied Pilots Association, Order of Contempt, U.S. District Court for the Northern District of Texas, Wichita Falls Division, Case no. 7:99-CV-025-X, 3.

14. K. Fairbank, "Pilots Union Fined 45.5 Million for Sick-Out," *Philadelphia Inquirer,* April 16, 1999, C1.

15. Hageman, "Dysfunctional Airline/Union Relations 101."

16. Drew Engelke, "Reno Air: Overview of the Current Situation," Memorandum from the Communications Committee of the Allied Pilots Association to all members, February 8, 1999, APFAA.

17. International Brotherhood of Teamsters, "Reno Air Teamsters Merger Committee Newsletter," April 12, 1999, APFAA.

18. "TWA/American Airline Workforce Integration," 65, 67.

19. Ibid., 10, 83–85.

20. "Airline Mergers and Acquisitions: The Question of Labor Protection," Hearing before the Subcommittee on Aviation of the Committee on Commerce, Science, and Trans-

portation of the U.S. Senate, November 21, 1985 (Washington, DC: Government Printing Office, 1986), 22, 37, 63–65.

21. These seniority data were taken from a series of charts produced by APFA for union leaders. Many flight attendants interviewed for the book noted that the charts were widely circulated among front-line flight attendants either via union listservs or in management briefings. Data taken from Association of Professional Flight Attendants, TWA merger information packet for union leaders, approximately March 15, 2001, APFAA.

22. Tommie Hutto-Blake, Letter to the APFA Board of Directors, March 21, 2001, APFAA.

23. Susan French, Letter to John Ward, February 23, 2001, APFAA.

24. Susan French, Letter to Steve Moldof, February 19, 2001, APFAA.

25. Tommie Hutto-Blake, Letter to the APFA Board of Directors, March 18, 2001, APFAA.

26. Patt Gibbs, Letter to John Ward, March 3, 2001, APFAA.

27. Association of Professional Flight Attendants, "Resolution 4," Minutes from the March 18 to March 22, 2001, Board of Directors Meeting, March 22, 2001, 1, APFAA.

28. Association of Professional Flight Attendants, "Resolution 4," 2.

29. The March 22 Protocol demanded full company seniority for TWA flight attendants, recognizing their years of TWA service for pay and vacation purposes. APFA's decision to deny TWA flight attendants' classification seniority is ultimately what set TWAers up to be laid off.

30. For a particularly poignant example of the internal debates within unions during seniority mergers, see the arbitration decision from the 1982 merger of Republic Airlines and Hughes Air West: Arthur Stark, "Opinion and Award of Arthur Stark, Arbitrator, in the Seniority Integration Dispute between the Flight Attendants of Republic Airlines and the Flight Attendants of Republic West," April 27, 1982, APFAA.

31. The Reno Air flight attendant seniority merger was itself an anomaly. In all previous mergers, flight attendants were awarded classification seniority at their new employer based either on their original date of hire or on a mathematical formula determined by a neutral arbitrator. In all of these cases, flight attendants got at least some actual bidding power from their years of service. In the Reno Air case, flight attendants got no seniority credit but were compensated in cash for their seniority. Though many flight attendants from Reno Air were angry about the deal, the severity of their case was mitigated by the overall junior status of all Reno Air flight attendants. Given that Reno Air was a new airline, its most senior flight attendant had flown for only six years. The TWA case was vastly different, as the most senior flight attendant had started in 1955, and 25 percent of TWA flight attendants had flown for over thirty years on the date of the American-TWA merger.

32. All TWA flight attendants interviewed for this project expressed anger and resentment at the IAM's choice to voluntarily waive TWA flight attendants' scope clause and Allegheny-Mohawk LPPs. For a particularly thorough and ongoing commentary on the situation, see the "Ladybug" newsletters of flight attendant Kaye Chandler and the transcript of her personal interview (August 6, 2008) for this book, Kaye Chandler private collection.

33. Robert Roach, Letter to John Ward, March 23, 2001, APFAA.

34. Robin Dotson, Letter to John Ward, April 18, 2001, APFAA.

35. Independent Union of Flight Attendants, "IUFA Update," February 17, 1981, Tamiment Library Wagner Labor Archives, New York University.

36. Robin Dotson, Letter to Richard Kasher, April 20, 2001, APFAA.

37. Robert Roach, Letter to Robin Dotson, April 23, 2001, APFAA.

38. John Ward, Letter to Robin Dotson, April 23, 2001, APFAA.

39. John Ward, Letter to Robert Roach, March 26, 2001, APFAA.

40. Since seniority summits were required by federal LPPs, they took place in every merger until 1985, when the Department of Transportation stopped enforcing LPPs. The airline industry then entered an intense period of consolidation in 1986 and 1987, most notably with the Delta-Western, Northwest-Republic, Ozark-TWA, USAir-PSA, and American-AirCal deals. Seniority summits took place on a voluntary basis in all of those deals as management continued to use the LPP system as a basic standard. Mergers at the major airline level then tapered off until the late 1990s, when American's unions avoided the summit system in both the TWA and Reno Air deals.

41. The National Labor Relations Board interprets and enforces the Wagner Act of 1935 and subsequent amendments. The board has no jurisdiction over airline workers because they are governed by the National Mediation Board, the interpreter and enforcer of the Railway Labor Act of 1926. The Riser case therefore has no official bearing on APFA's treatment of American flight attendants. It was, however, regularly cited in APFA's defense against the series of Duty of Fair Representation (DFR) lawsuits that Reno Air and TWA flight attendants filed against APFA and likely helped APFA win all DFR cases that have been decided to date. For more information, see Eleanor McNamara-Blad, et al. v. The Association of Professional Flight Attendants, Case no. 00-15846, U.S. Court of Appeals for the Ninth Circuit, filed January 11, 2002.

42. The text of the following NLRB decision thoroughly describes the legal precedents for the "time bind": Riser Foods, Inc. and Douglas F. Schreiber, and the International Brotherhood of Teamsters, AFL-CIO, Case 8-CA-21686, Case 8-CB-6465, National Labor Relations Board, November 30, 1992.

43. See http://www.iata.org/pressroom/facts_figures/traffic_results/Pages/2003-07-02-02.aspx, accessed August 2010.

44. Tommie Hutto-Blake, "All Call," March 4, 2001, APFAA.

45. Since standard industry practice—and the APFA March 22 Protocol—would grant company seniority to incoming TWA flight attendants, and since they were a largely senior group, they would be comparatively expensive to employ. Denying classification seniority to TWAers would allow the company to furlough employees at the top of the pay scale, a cost savings that other carriers were prevented from exercising due to seniority language in their union contracts.

46. Association of Professional Flight Attendants, "Agreement Prohibiting the Leveraging of TWA-LLC against APFA," December 17, 2001, APFAA.

47. Association of Professional Flight Attendants, "Agreement on Seniority Integration and Related Matters between American Airlines, Inc., and Association of Professional Flight Attendants Representing the Flight Attendants of American Airlines, Inc.," December 17, 2001, APFAA.

48. For a thorough description of the legal battle that took place over the concessionary settlement of April 2002, see the court records for Sherry Cooper, et al. v. TWA Airlines, LLC, American Airlines, Inc., and the Association of Professional Flight Attendants, 02-CV-3477 (NG) (KAM), U.S. District Court for the Eastern District of New York, 2005 U.S. Dist. LEXIS 41007, decided July 18, 2005. See also Ann M. Marcoux, et al. v. American Airlines, Inc., AMR Corp., and the Association of Professional Flight Attendants, 04-CV-1376 (NG) (KAM), filed November 13, 2006.

49. All of the data on TWA flight attendants' age and seniority were collected, analyzed, and submitted to the court by Thomas DiPrete, a Columbia University professor

contracted to assist TWAers in their class action age discrimination lawsuit against American and APFA. His research originally appeared as evidence submitted by the plaintiffs in the case *Margaret Anthony et al. vs. AMR Corporation dba American Airlines and Association of Professional Flight Attendants.* The age discrimination charge was later withdrawn and the claim rolled into the broader *Sherry Cooper, et al.* DFR lawsuit. That case was dismissed. TWAers' only remaining claims against APFA remain in the *Marcoux et al.* DFR case. See Thomas DiPrete, Declaration in the Margaret Anthony Case, 1–5, available at http://www.justice4twa.com/pdf/Columbia%20University.pdf, accessed August 2010.

50. For an analysis of how corporations have embraced the workplace racial and gender diversity that was a consequence of the 1964 Civil Rights Act, see Frank Dobbin and John R. Sutton, "The Strength of a Weak State: The Rights Revolution and the Rise of Human Resources Management Divisions," *American Journal of Sociology* 104.2 (1998): 441–476.

51. Roger Graham, personal interview, March 31, 2008.

52. Timeline and summary of the McCaskill interactions come from my personal interview with Roger Graham, who coordinated the Missouri effort.

53. For details of that commitment, see Claire McCaskill, Letter to former TWA flight attendants, October 30, 2006, APFAA.

54. Roger Graham, photograph, October 30, 2006.

55. "McCaskill Brokers Deal to Save 1,200 Jobs at American Airlines," *U.S. Senator Claire McCaskill,* December 22, 2007, available at http://mccaskill.senate.gov/?p=press_releases.

56. "The McCaskill-Bond Amendment," *Association of Flight Attendants Official Website,* Association of Flight Attendants–CWA, AFL-CIO, August 18, 2010, available at http://afaonevoice.org/images/McCaskill%20Amendment%20explanation%20FINAL%20for%20WEB.pdf.

57. Mouffe, *Democratic Paradox,* 99–105.

EPILOGUE

1. Dave Jamieson, "Virgin America Flight Attendants Vote to Join Union," *Huffington Post,* August 14, 2014, available at http://www.huffingtonpost.com/2014/08/13/virgin-america-union_n_5676228.html, accessed June 15, 2015.

2. Transport Workers Union, "Our Negotiating Committee," available at http://www.twuvx.org/OurUnion/tabid/1493/Default.aspx, accessed June 24, 2015.

3. Transport Workers Union, "2015 Industry Pay Comparison," available at http://www.twuvx.org/LinkClick.aspx?fileticket=WcjWCV7SHFw%3d&tabid=1534, accessed June 24, 2015.

4. Anna Marie Erwert, "Depressing San Francisco Median Rent Map Shows Rents Up All over the City," *San Francisco Chronicle,* March 9, 2015, available at http://blog.sfgate.com/ontheblock/2015/03/09/depressing-san-francisco-median-rent-map-shows-rents-up-all-over-the-city/, accessed June 15, 2015.

5. Jeanne Boydston, *Home and Work: Housework, Wages, and the Ideology of Labor in the Early Republic* (Oxford: Oxford University Press, 1994), 30–55.

6. John D'Emilio, "Capitalism and Gay Identity," in *The Material Queer: A LesBiGay Cultural Studies Reader,* ed. Donald Morton, 263–271 (Boulder, CO: Westview Press, 1996).

7. Colin Johnson, *Just Queer Folks: Gender and Sexuality in Rural America* (Philadelphia: Temple University Press, 2013), 85.

8. Ibid., 86–88.

9. For a cogent analysis of the consequences of the family wage for women workers, and for women's participation in the labor movement, see Anna Clark, *The Struggle for the Breeches: Gender and the Making of the British Working Class* (Berkeley: University of California Press, 1995), 198–215.

10. Delta Airlines, "Ready Reserve Customer Service Agent," available at http://www.delta.com/about_delta/delta_employment_opportunities/customer_services_reservations/rr_customer_services/index.jsp, accessed June 10, 2015.

11. As members of the International Brotherhood of Teamsters, Allegiant Airlines pilots were threatening to strike during the summer of 2015. The job action, held up in a legal dispute, had not been resolved as this book goes to press. Work rules are a core issue in the dispute, and perhaps the most hotly debated work rules issue is the VDB base program. Airline Pilot Central, the largest online discussion forum for professional pilots, has had extensive debate about the VDB program, and several VDB pilots regularly post updates about the work rules dispute there. See Airline Pilot Central Forums, Allegiant Air, page 38, July 27, 2014, available at http://www.airlinepilotforums.com/major/75731-allegiant-air-38.html, accessed June 15, 2015.

12. Pilots from across the Allegiant system discussed the frequency of multiple-month VDB assignments, and the stress that VDB basing puts on families, on February 25, 2014. Ibid., 201, available at http://www.airlinepilotforums.com/major/75731-allegiant-air-201.html, accessed June 15, 2015.

13. Bethany Moreton, *To Serve God and Wal-Mart: The Making of Christian Free Enterprise* (Cambridge, MA: Harvard University Press, 2009), 100–124.

14. To understand how the evangelical Protestant activists of the 1970–2000 period framed and advocated for the economic role that the nuclear family should play, see Moreton's discussion in ibid., 114–115.

15. For a list of airlines represented by AFA-CWA, the largest flight attendant union, see Association of Flight Attendants–CWA, "Our Airlines," available at http://www.afacwa.org/our_airlines, accessed June 10, 2015.

16. Jad Mouawad, "JetBlue Airways' Pilots Vote to Join Union," *New York Times,* April 23, 2014, B2.

17. "National Mediation Board Elections for Flight Attendants" (Washington, DC: National Mediation Board, 1976), Tamiment Library Wagner Labor Archives (hereafter cited as TLWLA).

18. Dante Harris's narrative taken from Dante Harris, personal interview, August 17, 2006.

19. Frank Dobbin and John R. Sutton, "The Strength of a Weak State: The Rights Revolution and the Rise of Human Resources Management Divisions," *American Journal of Sociology* 104.2 (1998): 441–476.

20. Kathleen Morgan Barry, *Femininity in Flight: A History of Flight Attendants* (Durham, NC: Duke University Press, 2007), 116.

21. Ibid., 118.

22. Pension termination data from Patricia A. Friend, "Protecting Pensions," Testimony, Senate Finance Committee, June 7, 2005, *Congressional Quarterly Congressional Testimony* (Washington, DC: Congressional Quarterly, 2005), 2. See also Bradley D. Belt, "Protecting Pensions in the Airline Industry," Testimony, Senate Finance Committee, June 7, 2005, *Congressional Quarterly Congressional Testimony* (Washington, DC: Congressional Quarterly, 2005), 2.

23. Terry Sousoures, personal interview, August 18, 2006.

24. "The Stewardesses Stripped 2007 Calendar" (Los Angeles: The Stewardesses Stripped, 2006).

25. Georgia Panter Nielsen, personal interview, August 18, 2006.

26. See http://www.rafa-cwa.org/RAFA/Welcome.html, accessed March 20, 2014.

27. Ibid.

28. Delta Airlines, "Ready Reserve Customer Service Agent."

29. Port of Oakland, "Social Responsibility," available at http://www.portofoakland .com/responsibility/, accessed June 20, 2015.

30. To understand how discriminatory and often illegal employment practices have become widespread in many industries, especially in the service and agricultural sectors, see Ruben J. Garcia, *Marginal Workers: How Legal Fault Lines Divide Workers and Leave Them without Protection* (New York: New York University Press, 2012).

METHODOLOGICAL APPENDIX

1. For a compelling theory of both the challenges and the opportunities of doing social research in the context of neoliberalization, see Avery Gordon, *Ghostly Matters: Haunting and the Sociological Imagination* (Minneapolis: University of Minnesota Press, 1997). See also Herman Gray and Macarena Gomez-Barris, eds., *Toward a Sociology of the Trace* (Minneapolis: University of Minnesota Press, 2010).

2. For an analysis of the particular challenges of doing post-1973 history, see Kim Phillips-Fein, "1973 to the Present," in *American History Now,* ed. Eric Foner and Lisa McGirr, 175–200 (Philadelphia: Temple University Press, 2011).

3. Mary Jo Maynes, Jennifer L. Pierce, and Barbara Laslett, *Telling Stories: The Use of Personal Narratives in the Social Sciences and History* (Ithaca, NY: Cornell University Press, 2008).

4. Off-the-record conversation with a flight attendant before an interview; name withheld on request of the flight attendant. All other testimony about her activism is on the record.

5. The narrative of the fate of the IFFA archive was reconstructed from e-mail and phone conversations with Victoria Frankovich, Kaye Chandler, and Mary Ellen Miller. Particularly important in framing the fate of the archive was an e-mail volley I had with Frankovich in the fall of 2007. Victoria Frankovich, e-mail correspondence, November 15, 2007.

SELECTED BIBLIOGRAPHY

The scholarly sources selected for inclusion in this list are those that were most influential to the argument of this book and those that define such core concepts as the following: deregulation; family values; financialization; the ideology of domesticity; neoliberalism; the resurgence of U.S. conservatism; and women's, gay, and lesbian liberationism.

Amin, Ash, ed. *Post-Fordism: A Reader*. London: Wiley-Blackwell, 1995.

Barry, Kathleen Morgan. *Femininity in Flight: A History of Flight Attendants*. Durham, NC: Duke University Press, 2007.

Bell, Daniel. *The Coming of Post-industrial Society: A Venture in Social Forecasting*. New York: Basic Books, 1973.

Bluestone, Barry, and Bennett Harrison. *The Deindustrialization of America: Plant Closings, Community Abandonment, and the Dismantling of Basic Industry*. New York: Basic Books, 1982.

Boydston, Jeanne. *Home and Work: Housework, Wages, and the Ideology of Labor in the Early Republic*. New York: Oxford University Press, 1994.

Brecher, Jeremy. *Strike!* Rev. and updated ed. Cambridge, MA: South End Press, 1999.

———. *Strike!* Exp., rev., and updated ed. New York: PM Press, 2014.

Brier, Jennifer. *Infectious Ideas: U.S. Political Responses to the AIDS Crisis*. Chapel Hill: University of North Carolina Press, 2011.

Briggs, Laura. *Reproducing Empire: Race, Sex, Science, and U.S. Imperialism in Puerto Rico*. Berkeley: University of California Press, 2002.

Brown, Gillian. *Domestic Individualism: Imagining Self in Nineteenth-Century America*. Berkeley: University of California Press, 1990.

Canaday, Margot. *The Straight State: Sexuality and Citizenship in Twentieth-Century America*. Princeton, NJ: Princeton University Press, 2011.

Clark, Anna. *The Struggle for the Breeches: Gender and the Making of the British Working Class*. Berkeley: University of California Press, 1995.

Cobble, Dorothy Sue. *The Other Women's Movement: Workplace Justice and Social Rights in Modern America*. Princeton, NJ: Princeton University Press, 2005.

Craddock, Susan, and Alex T. Urquhart. "Target(ing) HIV Prevention." In *Queer Twin Cities*, ed. The Twin Cities GLBT Oral History Project, 269–304. Minneapolis: University of Minnesota Press, 2010.

Critchlow, Donald T. *Phyllis Schlafly and Grassroots Conservatism: A Woman's Crusade*. Princeton, NJ: Princeton University Press, 2007.

D'Emilio, John. "Capitalism and Gay Identity." In *The Material Queer: A LesBiGay Cultural Studies Reader,* ed. Donald Morton, 263–271. New York: Westview Press, 1996.

Dobbin, Frank, and John R. Sutton. "The Strength of a Weak State: The Rights Revolution and the Rise of Human Resources Management Divisions." *American Journal of Sociology* 104.2 (1998): 441–476.

Duggan, Lisa. *The Twilight of Equality? Neoliberalism, Cultural Politics, and the Attack on Democracy*. Boston: Beacon Press, 2003.

Edelman, Lauren B., Christopher Uggen, and Howard S. Erlinger. "The Endogeneity of Legal Regulation: Grievance Procedures as Rational Myth." *American Journal of Sociology* 105.2 (1999): 406–454.

Foner, Eric, and Lisa McGirr, eds. *American History Now*. Philadelphia: Temple University Press, 2011.

Fraser, Nancy, and Linda Gordon. "A Genealogy of Dependency: Tracing a Keyword of the U.S. Welfare State." *Signs* 19.2 (Winter 1994): 305–321.

Garcia, Ruben J. *Marginal Workers: How Legal Fault Lines Divide Workers and Leave Them without Protection*. New York: New York University Press, 2012.

Gibson-Graham, J. K. *The End of Capitalism (as We Knew It): A Feminist Critique of Political Economy*. Minneapolis: University of Minnesota Press, 2006.

Gilpin, Toni, Gary Isaac, Daniel Letwin, and Jack McKivigan. *On Strike for Respect: The Clerical and Technical Workers' Strike at Yale University, 1984–1985*. Urbana-Champaign: University of Illinois Press, 1995.

Gordon, Avery F. *Ghostly Matters: Haunting and the Sociological Imagination*. Minneapolis: University of Minnesota Press, 1997.

Gould, Deborah B. *Moving Politics: Emotion and ACT-UP's Fight against AIDS*. Chicago: University of Chicago Press, 2009.

Gray, Herman, and Macarena Gomez-Barris. *Toward a Sociology of the Trace*. Minneapolis: University of Minnesota Press, 2010.

Harris, Cheryl. "Whiteness as Property." *Harvard Law Review* 106.8 (June 1993): 1710–1791.

Hart, Gillian Patricia. *Disabling Globalization: Places of Power in Post-apartheid South Africa*. Berkeley: University of California Press, 2002.

Harvey, David. *A Brief History of Neoliberalism*. Oxford: Oxford University Press, 2005.

———. "Neoliberalism as Creative Destruction." *Annals of the American Academy of Political and Social Science* 610 (2007): 21–44.

———. *The New Imperialism*. Oxford: Oxford University Press, 2003.

———. *Spaces of Capital: Towards a Critical Geography*. Edinburgh, Scotland: Edinburgh University Press, 2001.

Ho, Karen Z. *Liquidated: An Ethnography of Wall Street*. Durham, NC: Duke University Press, 2009.

Hochschild, Arlie Russell. *The Managed Heart: Commercialization of Human Feeling*. Berkeley: University of California Press, 1983.

———. *The Time Bind: When Work Becomes Home and Home Becomes Work*. Rev. ed. New York: Holt Paperbacks, 2001.

Hochschild, Arlie Russell, and Anne Machung, *The Second Shift: Working Families and the Revolution at Home.* Rev. ed. New York: Penguin Books, 2012.

Hong, Grace Kyungwon. *The Ruptures of American Capital: Women of Color Feminism and the Culture of Immigrant Labor.* Minneapolis: University of Minnesota Press, 2006.

Jakobsen, Janet R. "Can Homosexuals End Western Civilization as We Know It? Family Values in a Global Economy." In *Queer Globalizations: Citizenship and the Afterlife of Colonialism,* ed. Arnaldo Cruz-Malave and Martin F. Manalansan IV, 51–72. New York: New York University Press, 2002.

Jakobsen, Janet R., and Ann Pellegrini. *Love the Sin: Sexual Regulation and the Limits of Religious Tolerance.* New York: New York University Press, 2003.

———. "Sex + Freedom = Regulation: Why?" *Social Text* 23.3–4 (Fall/Winter 2005): 285–308.

———. *Working Alliances and the Politics of Difference.* Bloomington: Indiana University Press, 1998.

Jennings, Kenneth M. *Labor Relations at the New York Daily News: Peripheral Bargaining and the 1990 Strike.* Westport, CT: Praeger, 1993.

Johnson, Colin. *Just Queer Folks: Gender and Sexuality in Rural America.* Philadelphia: Temple University Press, 2013.

Joseph, Miranda. *Against the Romance of Community.* Minneapolis: University of Minnesota Press, 2002.

Kahn, Alfred E. *The Economics of Regulation: Principles and Institutions.* Rev. ed. Cambridge, MA: MIT Press, 1988.

———. *Lessons from Deregulation: Telecommunications and Airlines after the Crunch.* Washington, DC: AEI-Brookings Joint Center for Regulatory Studies, 2004.

Klinenberg, Eric. *Going Solo: The Extraordinary Rise and Surprising Appeal of Living Alone.* New York: Penguin, 2013.

Krippner, Greta. *Capitalizing on Crisis: Political Origins of the Rise of Finance.* Cambridge, MA: Harvard University Press, 2012.

Krupat, Kitty, and Patrick McCreery, eds. *Out at Work: Building a Gay-Labor Alliance.* Minneapolis: University of Minnesota Press, 2001.

Laclau, Ernesto, and Chantal Mouffe. *Hegemony and Socialist Strategy: Towards a Radical Democratic Politics.* 2nd ed. London: Verso, 2014.

Lasch, Christopher. *A Haven in a Heartless World.* New York: Basic Books, 1977.

Leitner, Helga, Jamie Peck, and Eric Shepard. *Contesting Neoliberalism: Urban Frontiers.* New York: Guilford Press, 2006.

Lichtenstein, Nelson. *State of the Union: A Century of American Labor.* Princeton, NJ: Princeton University Press, 2013.

Martin, Randy. *The Financialization of Daily Life.* Philadelphia: Temple University Press, 2002.

May, Elaine Tyler. *Homeward Bound: American Families in the Cold War Era.* New York: Basic Books, 1988.

Maynes, Mary Jo, Jennifer L. Pierce, and Barbara Laslett. *Telling Stories: The Use of Personal Narratives in the Social Sciences and History.* Ithaca, NY: Cornell University Press, 2008.

McCraw, Thomas. *Prophets of Regulation: Francis Adams, Louis D. Brandeis, James M. Landis, and Alfred E. Kahn.* Cambridge, MA: Belknap Press of the Harvard University Press, 1984.

McGirr, Lisa. *Suburban Warriors: The Origins of the New American Right.* Princeton, NJ: Princeton University Press, 2002.

Milkman, Ruth. *Farewell to the Factory: Autoworkers in the Late Twentieth Century*. Berkeley: University of California Press, 1997.

Montgommery, David. *The Fall of the House of Labor*. Cambridge: Cambridge University Press, 1987.

Moody, Kim. *An Injury to All: The Decline of American Unionism*. London: Verso, 1988.

———. *Workers in a Lean World: Unions in the International Economy*. London: Verso, 1997.

Moreton, Bethany. *To Serve God and Wal-Mart: The Making of Christian Free Enterprise*. Cambridge, MA: Harvard University Press, 2009.

Morgen, Sandra, Joan Acker, and Jill Weigt. *Stretched Thin: Poor Families, Welfare Work, and Welfare Reform*. Ithaca, NY: Cornell University Press, 2009.

Mouffe, Chantal. *The Democratic Paradox*. London: Verso, 2000.

Mozdzanowska, Aleksandra. "Growth and Operating Patterns of Regional Jets in the United States." *Journal of Aircraft* 42.4 (July/August 2005): 858–864.

Murphy, Ryan Patrick. "The Gay Land Rush: Race, Gender, and Sexuality in the Life of Post-welfare Minneapolis." In *Queer Twin Cities*, ed. The Twin Cities GLBT Oral History Project, 240–268. Minneapolis: University of Minnesota Press, 2010.

———. "On Our Own: Flight Attendant Activism and the Family Values Economy." Ph.D. diss, University of Minnesota, Minneapolis, 2010.

Murray, Charles. *Losing Ground: American Social Policy, 1950–1980*. New York: Basic Books, 1984.

Nance, John. *Splash of Colors: The Self-Destruction of Braniff International*. New York: William Morrow, 1984.

Ong, Aihwa. *Flexible Citizenship: The Cultural Logics of Transnationality*. Durham, NC: Duke University Press, 1999.

Orenic, Liesl Miller. *On the Ground: Labor Struggle in the American Airline Industry*. Champaign-Urbana: University of Illinois Press, 2009.

Peck, Jamie, and Adam Tickell, "Neoliberalizing Space." *Antipode* 34.3 (July 2002): 380–404.

Perlman, Selig. *A Theory of the Labor Movement*. New York: Macmillan, 1928.

Phillips-Fein, Kim. *Invisible Hands: The Making of the Conservative Movement from the New Deal to Reagan*. New York: W. W. Norton, 2009.

Pierce, Jennifer L. *Gender Trials: Emotional Lives in Contemporary Law Firms*. Berkeley: University of California Press, 1996.

Pleck, Elizabeth H. *Not Just Roommates: Cohabitation after the Sexual Revolution*. Chicago: University of Chicago Press, 2012.

Polanyi, Karl B. *The Great Transformation: The Political and Economic Origins of Our Time*. Boston: Beacon Press, 2001.

Rachleff, Peter. *Hard-Pressed in the Heartland: The Hormel Strike and the Future of the Labor Movement*. Boston: South End Press, 1993.

Raeburn, Nicole. *Changing Corporate America from the Inside Out: Lesbian and Gay Workplace Rights*. Minneapolis: University of Minnesota Press, 2004.

Ramirez, Bruno. *When Workers Fight: The Politics of Industrial Relations in the Progressive Era, 1896–1916*. New York: Greenwood Press, 1978.

Reich, Robert B. *The Work of Nations: Preparing Ourselves for Twenty-First-Century Capitalism*. New York: Vintage Books, 1991.

Robinson, Jack E. *Freefall: The Needless Destruction of Eastern Airlines and the Valiant Struggle to Save It*. New York: Harper Collins, 1992.

Rosenberg, Emily S. *Financial Missionaries to the World: The Politics and Culture of Dollar Diplomacy.* Durham, NC: Duke University Press, 2004.

Rozen, Frieda S. "Turbulence in the Air: The Autonomy Movement in the Flight Attendant Unions." Ph.D. diss., Pennsylvania State University, State College, 1988.

Sassen, Saskia. "Economic Restructuring in the American City." *Annual Reviews of Sociology* 16 (1990): 465–490.

Schumpeter, Joseph A. *Capitalism, Socialism, and Democracy.* New York: George Allen and Unwin, 1976.

Self, Robert O. *All in the Family: The Realignment of American Democracy since the 1960s.* New York: Hill and Wang, 2012.

Spade, Dean. "What's Wrong with Trans Rights?" In *Transfeminist Perspectives in and beyond Transgender and Gender Studies,* ed. Anne Enke, 184–194. Philadelphia: Temple University Press, 2012.

Stacey, Judith. *Unhitched: Love, Marriage, and Family Values from West Hollywood to Western China.* New York: New York University Press, 2011.

Stahl, Jason M. *Right Moves: The Conservative Think Tank in American Political Culture since 1945.* Chapel Hill: University of North Carolina Press, 2016.

———. "Selling Conservatism: Think Tanks, Conservative Ideology, and the Undermining of Liberalism, 1945–Present." Ph.D. diss., University of Minnesota, Minneapolis, 2008.

Tiemeyer, Phillip. "Male Stewardesses: Male Flight Attendants as a Queer Miscarriage of Justice." *Genders—Online Edition* 45 (2007).

———. *Plane Queer: Labor, Sexuality, and AIDS in the History of Male Flight Attendants.* Berkeley: University of California Press, 2013.

Tsing, Anna Lowenhaupt. *Friction: An Ethnography of Global Connection.* Princeton, NJ: Princeton University Press, 2005.

Van Scyoc, Lee James. "Effects of the Airline Deregulation Act on Market Performance: Price, Capacity, and Profits." Ph.D. diss., University of Nebraska, Lincoln, 1987.

Weeks, Kathi. *The Problem with Work: Feminism, Marxism, Antiwork Politics, and Postwork Imaginaries.* Durham, NC: Duke University Press, 2011.

Whitelegg, Drew. "Cabin Pressure: The Dialectics of Emotional Labour in the Airline Industry." *Journal of Transport History* 23.1 (March 2002): 73–86.

———. *Working the Skies: The Fast-Paced, Disorienting World of the Flight Attendant.* New York: New York University Press, 2007.

Willis, Patricia K. "The Stewardesses for Women's Rights: Opening Closed Doors for Radical Change." Ph.D. diss., State University of New York, Albany, 2004.

Witeck, Bob, and Wesley Combs. *Business Inside Out: Capturing Millions of Brand-Loyal Gay Consumers.* New York: Kaplan Publishing, 2006.

INDEX

Ryan Patrick Murphy—a former San Francisco–based flight attendant for United Airlines and Council Representative for Association of Flight Attendants–CWA Council 11—is Assistant Professor of History and Women's, Gender, and Sexuality Studies at Earlham College in Richmond, Indiana.

www.ingramcontent.com/pod-product-compliance
Lightning Source LLC
Chambersburg PA
CBHW020345270326
41926CB00007B/321